ADVANTAGE CHINA

ADVANTAGE CHINA

Agent of Change in an Era of Global Disruption

Jeremy Garlick

BLOOMSBURY ACADEMIC

LONDON • NEW YORK • OXFORD • NEW DELHI • SYDNEY

BLOOMSBURY ACADEMIC
Bloomsbury Publishing Plc
50 Bedford Square, London, WC1B 3DP, UK
1385 Broadway, New York, NY 10018, USA
29 Earlsfort Terrace, Dublin 2, Ireland

BLOOMSBURY, BLOOMSBURY ACADEMIC and the Diana logo
are trademarks of Bloomsbury Publishing Plc

First published in Great Britain 2024

Copyright © Jeremy Garlick, 2024

Jeremy Garlick has asserted his right under the Copyright,
Designs and Patents Act, 1988, to be identified as Author of this work.

For legal purposes the Acknowledgements on p. vii constitute
an extension of this copyright page.

Cover design and illustration by Grace Ridge

A catalogue record for this book is available from the British Library.

Library of Congress Cataloging-in-Publication Data
Garlick, Jeremy, author.
Advantage China: agent of change in an era of global disruption / Jeremy Garlick.
London; New York: Bloomsbury Academic, 2023. |
Includes bibliographical references and index.
LCCN 2023010995 (print) | LCCN 2023010996 (ebook) |
ISBN 9781350252318 (paperback) | ISBN 9781350252325 (hardback) |
ISBN 9781350252332 (epub) | ISBN 9781350252349 (pdf) | ISBN 9781350252356
LCSH: China–Foreign economic relations. | China–Economic
conditions–2000- | Yi dai yi lu (Initiative: China)
LCC HF1604.G368 2023 (print) | LCC HF1604 (ebook) |
DDC 337.51–dc23/eng/20230808
LC record available at https://lccn.loc.gov/2023010995
LC ebook record available at https://lccn.loc.gov/2023010996

ISBN: HB: 978-1-3502-5232-5
PB: 978-1-3502-5231-8
ePDF: 978-1-3502-5234-9
eBook: 978-1-3502-5233-2

Typeset by Integra Software Services Pvt. Ltd.

Printed and bound in Great Britain

To find out more about our authors and books visit www.bloomsbury.com
and sign up for our newsletters.

CONTENTS

Figures and Tables

Figures

Tables

ACKNOWLEDGEMENTS

This book would not have been possible without the assistance of those who believed in the project and ushered it towards completion.

At Bloomsbury, I would like to thank David Avital, who was the first to see the project's potential and was unfailingly supportive throughout the lengthy process of preparing the manuscript. Olivia Dellow provided practical advice on vital matters of detail and was always available when needed. Their guidance enabled me to transform the bare bones of an idea into the fully-fleshed-out corpus of text you hold in your hands.

I greatly appreciate the support of the Czech Science Foundation, whose generous grant funding gave me the time to conduct the research and complete the writing of the book. At Prague University of Economics and Business, Štěpánka Zemanová and Radka Druláková were instrumental in providing me with the support, resources and time to work on the manuscript.

The input of many scholars – too numerous to mention – has provided stimulating food for thought and allowed me to construct the arguments in the book. Rather than mentioning them all here, I recommend looking for recurring names in the endnotes.

I would also like to thank an anonymous reviewer whose criticism of certain points enabled me to reshape the argument in what I hope is a stronger form. I don't know who you are, but I appreciate both the encouragement and the invaluable corrections you provided.

Last but not least, my family has always been tolerant of my extended sessions at the computer. None of this would be possible without them.

Funding: This work was supported by the Czech Science Foundation (Grantová Agentura České Republiky, GAČR), as part of the research project 'China's regionalising normative influence in Asia and Europe', project no. 22–12355S.

ABOUT THE AUTHOR

Jeremy Garlick, PhD, is an associate professor at Prague University of Economics and Business and the director of the Jan Masaryk Centre of International Studies, a research centre within the university. He specializes in China's international relations, focusing primarily on the progress and regional implementation of the Belt and Road Initiative (BRI). His first book, *The Impact of China's Belt and Road Initiative: From Asia to Europe*, was published by Routledge in 2020. His second book, *Reconfiguring the China-Pakistan Economic Corridor: Geo-Economic Pipe Dreams Versus Geopolitical Realities*, will be published by Routledge in late 2021. In addition to publications on EU-China relations, he has also published numerous articles on a diverse range of topics related to the BRI, including China's economic diplomacy and regionalizing foreign policy. These publications include papers on the China-Pakistan Economic Corridor (CPEC), China's economic diplomacy in the Czech Republic, China's strategic hedging in the Persian Gulf, China's normative power drive in Central Asia and China's relations with India. Dr Garlick has taught and lectured for two decades at institutes of higher education in Asia and Europe including the University of the Chinese Academy of Sciences (UCAS) in Beijing and Ewha Womans University in Seoul.

INTRODUCTION

The rise of the People's Republic of China since Deng Xiaoping took the reins of the Chinese Communist Party in the late 1970s has been remarkable. Moving on from the chaos of the Maoist Cultural Revolution and a command economy that was almost entirely closed off from global trade and financial systems, development has been staggeringly swift. From 1978 onwards, China's gross domestic product rose on average by 10 per cent a year for three decades.[1] In 2010, China overtook Japan to become the second biggest economy in the world according to gross domestic product (GDP).[2] Measured by purchasing power parity (PPP), the GDP of the People's Republic has already overtaken the United States.[3] China's military spending is also the second highest in the world after the United States: $293 billion was allocated to defence expenditures in 2021, compared to a figure of $801 billion for the United States.[4] China is the world's factory, since 2010 the source of more industrial goods than any other country on earth. In 2019, China accounted for 28.7 per cent of global manufacturing, over ten per cent ahead of the United States.[5] There are now more dollar billionaires (819) in China than in any other country, including the United States (571).[6]

To cut a long story short, China's economic growth is ineluctably pushing the country to a position of global pre-eminence. This is especially true of its engagement with the developing world: in many countries of the global South, China is already the foremost provider of finance for infrastructure construction projects. China often invests in risky countries – such as Sri Lanka and Tanzania – where others fear to tread.[7] Beijing sends out its construction companies – of which there are too many in China – to build infrastructure financed by Chinese state lenders.[8] During the presidency of Xi Jinping, many of these overseas investments and infrastructure projects have been subsumed under the label of the Belt and Road Initiative (BRI).

Yet the reasons why China has gone from recipient of aid to development titan in such a relatively short space of time – just four decades – are not necessarily well understood in the West.[9] There is little or no attempt to learn from the relative success of China's strategies for growth and global expansion via the BRI and its predecessor, the 'Going Global' strategy. Western commentators frequently imply that China's economy is a bubble, or that China needs to Westernize in order to keep its economy growing, or that Beijing cannot sustain the present system without democratization or that the PRC's success is some kind of accident. There is also an inbuilt assumption that the BRI is faulty and destined to fail, even though it is steadily replacing Western development initiatives in many parts of the global South. It is neither understood nor accepted that China's success has not happened by chance but is due to a unique set of strategies that the West does not pursue and attributes that the West does not possess. In an era of global disruption, amid pandemics, climate change, wars and economic upheaval, these are giving China an edge which has not been well understood in the United States and Europe.

Of course, not every action that the Chinese government takes is perfectly coordinated. Some international relations (IR) scholars point out that China is not as much of a monolithic entity as it may appear because there are many actors contesting Chinese foreign policy.[10] However, it is essential not to overstate the extent of what is sometimes called 'fragmented authoritarianism'[11] or 'state transformation'.[12] Despite its plethora of actors pushing their own interests in an era of economic globalization, policy initiatives remain very much top-down rather than bottom-up in their conception and implementation, as the case of China's investments in Brazil demonstrates (for more on this, see Chapter 6). Discussing China's engagement with Brazil, an official from the Ministry of Foreign Affairs stressed the centralized, top-down character of economic cooperation, as implemented from the Chinese side.[13]

While it is true that commercial transactions are negotiated and renegotiated between many actors, China's overall strategy is planned behind closed doors in Beijing. The Chinese government classifies the details of its overseas development strategy as a state secret, which explains why details can be hard to come by and it can appear to casual observers that there is no clear strategy.[14] Economic agreements are also generally implemented non-transparently in bilateral negotiations with the leaders of other states. Dreher et al note that 'China has a track record of using aid strategically: to attract political support at high-level diplomatic events, to influence the voting behavior of recipient governments in various international fora, and to secure diplomatic recognition for the People's Republic of China at the expense of Taiwan.'[15] Commercial actors who step out of line can be quietly removed at the behest of the Chinese government and replaced with others: this happened in the Czech Republic, where the private company CEFC Energy went rogue and was replaced by the state-owned enterprise CITIC (more on this in Chapter 6).[16] Thus, while it may be true that China is not as unitary an actor as it first appears, its one-party system, authoritarian governance and top-down implementation of economic relations with partner countries mean that it is still far more unitary than Western democracies, in which many actors compete to promote policies which support their interests.

The Chinese strategy includes the possibility of failure and reassessment. Since the Deng Xiaoping years, the Chinese government has been pragmatic in the pursuit of growth and the establishment of China as a true world power. Chinese leaders from Deng onwards have understood that the road to a prosperous future is long, complex and winding. There have been many mistakes on the way to achieving China's economic 'miracle'. But the possibility of erroneous policy decisions has been included in Chinese calculations. Deng employed the frequently quoted maxim 'crossing the river by feeling for the stones' to describe the trial-and-error process of experimentation in economic reforms he believed necessary.[17] Deng's pragmatic and relatively flexible approach laid a foundation for China's leaders to figure out what worked and what did not without being unnecessarily fixated on ideological precepts as Mao had been.

Since the turn of the century, prominent Western observers have frequently viewed the People's Republic as fragile[18] or predicted that its Communist regime will soon collapse.[19] Yet the PRC, despite these perceived shortcomings, has stubbornly persisted – and has continued to grow economically. In fact, the Chinese Communist Party (CCP) has long been keenly aware of China's strengths and weaknesses. It knew about the property bubble, taking steps to deflate it gradually before the housing crisis of 2021–2, during which the extent of the property company Evergrande's debts became public knowledge.[20] It knows about the global environmental catastrophe caused by industrialization due to its negative impact on China's air and rivers: that is why Beijing is investing in green technologies and renewable energy.[21] It knows about the threats to China's internal cohesion: that is why Chinese security forces have clamped down with great force in Xinjiang, Tibet and Hong Kong.[22] And it knows about excessive debt and over-capacity in the state-owned sector: this is one of the main reasons for launching the 'Going Global' initiative in the late 1990s and expanding China's global expansion through the BRI from 2013 onwards.[23]

In short, the Party seeks to minimize its weaknesses and threats to its governance. It tries to neutralize them or turn them into strengths if possible. It also aims to exploit China's advantages, including the country's massive and relatively homogeneous population, the people's patriotism and their capacity for hard work and long hours in often less than ideal conditions.[24] It hand-picks the CEOs of state-owned companies and controls the purse-strings of state finance through state-owned banks.[25] Due to the strong hand of the state in allocation of finance, contracts, positions and resources, Chinese leaders are able to minimize the effect of volatile market forces – a luxury which Western countries do not necessarily have.

The West, on the other hand, arguably overestimates its strengths and underestimates its weaknesses. The West also systematically underestimates China. This might be called hubris; but it is better classified as a straightforward mistake of judgement due to lack of knowledge about China among Western elites. Western assessments of China are often simplistic, static and wide of the mark. The West simply does not grasp why China has the advantage because it has not taken the time to understand China well. Arguably, as I will seek to show, the West does not even grasp its own disadvantaged situation in the global marketplace of development. Democratic institutions are assets which China lacks; but transparency can produce inefficiencies in business when checks and balances slow down the awarding of contracts, allocation of finance and implementation of project initiatives. This explains why China resists making its financing of the BRI transparent: by keeping the details secret, China can negotiate directly with heads of state behind closed doors and implement deals faster than the West. To Western critics, lack of transparency looks like a problem; but for Beijing it is an asset when it comes to swift implementation and the generation of influence with authoritarian regimes.[26]

Clearly, China is expanding its influence outwards beyond its borders. But, despite frequent Western assertions to the contrary, the Chinese strategy for expansion is not especially aggressive by the standards of historical warfare. Rather than military invasions, over the last four decades the Chinese have pursued a strategy of gradual gains requiring a minimum of risk. This approach has been called 'salami slicing': opportunistically acquiring extra territory, for example in the South China Sea, in 'a slow accumulation of small actions, none of which is a casus belli'.[27] The PRC has not attempted a military invasion since its brief border war against Vietnam in 1979.[28] Nor has China rushed to place its armed forces in new bases overseas on a large scale. Instead, the Chinese approach to statecraft can be characterized as cautious, pragmatic and patient. Unlike the United States (which invaded Afghanistan and Iraq in the early 2000s), Beijing uses primarily economic and political tools rather than military ones. Instead of tanks and bombs, there are loans and investments. China makes bilateral deals, builds up influence, establishes new markets for its companies. As Rush Doshi has noted, the Chinese play the long game, biding their time and building their strength, while steadily working to undermine US dominance in the international system.[29]

Around the turn of the millennium, some observers based in the United States expected China to democratize – in other words, to Westernize.[30] They predicted that the Chinese Communist Party would lose power if it did not loosen its grip on China's political system. The economy would stagnate under a Leninist system of top-down control. China could not keep going in the same direction and hence would collapse.[31] These kinds of predictions followed on from Francis Fukuyama's hypothesis that the 'end of history' was manifested in the Western international order.[32] Those who supported Fukuyama's hypothesis agreed that all countries would turn to democracy eventually, in an inevitable wave of globalized liberalization based on acceptance of Western norms and values.

And yet China's course has defied such expectations over the last two decades. Ignoring Western pressures, China *has* maintained the same course under Chinese Communist Party (CCP) leadership. Not without bumps in the road, not without steadily slowing economic growth; but the Chinese juggernaut has kept rolling forwards. And it has done so without Westernizing its politics or society. China has been able to continue in this way because, despite frequent Western assertions to the contrary, it has certain advantages that the West lacks. It has a large, relatively homogenous population with a shared sense of history, culture and national destiny: over 90 per cent of China's 1.4 billion people identify as Han.[33] It has a stable governance structure that allows for long-term strategic planning. It has leaders who have, between them, a reasonably good understanding of the complexities of economic development and international affairs and have managed – so far – to steer the massive Chinese ship through the turbulent waters of a rapidly changing world.

It is not my intention in this book to depict China as a villain or a hero. There are plenty of others doing that already. Readers can make up their own minds on their view about whether China's rise is a force for good or evil, or – as an AidData research team has demonstrated through in-depth analysis of Chinese investments in the developing world – something in between.[34] Instead of engaging in values-based polemic, I hope the data-driven analysis in this book will present readers with a critical perspective contrasting China and the West's respective approaches to global development and international affairs. The intention is to show how China's approach is distinct from the West's, and how this approach gives the PRC certain advantages when trying to forge a route through the complex and turbulent times in which we live.

I have two primary aims in writing this book. The first is to lay out the characteristics and implementation of China's relations with the nations of the global South under the label of the Belt and Road Initiative (BRI). The second is to demonstrate that the West – shorthand for the United States and the EU – needs to understand why China is gaining influence in the developing world. If the West decides – as it almost certainly already has – that it is not possible to cooperate with China, it will have to put all its energy into the alternative route: effective competition. Put simply, the West needs to learn the lessons of the Chinese approach to international development and change its approach. Instead of assuming that it can continue with the same policies, the West needs to find new ways to compete involving a fresh set of ideas consistently applied.

I have three key and closely linked contentions. The first is that China's approach has altered the landscape within which international development takes place. China is setting new norms and practices for interactions with other countries, especially in the global South. These new norms are radically different from the Western-dominated international system established at Bretton Woods in 1944 which has guided the progress of international affairs ever since. The Chinese approach involves a very different use of financial resources and commercial enterprises than that to which Westerners are accustomed. It is much more top-down and directed with broad but specific strategic aims in mind over the long term. China's approach to international development, national security and influence-building is certainly not without flaws; but it does produce advantages for China and its developing world partners with which the West remains stubbornly reluctant to engage. I argue that it is not enough simply to acknowledge the need to compete with China. The West also needs to recognize that its approach, as it currently stands, is not competitive and needs to change more radically than most Western observers have so far been willing to contemplate.

My second contention, linked to the first, is that the West is failing to acknowledge the reasons why China's approach to the global South is more successful. The United States and Europe have difficulty facing the unpleasant truth that China is winning the influence battle in many parts of the world. Unpopular as this idea may be, the West needs to draw on developing countries' experience of China in resetting its approach to engagement with the global South. Despite the Western perception that the Chinese approach cannot work, it is in fact giving Beijing a great deal of influence in the developing world. It is also setting new norms for how bilateral relations can work, even if there are many flaws in the implementation. If it wants to compete, the West therefore needs to make up its mind exactly how it is going to establish an alternative programme which is more attractive to potential partners than the Chinese offer. Or, if this proves difficult, how it can find ways to work with China to avoid a global bifurcation into two competing systems.

My third contention is that the main reason why China's approach to investment in the developing world is successful is because it is better coordinated and more consistent than anything the West has been doing. Despite some perceptions to the contrary among Western scholars, experts and politicians, China has the advantage of being able to coordinate its financial institutions and corporations quite effectively under the relatively monolithic structure of the CCP. Unlike the West – meaning primarily the United States and Europe – where there are frequent changes of government, U-turns in foreign policy and a tendency to favour words over actions with respect to the global South, China has also been able to implement a relatively consistent approach to its relations with developing countries. The Chinese approach offers clear benefits to partners in the global South, even if they are often reluctant to be subsumed into a Chinese-led economic and political order that falls outside standard international norms.[35] The benefits offered by cooperating with China are simply not available from any other source – including the West. In an era of global disruption, amidst pandemics, wars and economic strains, in an era when the West lacks coordination and consistency, China is many impoverished countries' best option for development finance and practical assistance. China has gained the advantage in the marketplace of development ideas and implementation, and the United States and Europe are going to have to work hard to take it back.

Within this framework, the book presents seven main arguments, summarized as follows:

1) Under the overall label of the BRI, China is employing a relatively consistent set of policies for engaging with the global South. These include the following:
   - obtaining energy supplies and other resources by signing deals and building relations with regimes in resource-rich countries such as Saudi Arabia, Brazil and Venezuela;
   - building loan-funded infrastructure using Chinese companies;
   - engaging with countries at the regional and bilateral levels simultaneously;
   - creating new markets for Chinese companies; and
   - generating political influence in the global South at the elite level.
2) China is a catalyst for change, even if the course of that change may take an uncertain route. China has altered the landscape of how investment and development in the global South can be done. Its economic clout has altered the landscape of global commerce. Its influence-building activity has also changed the international political environment. There seems little reason to believe that the processes of change set in motion by China's rise can be reversed with the aim of maintaining the Western-led liberal international order indefinitely in its traditional form.

3) Complexity thinking reveals that, in an era of global disruption producing outcomes which are hard either to predict or control, it is necessary for countries to approach international affairs flexibly and pragmatically. China's practical approach to building relations within a relatively consistent overall strategic framework gives it an advantage over the West, which insists on sticking to the 'rules-based' international order set up at Bretton Woods in 1944 – even if this may no longer be the best way forward (or needs to be better adapted to the needs of developing countries).

4) The West has been very slow to react to the BRI and other aspects of China's influence and activity in the developing world. In its first few years the BRI (introduced in 2013) was dismissed as vague and over-ambitious, an empty shell with no real content. However, as it has become apparent that China is building infrastructure, increasing trade and gaining influence across the global South, the West belatedly started talking about counter-initiatives in 2021, most notably Build Back Better World (B3W), Partnership for Global Infrastructure and Investment (PGII) and the EU's Global Gateway. However, these so far lack substance.

5) Western initiatives are uncoordinated in comparison to Chinese ones. In business, the West relies on commercial actors rather than state-led initiatives to forge a path. In contrast, there is a strong top-down aspect to the BRI, especially in terms of the signing of bilateral deals between the Chinese government and partner countries' regimes. The West is also uncoordinated within itself: for instance, the United States and the EU often appear to be on different policy tracks. Even within the EU there are substantial divisions and individual countries such as Germany appear to be making foreign policy unilaterally despite their supposed obligations to the EU. The West's fragmented approaches to foreign policy and the global South undermine efforts to counter or respond to China.

6) Even if China has significant weaknesses, and its economy is under strain, its economic clout and political clout in the global South have been increasing rapidly while the influence of the West has been stagnating or declining. Developing countries may be suspicious of Chinese intentions, but many of them are also suspicious of the West due to historical reasons. This gives China – which portrays itself as a leader of the global South rather than a member of the global North – an advantage when building ties with countries which were former European colonies and still feel disadvantaged in the international system.

7) It would be far better for the future of the world if the West and China could work together on solutions to problems such as development, global warming, energy, resources, over-population and the weaknesses inherent in the current economic system. However, given the entrenched geopolitical rivalries and lack of mutual understanding this seems highly unlikely. It is difficult to be optimistic about cooperation between China and the West, even though this seems essential if good solutions to the planet's problems are to be found. It even seems unlikely that the West can coordinate its own response effectively; but it will have to if it intends to compete with China by presenting an alternative to the Chinese approach to development.

This book tells the story of how the People's Republic of China has managed not only to survive but – despite Western expectations – to thrive in the global marketplace of ideas and economics. It explains how and why China has come to dominate the development landscape in the global South, forcing a reaction out of the West. It explores the characteristics of China's global expansion under the umbrella of President Xi Jinping's Belt and Road Initiative. And it examines what the West should learn from China and how it should engage with China's increasing global influence: by developing and implementing coordinated long-term strategies which engage with the reasons underlying China's success rather than assuming the BRI will fail.

Chapter 1

CHINA AND THE WEST

In the third decade of the twenty-first century, the conventional wisdom shared by many opinion-makers and experts in the United States and Europe is that the People's Republic of China (PRC) is a threat to Western civilization, norms, and moral leadership. China has a communist, authoritarian government which seeks insidiously to spread its influence internationally. The Party elites in Beijing attempt to undermine Western democracy, institutions and values. Indeed, experts on China have presented substantial evidence supporting the assertion that the PRC actively seeks to counter Western norms and the so-called 'liberal international order'.[1] At the same time, in the collective Western subconscious, through the prevailing discourse emanating from experts and the media, an image of China is formed as a dragon at the gates, a red threat, possibly, subconsciously, even a 'yellow peril'.[2] Communist China is threatening to tear down Western defences, loot our property (physical and intellectual), undermine our values and take over our societies.

China is therefore automatically depicted as a threat, as the enemy. While this assumption is understandable and not entirely without merit from a Western perspective, it also creates a stereotyped, somewhat under-informed image of China. China is depicted, despite Edward Said's much-quoted warnings about orientalism, as strange, inscrutable, other.[3] As John Hobson demonstrates, Eurocentrism creeps, often unconsciously, into Western depictions of international affairs.[4] Europe is wiser and more moral, the EU a 'normative power' for good, dispersing European values to the world.[5] It is assumed that Europeans and their descendants, who have shaped the direction of global affairs over the last few centuries through imperialism and colonialism, will continue to bear the burden of inculcating their impoverished former colonies with wise European norms. From the American perspective, the assumption is that the United States represents a 'shining city on a hill': a beacon of democracy and freedom whose duty is to proselytize American values to the world, nobly scattering the seeds of the American dream into the semi-arid wastes of the developing world. The possibility of non-Western agency in the shaping of the international order is excluded.[6]

In reality, there is no sense or logic to assuming that the West has all the answers to the world's problems. Yet that is precisely the unthinking assumption that

 Advantage China

many Westerners tend to make: that Westerners, the children of the renaissance, liberalism, capitalism and the industrial revolution, are the world's opinion-formers, leaders, teachers and inventors. It therefore follows naturally that all the 'others' – the Asians, Africans and so on – ought to listen to what we have to say. And this assumption that we have the right to dictate to the rest of the world includes the assumption that we have the right to instruct China how to approach its domestic and international affairs, just as it is our duty to teach impoverished countries – most of them former European colonies – how to develop.

Thus, the possibility of a China endowed with material as well as normative power – defined as the ability to shape the future in one's own image – is something which Westerners are not able to recognize or acknowledge. It is not even on the radar of Westerners that perhaps, just perhaps, there might be some lessons to be drawn from the rise of China – and from other rising economies in Asia and elsewhere. So used are Europeans and their colonial descendants in North America and other parts of the world to automatic global dominance that the idea that they might have something to gain from listening to other occupants of this planet is barely considered – even though there is evidence that China and other countries in the global South are already creating their own regional orders and norms independent of Western influence.[7]

The idea of Chinese agency does not compute because there is obviously something wrong with China. The PRC is not democratic, not liberal – not Western. China does not listen to us in the West – on Hong Kong, Taiwan, Tibet, Xinjiang and a host of other issues. If only we could change China, Western experts exasperatedly sigh – just as they have sighed for centuries. As the late, great historian of China Jonathan Spence demonstrated in his book *To Change China*, Western attempts to influence the development of the Middle Kingdom have always come to naught.[8] The idea that instead China might have agency and might change the West is beyond the bounds of the acceptable. It cannot be allowed to happen. Therefore, the West must keep on pushing back against China, striving to change it. As US Secretary of State Mike Pompeo put it in July 2020, 'If the free world doesn't change Communist China, Communist China will change us.'[9] The possibility of being changed by China is unthinkable, too horrible to contemplate.

But the reality is that the Chinese stubbornly refuse to become Western. The historical record – outlined masterfully by Spence – shows that Western attempts to steer the Chinese towards a European worldview have consistently failed.[10] In the present day, China – in the form of the ruling Chinese Communist Party (CCP) – persistently refuses to listen to Western admonitions and change its behaviour to suit the West.[11] And the likelihood is – as Beijing's refusal to let the West dictate the management of Hong Kong demonstrates – that the Chinese will not adopt a fully Westernized approach in the future either. Under President Xi Jinping, the CCP has promoted a vision of China as Chinese rather than Western: it has pushed back against Western influence by propagating to the Chinese people the idea of national rejuvenation based on traditional Chinese values.[12]

Ever since I began researching, writing and teaching about China, my primary goal has been to contribute in some small way to bridging the gaping communicative chasm between China and the West – and more particularly between China and Europe. As a European who has spent a considerable chunk of his life living and working in various countries on both continents, I feel the mutual lack of understanding between Asia and Europe keenly. It is an obstacle to the peoples of these two great continents – which in fact are part of one landmass – understanding each other. It has always therefore been my hope – probably over-optimistic, even utopian – that establishing better understanding and improved channels of communication between China and Europe would encourage the evolution of peaceful cooperation and mutually beneficial relations rather than zero-sum games played by powerful elites.[13]

Now, however, it seems to me that the case for investing substantial amounts of time and energy into trying to encourage better mutual understanding is a weak one. In the wake of Donald Trump's trade war and the coronavirus epidemic, the lack of trust between China and the West is so great that it is a task of Sisyphean proportions to push relations uphill and onto a more collaborative footing. Once again, after the first wave around the late 1990s and early 2000s, there is a prevalence of 'China threat' discourse in Western scholarly literature and mainstream media.[14] Publications about Chinese attempts to gain political influence in individual European countries proliferate.[15] Although it is perfectly valid to have such discussions, there is a tendency for some think tanks in Europe to persist in 'othering' China, establishing securitized threat perceptions which must be causing Edward Said to turn in his grave.[16] In a metaphorical sense – but one which pervades much European think tank and media discourse – China is depicted as a dragon at Europe's gates, plotting to invade us.[17]

Thus, if one does not want, like Sisyphus, to be continually rolling a rock labelled 'trust' up a hill, only to see it slip from one's grasp and roll back to the bottom again, one has to take a different approach to the problem of Sino-Western relations. It is time to take a pragmatic approach to China, one that accounts for the evolving global situation rather than the vision of what one would like to occur. The simple fact is that, whether we like it or not, the 'dragon' is already metaphorically 'at the gates' – and action, concerted action, is needed. Whether one perceives China as a threat or an opportunity, it is necessary for the West to construct a coordinated and coherent response to the dragon's presence.

This is especially the case in the countries of the global South where the Belt and Road Initiative (BRI) is being implemented through investments and infrastructure construction. The West's response should be not only reactive but also proactive, implementing a carefully designed set of policies for assisting the developing world as far as possible. The problem is that amid disintegrative tendencies and policy incoherence, both the United States and the EU remain far away from developing and coordinating a cogent and unified China policy, let alone a clear strategy for the development of the global South that can compete with China's BRI. That they are each unable to do this within their own polities does not bode well for them being able to coordinate policy together; yet, I argue, this is what they must do if they wish to counter China. The West must accept that China is not going away. The Middle Kingdom is an agent of change to the existing international order. As a result, it is necessary to take pragmatic steps to adjust to the rise of an increasingly influential China.

In recent decades, since the start of the new millennium, the EU has lost sight of the goal of being an international actor invested with agency. Instead, Brussels has (understandably) become preoccupied with damping down the flames billowing out of the latest crisis – whatever it may be. The 2007–8 recession, migrants, Brexit, coronavirus – no sooner is one crisis partly extinguished than another ignites on top of the half-burnt remains of the last. On each occasion, Brussels staggers unsteadily into something like action, drops a couple of buckets of water on the ever-growing inferno and hobbles off for a sit-down and a cup of tea. The EU's norm seems to be crisis management in its neighbourhood rather than long-term strategic thinking regarding its global role. There is, in particular, a lack of vision regarding the EU's engagement with the global South, from whence unwanted waves of refugees and migrants seeking a better life continue to pour into Europe.

As regards the EU's approach towards China: well, frankly there isn't one coherent, cohesive strategy. There is a lack of vision or clear policy concerning the decades to come. Since the beginning of the twenty-first century, Europe has swung discombobulatedly between the diametrically opposed poles of cooperation and competition with China. The EU has labelled China a 'systemic rival',[18] yet there have also been a string of documents such as the *EU-China Strategic 2020 Agenda for Cooperation* (published in 2013)[19] and the *EU-China Roadmap on Energy Cooperation (2016–2020).*[20] These documents, worth little more than the paper on which they are printed, betray no sign of a long-term strategy to engage with the Chinese challenge which would frame European action clearly or present a united face to the world. EU policy, on China as on other issues, should be something more than a facade of cooperation which results in no action. It should also not be about fighting fires when they break out. Instead, it should be about shaping the international political and economic environment so that there are fewer fires in the first place.

Similarly, the United States has lacked a coherent and consistent China policy over the last decade despite frequent attempts to design and implement one. The US approach to the global South is even less defined. From the Obama administration's 'pivot to Asia' to Donald Trump's trade war to Joe Biden's Build Back Better World (B3W) and Partnership for Global Infrastructure and Investment (PGII), US initiatives concerning China and the rest of the global South have come and gone, lacking substance, detailed planning or proper implementation. As administrations change, so does China policy. In addition, the United States does not have a coherent approach to development in the global South. The lack of continuity and long-term strategy is clear and contrasts strongly with China's relatively more consistent approach to engagement with the global South via the BRI and its predecessor, the 'Going Global' strategy, which was developed in the late 1990s.

The question thus becomes – twisting Mike Pompeo's words quoted earlier in this chapter – not how we in the West should change China, but to what extent China's global expansion will change the West. But there is also a second part to this question: how should the West actively and pragmatically change its approach to the Chinese presence on the global stage by adapting constructively to a world in which China plays a leading role, especially in the global South? In other words, it is time for the West to rethink its approach to a future which contains a China which Westerners may not like but with which they have to co-exist.

We live in an era in which the world seems to lurch unsteadily from one crisis to another. Whether it be a financial crisis or a pandemic, the election of populist demagogues or an uncontrolled influx of refugees, the West increasingly seems unable to cope. The onset of the coronavirus pandemic in 2020 brought home the stark reality of the West's muddled and ineffective approach to long-term planning. Although pandemics had been a common trope in Hollywood movies and popular culture since the 1990s or earlier, there was a lack of preparedness for Covid-19.[21] Of course, China was also unprepared for the virus, which originated in the city of Wuhan. There was a period of confusion and localized attempts to cover up the seriousness of the situation during the early stages of the outbreak. The Chinese government – central and local – did not emerge from the first three months of the crisis smelling of roses. Yet once the machinery of state did grind into gear, the Chinese response was coordinated and brought the spread of the pandemic under control. On the other hand, Chinese vaccines turned out not to be as effective as US and European ones, indicating that a research gap still separates China and the West. The PRC was also slow to implement a vaccination programme, necessitating a 'zero-COVID' approach deep into 2022, followed by a sudden relaxation of the rules and the rapid spread of the virus among a population which lacked herd immunity. Overall, it seems that both China and the West have strengths and weaknesses when it comes to crisis response. Ideally, they would learn from each other and cooperate more; but given present tensions this does not seem likely to happen.

The primary argument in this book is that the United States and Europe should attempt to draw lessons from the rise of China and respond to it in a pragmatic fashion. In 1978, at the behest of Deng Xiaoping, China pragmatically began to use foreign investment, capitalism and entrepreneurship to overcome a century or more of weakness and get rich.[22] This monumental effort, while not without inherent problems – most notably, the contradiction between capitalism and communism inherent in China's rise – has been broadly successful in raising China's economy, status and power in the world, especially in the global South. The West needs to acknowledge the fact that it can – and must – learn from China's success in emerging from the ruins of Maoist isolationism into growing global influence in the space of less than half a century.

Of course, the idea that Westerners should learn from China is not an easy pill to swallow. The West is used to being at the top of the tree, the proud creator of industry, modern science, globalization, capitalism, democracy and the so-called liberal international order. The notion that Westerners should stoop so low as to take lessons from the Chinese is offensive to their inherited sense of superiority. Yet if the West wants to maintain something like its old influence, it needs to bite the bullet and acknowledge its growing weakness with an attention to detail rather than just generalities. The West has to face up to the need to learn from the success of those – such as China – who are challenging Western dominance in the global economic and political order by studying in more depth how this is happening.

Some might say that transforming the West according to an Asian model is neither desirable nor possible. Westerners are not Asians, nor do they wish to be. Yet the West would do itself a service if it came to the realization that the people of East Asia, from the nineteenth century onwards, had to go through precisely such a process of mental and physical readjustment in reaction to the West's obvious superiority. First, over a century ago, Japan, influenced by its long contact with Europeans from the fifteenth century onwards, decided in a coordinated fashion to transform its military, westernize its education system and learn from European science and industry. Based on this deliberate programme of westernization, Japan was able to destroy a Russian navy and invade much of Asia before rising a second time after the Second World War to become a global economic powerhouse. China underwent a long 'century of humiliation' from the 1840s onwards, during which its navy was smashed by the British and its territory was invaded by the Japanese. Yet it took until Deng Xiaoping assumed power in 1978 that the Chinese acknowledged the need to learn from the West and reconstruct their industry, economy and society. In contrast to the traumatic transformation processes which Japan and China had to endure, it would be wise if Westerners adjusted to the rise of their competitors and learnt from them in a shorter time frame.

This is not to say that all the lessons should be positive ones. It is perfectly all right to conclude that one does not like everything China represents. It is correct to strongly object on moral grounds to the approach taken by the Chinese Communist Party in Xinjiang, Tibet and elsewhere. It is natural to decide that many elements of the Chinese approach cannot – and should not – be implemented in the West. It is logical to conclude that the Chinese way is intrinsically unsuitable for Western societies and that acceptance of Chinese norms would undermine Western values. It is valid to weigh up the evidence and decide that China is a threat to the West and action should be taken to halt its advance by strengthening the West's position in the face of the Chinese challenge.

But before coming to such conclusions Westerners first need to understand and accept that they do not hold all the aces and that the People's Republic of China has trumped the West in many aspects. If Westerners see China as a threat to our democracies and their liberties, then fine; but they need to think more deeply about what we are presenting as an alternative to the Chinese version of the future. The time when the West could assume that it was in a position of superiority from which it could lecture China about its aberrant behaviour is gone. Now is the time to react to China by developing a Western vision for the twenty-first century: one that does not simply repeat the mistakes of the past by dogmatically repeating the mantra that the Western way is automatically the best.

In order to do so, the West needs to understand clearly what China does and how it does it. Westerners need to evaluate the lessons of China's rise and its spreading global influence, drawing on the example of China's successful adaptation to Western hegemony. They need also to acknowledge weaknesses inherent in the

Western approach, such as the continued reliance on exploitative capitalism at the expense of developing countries. Westerners need to think whether there are any aspects of China's success which we can adapt to their own use, remaking them in their own image. They need to acknowledge that the Western way of doing things may not always be the only way, and that maybe – just maybe – China now does some things better.

Of course, both China and the West have their strengths and weaknesses. But it is only by understanding the differences between them and how they impact mutual relations that the West can construct for itself a more coherent response to the Chinese challenge. In the next two sections I will outline some advantages China has over the West which emerge from the nation's history and its present-day circumstances.

The impact of the past

This is not a history book. Its primary focus is on the present and future, not the past. Yet in order to understand the present and future it is necessary to acquire a solid understanding of how China and the West have arrived where they are today. Doing so demands an examination of the historical reasons underlying China's increasingly influential role on the global stage. Although it is not desirable to cover the entire complex sweep of Chinese history, understanding China today demands at least a brief look backwards.

From the fifteenth century onwards, Europeans fanned out across the world, exploring, conquering and colonizing. The renaissance and the industrial revolution provided Europeans with the scientific, technological and economic tools to dominate all other global regions. These included regions such as Asia in which other powers – India and China – had long been hegemonic. The dominance of the West forged an international system of nation states and free market capitalist economics based on colonialism, industry and the exploitation of natural resources.

In the mid-nineteenth century, Britain smashed the Chinese navy and sacked the emperor's Summer Palace in Beijing. At the point of a gun, the Chinese were forced to hand over Hong Kong and allow the British to sell opium. The Qing dynasty was irrevocably weakened and eventually collapsed in 1911.[23] Defeat at the hands of the British forced China to react to the Western-led system and to try to adapt to it as the Japanese had done during the Meiji restoration. However, initial Chinese efforts at adaptation were not as successful as those conducted by the Japanese. Most importantly, the first attempt to set up a republic after the collapse of the Qing dynasty in 1911 led to a period of chaos, Japanese occupation and civil war which was only resolved when the Chinese Communist Party (CCP) seized power in 1949.

In short, the actions of a few Europeans off the eastern coast of China had triggered the downfall of an empire which had endured for 2000 years. The attempt to establish a Chinese republic failed and China was divided into warring provinces. The Japanese saw their opportunity and invaded north-east China – Manchuria – in 1930. China had always assumed it was superior to Japan; now indignities were being heaped upon it by its relatively diminutive neighbour. The worst of all, in Chinese eyes, was the Nanjing massacre of 1937–8 in which between 50,000 and half a million Chinese – mostly civilians – died.[24] The Japanese were only expelled when they lost the Second World War.

Once the Japanese had been expelled, a civil war broke out between Chiang Kai-Shek's nationalist Guomindang (Nationalists) and Mao Zedong's communists. The two parties had cooperated in the struggle against the Japanese, but the departure of the Japanese had reopened a power vacuum and caused them to renew their entrenched opposition of the interwar years. In 1949, after four years of bitter conflict, Mao won and reunited the country under the new name of the People's Republic of China (PRC). Chiang fled to Taiwan with a million followers, including 300,00 troops, and a hoard of treasure and ancient artefacts.[25] There he installed the Republic of China (ROC). Since the ROC was still recognized internationally as the legitimate government of China, Taiwan was granted China's permanent seat on the United Nations Security Council. The seat was handed to the PRC only in 1971 after a vote in the UN, whereupon Taiwan was expelled from the organization.[26] In 1972, Nixon visited Beijing and a rapprochement of sorts took place between Washington and Beijing. Engineered by Henry Kissinger, the purpose of the rapprochement from the US perspective was to exploit an ideological split between Beijing and Moscow which had emerged in the late 1950s and solidified in the 1960s. The two sides would subsequently share intelligence about the Soviet Union and – at least for a while – form a wedge against it.[27]

By the 1970s, China was united but economically impoverished and in need of modernization. The Mao years (1949–76) were an era of upheaval and tragedy in which millions died, but also one in which China remained united, shook off many out-of-date customs (such as the foot-binding of women) and acquired nuclear weapons.[28] The Cultural Revolution (1966–76) was a destructive period in which many lives and cultural treasures were destroyed; but it was also a period which erased much of the past and created something like a tabula rasa for the state-led capitalist development which was – surprisingly – to follow under the rule of China's next president, Deng Xiaoping.

When Deng took power after the death of Mao, China was cut off from the world. The PRC's economy, neglected because of Mao's focus on perpetual revolution and class warfare, was in the doldrums.[29] Deng's view was that China above all needed economic development, no matter what it took to achieve it, including casting off Maoism. His pragmatism took the form of allowing previously unheard-of economic reforms, including foreign investment and individual entrepreneurship as a supplement to the traditional top-down approach of a socialist command economy.[30]

China's rise was rapid. From 1978, when Deng took control, until the early 2010s, China's economy, measured by GDP growth, expanded at an average of about 10 per cent per year.[31] China's ability to take foreign investment capital and generate vibrant industrial clusters resembled the economic 'miracles' which occurred after the Second World War in other East Asian countries such as Japan and South Korea. For instance, the Shenzhen Special Economic Zone (SEZ), set up in 1980, demonstrates the rapidity of development. A city with an official population of over 12 million people emerged from a county town of less than half a million to become a centre for the production of electronics and other goods for domestic and international markets.[32]

There have arguably been three stages in China's economic miracle, which has also inevitably included a transformation of society. The first was to accept the circumstance that China was economically weak and needed to learn from the West. This happened at the end of the 1970s and in the early 1980s. Then followed a period of adjustment and adaptation. From the late 1980s onwards, and particularly in the 1990s and 2000s, Chinese society and industry transformed, shifting from a command economy to a new model of political economy often called state capitalism. In the third decade of the twenty-first century, under Xi Jinping's leadership, China has reached a new stage: it is in the process of becoming an agent of change, taking advantage of shifting global currents to try to position itself as a global economic and industrial leader.

The 'century of humiliation' and the China dream

As the previous section demonstrates, China did not come to terms with the West's dominance overnight. Famously, in 1793 the Qianlong emperor rejected a British diplomatic mission seeking to open up China to trade.[33] The Qing emperors continued forlornly to resist change right up to the collapse of the dynasty in 1911. All in all, it took the Chinese over a hundred years to accept that their once great empire had been overtaken by the industrial and military might of European powers. The official term for this period of Chinese history is the 'century of national humiliation'. The concept was conceived in the 1920s and revived in the wake of the 1989 Tiananmen Square incident.[34] The century of national humiliation is officially defined as lasting from the beginning of the Opium Wars in 1839 to the founding of the People's Republic of China in 1949.

Even after that, China continued to go its own way, remaining sealed off for the most part from the rest of the world through the Mao years. The Chinese went through a long period of denial before they were ready to swallow the bitter pill: that they had been overtaken and needed to make radical changes. It was only with the accession to power of Deng Xiaoping in 1978–9 that the decision was finally made to emulate the economic methods that had made the West wealthy. Former US Secretary of State Henry Kissinger memorably describes hearing Deng express this intention during a 1979 banquet during a visit to Beijing: as Deng began to talk, the room fell silent as everybody pricked up their ears to listen to his startlingly radical – and Western-influenced – vision for China's future.[35] There followed an extended period of economic and social development which is still in progress today. Once this process is complete, China's leaders will be able to restore the Middle Kingdom to its former glories. Perhaps, in their minds, that time has already arrived.

China's traumatic history has – counter-intuitively – endowed it with some advantages. One of these is a strong collective motivation to revive what are now perceived as the glories of the past: the days when China had a powerful empire which was hegemonic in East Asia. It should be noted here that the Chinese have a relatively strong sense of collective cultural, racial and civilizational roots, which is permeated by ideational elements drawn from Confucian philosophy. The notion of having a shared history, language and heritage binds together the Han Chinese, who constitute about 90 per cent of the population.[36] The government's reinforcement of the Chinese sense of national collective identity with lessons about what is called the 'century of humiliation' at the hands of Europeans and the Japanese produces, as American scholar William Callahan points out, a potent *yin-yang* mix of optimistic and pessimistic elements. These drive contemporary Chinese nationalism and the desire to realize Xi Jinping's vision of renewed world-leading status.[37]

Understandably, China's turbulent history over the last two centuries has had a great impact on the collective national psyche. It has also provided fuel for the CCP's goal of restoring the nation to what it portrays as its rightful seat at the table of leading global powers. The CCP needs to mobilize the population behind its efforts at social transformation and economic progress. Contrary to stereotypes prevalent in the West, the Party cannot simply dictate to the people, but needs the tacit consent of most of the citizenry to sustain effective governance.[38] Thus, for decades the CCP's domestic public relations campaign in support of its policy goals has largely been based on the idea of China's collective experience of national humiliation at the hands of outsiders. This nationalistic propaganda – and the Chinese have no hesitation in labelling it as such – finds its way even into school textbooks in the form of what is called a 'patriotic education campaign'.[39]

The sense of common destiny and mythologized suffering generated by the 'patriotic education campaign' leads to a greater tendency to collectivism than in the West. It enables the government to use slogans such as the 'China dream' (*zhongguo meng*) to mobilize the Han Chinese citizenry in the service of the state. For instance, in the coronavirus crisis of 2020, Chinese people adhered to the rules of lockdown to an extent unimaginable in the West. As much as sections of the Western political class and media might wish otherwise, cases such as these owe as much to the Chinese people's notion of collective responsibility as to top-down enforcement. Indeed, research reveals that most Chinese people broadly support the government. As Bruce Dickson demonstrates in his rigorously quantitative and objective survey of Chinese public opinion carried out over several years, upwards of 70 per cent of the Chinese population are in favour of the goals presented to them by the Chinese state.[40]

Thus, Xi Jinping's 'China dream' needs to be understood in the context of China's complex history of a humiliating fall from grace and return to regional and global prominence. Most Han Chinese tend to buy into the dream – even if many of them may have private reservations – because they see its material benefits for themselves and for their nation. Their support for the common goals for development set by the Chinese government is underwritten by a drive to re-establish what they have been taught to see as China's historical right to global status and recognition.[41]

The West has now entered a similar process of denial to that experienced by the Chinese during the Qing dynasty. Long used to hegemony, it is difficult for Westerners to accept the idea that the centre of global economic gravity has shifted to Asia, and that geopolitical influence, still with the West, is steadily shifting eastwards too. Perhaps it is too much to hope that less than a hundred years pass before the West accepts that it is being overtaken and starts the process of adjustment and adaptation. Indeed, it would be a good idea to begin adjusting while China is still in the process of overtaking rather than when it is already hegemonic.

China's advantages

China has some innate advantages over the West. First, there is China's sheer size. With a population of 1.4 billion, competitive pressure produces not only a high statistical chance of multiple innovations but also takes place in an environment which has the inbuilt advantage of producing economies of scale. In other words, when you have a big marketplace with a lot of competition for consumers' wallets, volumes of sales can quickly go higher and both costs and prices are driven down. Many companies go out of business; but those that succeed have an almighty advantage in terms of their domestic base which serves as a good foundation for expansion into overseas markets. Kai-Fu Lee, who has held executive positions at Google, Microsoft and Apple, points out that China is becoming an 'AI superpower' thanks to the need for companies to adapt and innovate in order to meet the rapidly shifting demands of the Chinese market.[42]

Some will object to this assertion on reputational grounds. It is true that as Chinese companies go out into the world, they have trouble being accepted because of China's generally poor image, especially in the West. For instance, the Chinese company Huawei has been suspected of espionage through its 5G internet technology. The company's ability to implement 5G in Europe and the United States has been seriously impacted. By 2022, its share in the global smartphone marketplace had also severely declined.[43] Still, this is not the whole story: by 2021, as Chapter 6 will demonstrate, the Chinese smartphone manufacturer Transsion had acquired an almost 50 per cent share in the African market.[44]

At any rate, the mere fact that Chinese companies have penetrated global markets in numbers is a sign of things to come. Up to 2010 there were no Chinese companies with an international reputation. By 2020 there were at least six well-known ones: Huawei, Lenovo, Xiaomi, Alibaba, Tencent (owner of WeChat) and ByteDance (owner of TikTok). By 2030 there are likely to be exponentially more. They will reach prominence inexorably due to the advantages they gain from their base in the huge Chinese domestic market – and, of course, the support they receive from the Chinese state. As an example of what is possible, look at the case of TikTok: since Donald Trump attempted to ban it in the United States, it has gone from strength to strength, even if it continues to be the object of suspicion.[45] Indeed, as of 2022, TikTok is dominating the youth social media marketplace, forcing Instagram, YouTube and Facebook to revamp their platforms in an effort to compete. It may be a hard pill for Westerners to swallow, but US companies are changing their approach to keep up with the rapid growth of a Chinese competitor.[46]

In short, China's size, allied with the backing of the state and its ability to mobilize people, gives its commercial actors an advantage over all competitors except India, which has a similar population size. To be sure, India's population is still growing rapidly, while China's is beginning to decline.[47] However, India still lags developmentally and structurally far behind China. China can continue its rise because of its ability to mobilize its huge population behind national goals using the notions of national humiliation and the China dream. Drawing on the nation's history to motivate its people, the Chinese government has so far been able to turn its huge citizenry into an asset of unprecedented proportions.

Another important advantage China has over the West, unpleasant as it may be for Westerners to acknowledge, is continuity of governance under one party. China has been run by the CCP since 1949. For seven decades, the Party has developed sophisticated systems – political, economic and military – through which to maintain an iron grip on Chinese society. It has learnt lessons from the fall from power of communist parties in other countries – most notably Russia – and, despite outward appearances, evolved and adapted to domestic pressures and changing circumstances.[48] This gives China the advantage of stable, relatively consistent governance which has not been challenged by sudden changes of government in democratic elections or the coups experienced by many other autocratic countries.

Under Xi Jinping, the CCP's grip on power has been steadily tightened. Challenges to CCP rule are undermined before they even gather much momentum. Public opinion, allowed to flourish to an extent on the Chinese internet, is closely monitored and censored by squads of online observers. A 'fifty-cent army' of paid commentators pushes discussions in the direction the government prefers.[49] Discussions which are viewed as relatively harmless – even if they do not adhere to communist orthodoxy – are permitted to continue; but viewpoints which might be troublesome are quickly stamped out. Likewise, the media and academics are under close control and can propagate only views which adhere to Party orthodoxy. Debates can take place but must remain within the bounds of what the Party allows. Like it or not, this system of control gives China the advantage of a relatively stable governance structure untroubled by having to deal with extensive public debates expressing disagreement with official policy.

The CCP does not, unlike Western democracies, face democratic elections which could oust the Party from power. This gives the CCP the ability to plan long-term and to implement decisions which may be unpopular with significant sections of the population – such as the Uighurs, Tibetans, citizens of Hong Kong or the students in Tiananmen Square in 1989. Unpopular as they may be with some Chinese citizens and many Westerners, the decisions taken by Chinese leaders over the last four decades have arguably given China stability by promoting and maintaining state-led economic growth.

The CCP has also managed to overcome internal divisions – as in the Tiananmen massacre in 1989, where Deng Xiaoping took the decision to crack down on pro-democracy protestors as well as dissenters within his own administration – and maintain both control and legitimacy. Notably, unlike in almost all other autocratic countries, there have been no coups since 1949. There have undoubtedly been internal power shifts within the Party; but the CCP has always managed to right the ship and maintain control. Thus, China has avoided the sudden disruptions to governance and consequent instability experienced by many developing countries in Africa, Latin America, Central Asia and the Middle East. Yuen Yuen Ang argues that China manages this because it has a different type of autocratic regime: one which is responsive to public opinion, capable of adaptation and hence able to maintain the support of the majority of its citizens.[50] These characteristics generate a political stability which has allowed China to develop economically over four decades. It is also likely to permit China to continue expanding its influence worldwide – especially in the global South – for the foreseeable future.

Thus, this book's argument is that China has three significant advantages over the West which are enabling it to establish global influence – especially in the developing world – by implementing the goals of the Belt and Road Initiative (BRI). The first emerges from historical experience and the Party's 'patriotic education campaign': the shared vision (now called the China dream) of overcoming past humiliation and reclaiming China's leading position on the world stage. The second advantage is obtained from the country's sheer size, which gives it economies of scale and the ability to send its companies out to establish market share across the world. The third advantage is a stable governance system (whether one approves of it or not is irrelevant here) established over seven decades. These three advantages are not possessed in this specific combination by any other country on Earth. As China goes out into the world, investing and constructing under the umbrella of the Belt and Road Initiative (BRI), these three core advantages enable it to implement economic foreign policy relatively efficiently – at least compared to the West. As a result of better policy coordination and implementation, China gains a degree of influence in the developing world which is enabling it to leave the West behind.

If Western countries intend to compete with China, they need to understand and acknowledge this package of advantages. They should also study the relative success of the BRI in expanding Chinese influence (which I will examine in Chapters 5 and 6). By understanding how China has established its strengths, they will be better able to decide what they are going to do in response. There is no sense in falling back on repetitive and ill-founded criticisms of China amid expectations that it will change according to Western demands: it will not. As far as the West is concerned, the situation demands a coordinated, informed, well-thought-out response which takes China for what it is rather than what the West would wish it to be. Wishes are not horses – the West needs some steeds it can ride into the future, rather than a mismatched collection of fears and hopes.[51] Dependence on what ifs rather than a clear strategy of response is likely to lead only to the West continuing to decline relative to China.

How the West needs to react

Although it is important not to 'flatten' either China or the West by overgeneralizing, it is still necessary to draw out the shape of international affairs at a broad level. This can only be done by pointing out the overall trends and tendencies on each side of the China/West divide. While it is true that 'the West' is a somewhat unsatisfactory term since, for instance, Australia, New Zealand and Japan are not geographically in the west, it can still meaningfully be used to encompass the globally dominant countries which possess liberal democratic systems intertwined with free market capitalist economics. Although obviously 'the West' includes many different countries with different traditions and languages, it is still essential for the purposes of analysis to explain broad characteristics in order to draw out the contrast with China.

Accordingly, we can state that 'the West' now divides into two main camps. The first is the US-led one. This certainly includes Japan (where the United States has had military bases since the Second World War), and probably includes (despite some uncertainties during the Trump presidency) the UK, Canada, Australia and New Zealand. The second is the European sphere in which Germany and France take the lead in the EU (minus the Brexited UK). The Trump presidency revealed and deepened the divides between the United States and Europe, meaning, despite the existence of the North Atlantic Treaty Organization (NATO), that the EU is currently deciding its foreign policy without paying as much attention to the United States as previously. This means that the United States and the EU have not developed a clear and united China policy together. Ideally, they would cooperate on one; but the day when they might be able to coordinate that seems far away. Even within each bloc, the United States and the EU, there are many differences of opinion and approach between countries which undermine the development of a consistent and coherent approach to China.

In this section, I explain why I believe that there is somewhat more chance of the EU developing a strategy which actively engages with the challenge from China rather than seeking merely to oppose, constrain and undermine it. I also outline a rough framework for an adaptive approach to China which accounts for present circumstances rather than pointlessly trying to turn back the tide of time.

It is clear that – no matter who is president – the US government is going to take a securitized, zero-sum approach to China. For instance, the Biden administration's reaction to the 'Chinese spy balloon' scandal of February 2023 is a typical example of the US knee-jerk response to China.[52] Put simply, the Washington consensus is that China is a threat to US global dominance and there is only room for one kid on the block. Therefore, the United States will do its best to beat China down by a variety of means including trade sanctions and military posturing. During the Trump presidency, measures included the infamous trade war, moves to block Huawei's 5G networks and pressure in August 2020 on Chinese company ByteDance to sell the US version of its popular TikTok social media app to Microsoft.[53]

China, understanding the US approach only too well, tends to respond in kind. Beijing beefs up its military and tries to wrest control of the South China Sea, the Taiwan Straits and other coastal areas where it feels vulnerable. The Chinese government also does its best to increase influence and leverage in crucial partner states, for instance those that supply it with oil and gas such as Russia, Kazakhstan, Turkmenistan, Iran and Saudi Arabia. Since 2019, Chinese ambassadors in the West have been instructed to push back assertively by showing more 'fighting spirit' against criticism emanating from the countries in which they are located.[54] US trade tariffs on Chinese exports are met with tit-for-tat equivalent tariffs on US exports to China. Mutual suspicions thus overrule mutual need and possible cooperation on the environment, nuclear proliferation, trade and other issues. Tensions build, and both sides, while not actively seeking military conflict, prepare assiduously for that eventuality.

This is what the influential US international relations scholar John Mearsheimer calls 'the tragedy of great power politics', and what Harvard University's Graham Allison calls 'the Thucydides trap'.[55] In their view, a rising power is highly likely to end up in a military conflict with the top dog. Both will seek to end up top of the heap and the historical record shows that the result is usually (although not always) war.[56] Thus, according to these two senior scholars, there is a high probability of military conflict between the United States and China. This expectation is fed and maintained by the perception and portrayal of China as a threat. The assumption that China is not to be trusted and that war is likely feeds into a securitized approach to China which further fuels militarized build-up.

Such was the underlying assumption which formed the basis for China policy in both the Obama and Trump administrations. During his presidency, the liberal-leaning Obama unsurprisingly demonstrated a consistent suspicion of authoritarian China and generally sought to keep Beijing at arm's length. Thus, the Chinese correctly understood Obama's 'pivot to Asia' as an attempt to contain China.[57] Trump's trade war was a much more explicit attack on China, if only in economic form. Zero-sum thinking continues to be evident in US pressure on Huawei and TikTok. Given that President Joe Biden was Obama's Vice-President, there is little basis for the argument that the United States might take an approach to China that involves a higher degree of engagement. Since US public opinion towards China was increasingly negative during the Trump presidency there is little support for a US administration which would take a more cooperative approach: according to a survey conducted by the Pew Research Center, two-thirds of Americans have an unfavourable view of China.[58]

The EU, on the other hand, tends to be more conflicted. There are those who believe it is necessary to stand up to China in order to defend the EU's core values of human rights and democracy. In contrast, there are others who prioritize business interests and economic development: they hold that it is essential to engage with China.[59] This tug of war between the two main factions has led to a lack of clarity at the level of the EU, and even, in many cases, at the national level. The consequence has been, as in many other areas of policy, an absence of leadership and vision at the leadership level on the issue of what to do about China.

The European dithering does, however, leave the door open for the possibility of a coordinated China strategy which includes selective engagement as well as opposition. In fact, such has been the approach taken by some European countries, most notably Germany. While occasionally pausing to make a public point of criticizing China's human rights record, Angela Merkel led business delegations to China no fewer than twelve times during her chancellorship.[60] Chinese markets are crucial to German industry. German car manufacturers, for instance, are heavily dependent on Chinese sales, which continue to grow. Merkel's approach has been to classify China as both a 'strategic partner' and a 'competitor', but to refrain from labelling China – as the EU does – a 'systemic rival'.[61] This is important as far as Europe is concerned since Germany is the EU's single biggest economy. Although German foreign policy is not EU foreign policy, and thus not representative of the whole EU, it does reveal some understanding in elite Western European circles of the need to engage with China – albeit with a large pinch of hypocrisy, since Germany also continues to criticize China's human rights record.

While the United States seems incapable of admitting that it is no longer realistic to expect its president to attempt to direct global events from a pulpit in Washington, the Germans – and most other Europeans – have no such post-hegemonic hubris to overcome. Germany underwent a radical readjustment to its diminished place in the global order at the end of the Second World War and thus takes a pragmatic approach to foreign policy. Although the French, Spanish, Dutch and Portuguese had overseas empires, the decolonization process is now far enough in the past to mean that these countries are also pushed to take a pragmatic line into the future. With generally uncooperative Britain out of the picture after leaving the EU, there is arguably space for Europe to forge a more coordinated approach to China policy.

On the other hand, the contemporary European project has always involved a strong normative element. The European Union tends to see itself as a standard-bearer for human rights and democracy. This is a problem for engagement with China, which Europeans tend to identify above all as an autocratic abuser of human rights. Business interests and pragmatism conflict with European ideals and conscience. So how does Europe move forward in developing a China policy which adjusts to the reality of China's rise but does not end up sacrificing European idealism?

The coronavirus crisis has revealed that the European approach is often surprisingly uncoordinated. This creates a huge advantage for China. The EU therefore needs to address China's advantage by taking the Middle Kingdom's institutional, social and structural advantages seriously. The EU needs to study China's continued success in building up its economy, interests and influence, rather than dismissing the PRC as merely an evil communist state on the verge of collapse, as some commentators in the United States do.[62] Chinese scholars and leaders have closely studied the West for four decades – since Deng Xiaoping was appointed leader in 1978 – in order to cherry-pick what is useful for China.[63] The EU needs to do the same: pick out and apply specific elements of China's approach – such as state support for commercial actors, emphasis on collective interest and ability to mobilize the population in support of policy – in order to better compete with the Middle Kingdom. This may mean returning to Keynesian economics of top-down economic stimulus and more state control of assets vital to the national interest. Although this idea is not Chinese but Western in origin, it is one which the Chinese use consistently. In short, the EU would need to re-introduce the idea of strategic planning and proactivity in its approach to world affairs, rather than the generally ad hoc, reactive approach to economics and politics which has taken over in recent decades.

In its engagement with the developing world, Europe needs to study and learn from the Chinese case instead of dismissing it off-hand as incorrect or immoral. The at least partial success of the BRI in generating more Chinese influence in regions such as Southeast Asia, Central Asia, the Middle East and Africa reveals what the West should be doing: investing, or encouraging companies to invest, in the developing world through coordinated programmes, subsidized with corporate tax cuts or other incentives if necessary. Building up the economies and infrastructure of developing countries would address the problems of excessive migration and terrorism at source: if people see economic opportunities at home, they are far less likely to migrate or to turn to extreme solutions to their problems such as terrorism. A coordinated investment scheme would also generate more goodwill towards Europe and divert attention away from China's BRI. In the long term, investing in the global South can alleviate pressures on Europe such as massive influxes of migrants, and can produce economic benefits by building up new markets from which European companies can profit. Of course, this will take decades to achieve; but that is what long-term planning for the collective good is intended to do, as the Chinese well know. Indeed, the EU has an opportunity to coordinate investments in an altogether more transparent and effective way than China – which, after all, is still a developing economy – has so far managed.

Taking a leaf out of China's book, European countries need to collaborate and coordinate policy more closely. In the EU there needs to be more emphasis on collective action. This should include a complete rethink on the use of EU funds. Too much money has been spent on uncoordinated and unintegrated regional development containing a mass of small, disconnected projects. There needs to be a more integrated approach to transport infrastructure across the EU and beyond, for instance. Green energy and other environmentally friendly industries such as electric cars and recyclable packaging should be prioritized with a subsidized programme of investment. In the long term, it may be possible to create a profitable industry which can drive European economic growth through the remainder of the twenty-first century. At any rate, the climate emergency demands the attempt, as does the synergistic logic of identifying and exploiting an economic growth opportunity.

As regards the impact of Chinese companies in Europe, the EU needs to ensure that there is a consistent approach across the board instead of each country going it alone. This means developing a pan-European approach to investment from and trade with China. If it is deemed that Huawei's 5G networks are indeed a threat to European security, then there needs to be a coordinated approach to assessing foreign investment proposals in the EU. At present, the structures and systems in the EU are an obstacle to generating coordinated policy: for instance, having the EU presidency rotating between countries every six months only sows confusion as each country pushes its agendas for that period before handing over to the next. Without advocating any kind of swing to authoritarianism, a rethink of EU structures and processes is necessary to encourage more coordinated direction and decision-making.

Another option is for Europe to find ways to cooperate with China rather than trying to compete. This may prove difficult if China takes an uncooperative stance. Communication gaps and mutual suspicion are likely to undermine such efforts. In short, the prospects on this front do not look very promising. For this reason, it is probably best to assume that the optimum outcome that can be hoped for is that the EU and China find ways to put up with each other rather than allowing the situation to escalate into recriminations and confrontations such as the US-China trade war.

Overall, the optimum course would be for the West to reunite under one banner and develop a coordinated, collective approach to international affairs which will benefit the developing world as well. If this proves impossible due to US unwillingness to compromise, then, as I have suggested, the EU with urgency needs to find ways to pull together and utilize the potential of its collective strength. Europe needs to reconstruct its international image and establish a rival strategic initiative to the Chinese-led BRI. Europe's task is thus to establish what its vision is and then find ways to implement it. At the very least, a coordinated, coherent programme of long-term investment in the global South should be prioritized. This can generate genuinely win-win outcomes in terms of economic benefits and mutual goodwill.

As for the United States – well, it needs to adjust to a diminishment of its global power. This means adapting to a world in which other powers have enough influence to ensure that the United States cannot get what it wants merely by throwing its weight around and telling others what they should be doing. Conceding this point includes accepting that a powerful China is here to stay and that it would be better for the whole world to try to find ways to work with Beijing – as far as possible – rather than against it. But whether America is ready for such an adjustment of outlook – and what that would mean in practice when China and the United States seem unable to develop any degree of mutual trust – is highly uncertain. If competition continues, avoiding a US-China military conflict may be difficult. Noting this, it may end up being part of the EU's role to act as a middleman keeping the two combatants apart – and, normatively, to generate enthusiasm and create a blueprint for a new, more cooperative world order in which nations work together to solve common problems.

A complex world demands complex analysis

We are living through an era of dynamic and tumultuous change. Huge political, economic, cultural and environmental forces are in play, interacting with each other in complex ways which are difficult for the human mind to grasp. The size of the problems facing us is massive, their implications daunting. As the Covid-19 pandemic has demonstrated with its ability to disrupt what we consider our 'normal' lives, we are ant-like in the face of immense, impassive nature. Equally, economic phenomena such as the global financial crisis of 2007–8 – which was not predicted or prevented using standard economic models – show how we are at the mercy of complex man-made energies we do not fully understand. Sudden shifts in the political landscape – such as a change of leader or government after an election – can also bewilder us with their intensity and frequent unpredictability.

Straightforward analytical frameworks are therefore not sufficient to capture the energies which are shaping the future of our world in this time of transition. This means that using the language of linear causality – with its use of dependent and independent variables to try to show how *one* cause exerts *one* effect – does not do justice to the intersecting range of global impacts generating feedback effects and emergent phenomena. As Professor Emilian Kavalski has pointed out, linear thinking in the social sciences is outmoded: it is time for a new paradigm which fully accounts for complexity.[64] Just as Einstein replaced Newtonian physics with relativity theory, understanding international relations demands looking through a fresh lens: one which takes account of nonlinearity, unpredictability and risk. The complexity of our world demands answers based in a clear understanding of complexity itself. Such answers can be supplied using an analytical framework based on a combination of complexity theory (also sometimes called 'chaos theory') and analytic eclecticism – the idea that concepts from different theories can be used in a pick-and-mix fashion without assuming that they contradict each other.[65] It is also important to consider the idea of social evolution which has been developed by Professor Tang Shiping: the notion that human societies are subject to evolutionary forces similar to those which affect biological life.[66]

To avoid bogging the book down in an over-abundance of theoretical considerations, analytical concepts will be deployed at judicious intervals in the text where appropriate, using theories and concepts where they fit best, according to needs, rather than sticking to a single rigid analytical line.[67] For instance, when discussing the different approaches of Chinese and US leadership to global problems, we will refer to the concepts – taken from game theory – of zero – and positive-sum games. When studying the complex effects of unexpected events – such as pandemics or wars – and governments' responses to them, I will refer to the concepts of 'black swans' and 'grey rhinos': highly improbable events that can be anticipated and incorporated in strategic planning to at least a certain degree.[68] When examining the impacts of China's Belt and Road Initiative (BRI), we need to draw out not only the material impacts – economic, political, environmental – but also ideational ones, such as the effects of norm diffusion and normative power. In examining how the BRI is interpreted by publics in different parts of the world, we need to refer to the constructivist concept of identity being socially constructed.[69] When inspecting the differences between Chinese and Western leaders' approaches, we need to delve into the distinction between holistic patterns of strategic thought based on pragmatic principles (as in China) and those analytical ones based on breaking problems into their constituent parts (in the West).

The book's focus on pragmatism and complexity has direct parallels in the Chinese state-led approach to economic development. As Yuen Yuen Ang has demonstrated convincingly in her award-winning book *How China Escaped the Poverty Trap*, the Chinese are prepared to make adjustments on the fly as needs and circumstances demand. The government does not demand that companies and investors stick to a fixed approach imposed from above. Instead, it asks that they develop an approach which achieves the desired goals while avoiding descending into chaos. Thus, Chinese individuals and commercial actors are permitted flexibility within certain limits. This experimental but pragmatic and delimited approach generates outcomes which Deng Xiaoping called 'crossing the river by feeling the stones' and which Ang, using a term derived from complexity theory, calls 'co-evolution'.[70]

Jonathan Fenby sees the Chinese government as inflexible and incapable of using new ways of thinking to approach the problems of the twenty-first century.[71] However, Ang shows that it is not the case that the Chinese domestic political economy is incapable of adaptation to changing circumstances. In the last four decades, the Chinese government has used directed improvisation and influence rather than control to allow its many actors in cities and provinces to discover unconventional routes to economic development.[72] David Shambaugh also wrote an authoritative study of Chinese leaders' adaptation to circumstances while retaining the same political structures.[73] This process continues under Xi, but with further evolution in the development process, varying across specific locations according to circumstances. Thus, China's political economic system is not as monolithic and rigid as it appears to Western observers looking from the outside. It is adaptive and evolving, incorporating complex change in ways which we in the West are often slow to recognize. In short, Chinese leaders recognize that they must adapt to the transformation of our world by turning China into a catalyst of change rather than passively waiting to see what happens.

The remainder of the book is organized as follows. Chapter 2 outlines the complex characteristics of our era of global transformation with which we need to grapple – and why China is better equipped than the West to face the coming huge challenges which humanity will encounter, especially in terms of development in the global South. Chapter 3 compares the present circumstances of the United States, the EU and China in three aspects: economic development, political systems and security arrangements, within the context of the complex historical processes affecting each actor and the world. Chapters 4–6 focus on the Belt and Road Initiative (BRI) as a vehicle for the expansion of Chinese economic activity and political influence in the global South, outlining its characteristics and evolution. Chapter 4 examines at a broad level the role of President Xi Jinping's Belt and Road Initiative (BRI) in China's emergent global expansion in terms of both material and ideational impacts. Chapter 5 delves into the detail of China's relations with its economically developing neighbours in Central Asia, South Asia and Southeast Asia, and the implementation of the BRI in those countries. Chapter 6 moves on to the implementation and impacts of the BRI in the rest of the developing world, specifically Africa, Latin America, the Middle East, Central and Eastern Europe, and the Pacific islands. Chapter 7, the concluding chapter, summarizes the book's main arguments concerning China and the West's respective strengths and weaknesses, especially concerning international development. It charts the ways in which China will play a leading role in the developing world, before explaining how the West should adapt and react – if it can.

Chapter 2

CHINA, AGENT OF CHANGE

When my wife and I first visited Beijing in the summer of 1999, we were struck by the proliferation of bicycles and the relatively low number of cars. Hundreds of cyclists swept sedately along designated cycle lanes in close proximity to each other, maintaining the same speed as their neighbours to avoid bumping into each other. Occasionally there were collisions and spills at stop lights, but the general impression was of calm, coordinated pedalling along wide boulevards. A few cars rolled along the roads, often black and with opaque windows which concealed the occupants: these were generally used by Party members, supposedly on official business.

When we returned in 2008 shortly before the Beijing Olympics began, we were amazed to find that cars now dominated the city's road system. In fact, they were clogging up the brand new six-lane highways: traffic jams were now standard. Once when we took a taxi from one side of Beijing to the other, we got stuck in traffic for over an hour and barely caught our train: the subway would have been quicker. By this time, while bicycles were still present in considerable numbers, they were no longer the primary form of urban transport and were used mainly for getting to and from subway stations. Cars were now of similar types to those in the West: older models had disappeared from the roads entirely.

The shift from rusty old bikes to modern cars was a step forward technologically. As such, it was a necessary developmental step in a modernizing economy. But it was also a step which had clearly brought with it new problems: traffic jams and pollution. The pace at which these problems had appeared was staggering: a complete paradigm shift in just nine years. The switch from bicycles to cars as Beijing's main form of transport was indicative of the complex changes hitting Chinese society in an extremely compressed period.

From 2009 to 2010 we worked at a state university in the west of Beijing. My wife and I lived in a building which also served as accommodation for students. The students lived modestly, eating cheaply in the cafeteria on campus and rarely going out to eat or shop. They seemed to have little spare money for consumer products. They lived spartan lives by Western standards, sleeping four or six to a single-sex dorm room with rudimentary furnishings, but did not complain. In fact, they usually expressed gratitude for being allowed to come to Beijing to study at a prestigious university.

When we returned for a second stint at the same university from 2013 to 2015, we discovered that there had been a remarkable change in student lifestyles during the three intervening years. Delivery motorbikes pulled up outside the students' dormitories and disgorged mounds of packages from wheeled containers they towed behind them. Judging by the piles of discarded boxes we noticed cluttering the dustbins and stairwells each day, students were now able to buy goods ranging from computer monitors to mobile phones and other high-tech or high-value consumer goods. In just three years, the students' economic fortunes and expectations of their lives at university had clearly been utterly transformed.

These two stories – about changes in transport and students' lives – are just two small illustrations of the rapid developments which have occurred in China in the last few decades. They also show how the Chinese are able to adjust to such changes – and the complex modern world which comes with them – with startling rapidity. Indeed, the changes have been so rapid that from lagging far behind the West in every way in the 1990s China has now moved ahead in some areas. For instance, many Chinese have never owned credit or debit cards. Instead, they have bypassed the bank card phase of economic development to go straight to mobile phone payments. These are now so prevalent in China that you can buy vegetables in the market with your phone. For some transactions, it is no longer possible to use cash at all. China has completely hopped over a developmental stage in the history of financial transactions – bank cards – that has lingered in the West for half a century.

Over the last two centuries, the Chinese have got used to adjusting to rapid changes and sudden historical shifts. Around the beginning of the nineteenth century, Napoleon is apocryphally supposed to have referred to China as a sleeping giant which would shake the world when it was prodded awake.[1] Fortunately for the West, the Qing empire continued to doze through the industrial revolution, ignoring signs that modernization was necessary. When it collapsed in 1911, China collapsed with it. Chaos ensued as warlords ruled and the Japanese invaded and occupied large parts of China for over a decade. At the end of the Second World War, after the Japanese were expelled from China, a bitter civil war resulted in the victory of the Communist Party in 1949.[2]

Under Chairman Mao there were wrenching attempts at transformation of Chinese industry and society. First, there was the Great Leap Forward of 1958–62, in which millions died of famine as a result of an ill-conceived attempt to produce steel instead of food. Then there was the Cultural Revolution, in which the rich and intellectuals were persecuted, and most relics of historical China were destroyed. Upheaval followed upon upheaval in what Mao intended to be a perpetual people's revolution.[3]

Mao's death in 1976 changed everything again. Deng Xiaoping decided to focus on economic rather than political or cultural goals in order to construct a new, prosperous China. He guided the nation to capitalist industrial production based on investment. Hundreds of millions of peasants moved from the country to cities in search of better wages in China's new factories. New urban conglomerations such as the city of Shenzhen emerged within decades from the former site of rice paddies. China is unarguably still in the midst of a rapid economic transformation that has forced its people to be flexible in the face of extraordinary changes in Chinese society.

Such drastic shifts and alterations to the landscape of China – both physical and immaterial – mean that all present generations of Chinese, from teenagers to pensioners, are mentally adjusted to rapid change. They are used to living in a system with characteristics which emerge from the complex – and often seemingly contradictory – interaction of various phenomena which arise in conjunction with rapid economic shifts. Many have experienced both grinding poverty in the countryside and relative comfort in the cities to which they migrated for work. They have seen fishing villages turn into megacities within a generation. They have witnessed the destruction of traditional dwellings and the construction of fantastic new skyscrapers. They are prepared to face more of the same. They have good reason to believe that their rulers are able, despite wrenching shifts and disruptions to many people's lives, to maintain order and react to the changes in a remarkably orderly fashion. This even holds true for the Covid-19 pandemic. Despite early mistakes, stringent lockdowns, problems with the vaccination programme, then mass protests and a sudden loosening of restrictions in late 2022 leading to a rapid surge in infections, the majority respect for Xi Jinping appears to have held fast.[4] In a nation of 1.4 billion people, that is a remarkable achievement – and one which it is not surprising that the West finds it difficult to grasp. So, undoubtedly, do the Chinese – but since they live in a China which has been transformed beyond all recognition, they have been forced to embrace change rather than resist it.

Since the late 1990s, Chinese companies, many of which have maxed out their domestic market, have been expanding outwards into the world. The Chinese reaction to 'great changes unseen in a century' – which, since 2018, is the official interpretation of events within and outside China – is to embrace domestic and global economic shifts. China, for decades the world's workshop, is rapidly transforming into a leader in high-tech industries such as computing and mobile phones. The aim is to find ways to take advantage of the situation in whatever way possible and boost Chinese economic fortunes further.

This is where Xi Jinping's Belt and Road Initiative (or BRI) comes into the picture. It is an attempt to address three connected problems – outlined below – in one fell swoop, with a single integrated strategy based on a keen understanding of the interrelatedness of complex economic phenomena.[5] All three problems – and their accompanying solutions – relate to China's rapid economic growth since the late 1970s. Growth needs to be sustained in order to legitimize the continuing rule of the Chinese Communist Party. And, like other rising powers before it – such as the Roman or British empires – China needs to expand outwards into the world to sustain its growth.

The first problem facing China is that the nation has more companies than demand for their services, especially in construction. This is what is known as excess industrial capacity – more firms than the Chinese domestic market needs. The solution is to channel the excess industrial capacity overseas.[6] This helps to alleviate some of the pressure inside China's domestic economy, preventing it from overheating. The BRI does this by attempting to create new markets for Chinese firms to exploit. It especially focuses on the developing world, whose economic potential has long been ignored by the West.

Second, Chinese economic growth is slowing. The BRI supports China's continued drive to sustain growth by generating profits from commercial activity outside China. There are many emerging economies – developing countries – which lack funds but are desperately in need of investment and infrastructure. Their markets are small, their consumers short of disposable income. They lack energy, roads, ports, hospitals and railways. China kills two birds with one stone by granting loans to impoverished countries to fund infrastructure construction by Chinese companies, the same ones which had been encouraged to 'go out'. Chinese investment capital circulates from Chinese state-run financial institutions – such as Exim Bank – through the foreign government and into the coffers of Chinese construction companies, who obtain contracts to build new projects. The side effect is that the partner country runs up a debt that it has to pay back but hopes it will be able to fund using its newly acquired infrastructure to increase economic activity. Whatever happens, Chinese money ends up back in Chinese pockets, and Chinese companies get work. At the same time, Chinese business interests get established in the partner country, giving China long-term commercial opportunities as the partner – hopefully – develops its economy.

Third, China is simultaneously short of resources and friends. The BRI allows China to pursue a long-term strategy of steady global expansion, increased influence in partner countries and resource acquisition. Lending to emerging economies creates dependencies on China, particularly in countries which find it difficult to obtain funds elsewhere. Examples include oil-producing nations which have been generally shunned by the West, such as Angola, Sudan or Iran. Such dependencies can be transformed into leverage – influence – over the government of said country, enabling China to obtain favours or do deals which benefit China. These may include steady energy imports from the Persian Gulf, Central Asia or Africa, sometimes at a lower price. Thus, the BRI – which is often portrayed as a purely economic initiative – also has political aspects related to influence, especially in the global South. Essentially, Xi Jinping's flagship foreign policy initiative combines economic and political aims in the pursuit of increased Chinese leverage in the developing countries and regions where the BRI is being implemented in the service of China's national economic security.[7] At the same time, China obtains supplies of energy and other resources to fuel its economic growth.

We will examine the impacts of the BRI in more depth and detail in Chapters 4–6. In the meantime, let us look at some of the foundational aspects of China's rise which contribute to the nation's emerging role as an agent of change in our era of increasing global disruption and transformation.

'Great changes unseen in a century' – and other slogans

The Chinese love colourful proverbs and slogans. Since the foundation of the PRC in 1949, the Chinese Communist Party (CCP) has been happy to supply them. Each president needs to create an identity for himself. Attaching new slogans to his presidency allows each man – Chinese presidents have inevitably always been men – to differentiate his regime from his predecessor's and to communicate a vision for China's future. Although there are ongoing debates about the meaning and substance of leaders' slogans, there is little doubt that they have exerted extraordinary influence over the development of China under the rule of the Communist Party. In China, as elsewhere, words can be a form of action, transforming people's lives by introducing new practices, both discursive and non-discursive.[8] Coming from Chinese leaders, who are granted great influence by their position at the head of the Party and the political structure, short snippets of language, when reiterated in speeches and reproduced on posters around the country, acquire the power to change the course of history.

In 1956, Mao Zedong decided to 'let a hundred flowers bloom', encouraging intellectuals to express their opinions. He later changed his mind and cracked down on dissidents who had dared to challenge his wisdom.[9] He also exhorted Chinese people to 'dare to think, dare to act' and to 'smash the four olds': old ideas, old culture, old customs and old habits.[10] Such slogans represent the Maoist principle of perpetual revolution. This brought disastrous consequences during the Cultural Revolution of 1966–76, when youthful Red Guards were encouraged to destroy anything which smacked of tradition, including its human representatives such as landlords and intellectuals. Although wantonly cruel and inhuman, the destruction of the Maoist era did at least create something like a tabula rasa upon which Mao's successor, Deng Xiaoping, could build a new version of China.

Deng Xiaoping, who took power in 1978, became known for a range of striking proverb-like sayings. One of the most famous is 'crossing the river by feeling for the stones', by which he meant that Chinese companies should experiment with different approaches until they hit upon one that would work. He also said that China should 'hide its light and bide its time' – in Chinese, *taoguang yanghui* – meaning that China should be patient rather than assertive in foreign affairs until the nation had built up its strength.[11] He is also supposed to have said that 'it doesn't matter if a cat is black or white as long as it catches mice'. This slogan was used to reconcile the apparent contradiction in China's use of Western investments and a state-backed version of free market capitalism while still retaining an authoritarian political system based on Marxism-Leninism.

For Hu Jintao, who was appointed president in 2002, there were slogans derived from Confucianism such as 'peaceful development' and 'harmonious world'. There was also the rather vague notion of 'actively accomplishing something'.[12] These slogans sounded nice, relatively harmless and – even if empty of substance – were supposed to serve as an antidote to the idea, prevalent in the West, that China's rise represents a threat to regional and world peace.[13] Hu's presidency thus became associated with the *tianxia* school of thought, chiefly espoused by the philosopher Zhao Tingyang.[14] Based on traditional Confucian ideas about social harmony, *tianxia* claims that a peaceful world can arise by overcoming differences between nations and establishing government through a world institution. Although controversial because of the implication that the world should learn to live by Chinese example – and possibly under Chinese leadership[15] – *tianxia* represents an attempt at applying Chinese traditional thought to contemporary global problems.

Upon becoming president in 2012, Xi Jinping put forward the idea of a 'China dream'. This slogan connects personal and national prosperity to create a patriotic goal based on Chinese people's efforts to build better lives for their families. The 'China dream' thus connects to Deng's economic miracle by presenting a further justification for wealth generation based on capitalism: to make China rich and influential in the world.

Connected to the China dream – as well as *tianxia* theory – is Xi's call for a 'community of shared destiny' or 'community of shared interests'.[16] Although seemingly vague, the 'community of shared destiny/interests' slogan has been used with regard to China's cooperation with other countries through regional platforms such as the Forum for China-Africa Cooperation (FOCAC) and the China-Arab States Cooperation Forum (CASCF).[17] In a speech promoting the CASCF, Xi also talked of young Arab men becoming the embodiment of 'a perfect combination of the China dream and the Arab dream'.[18] These ideas are also connected to the Belt and Road Initiative (BRI), Xi's vision for a vast trade network based on Chinese investment and infrastructure building. The 'community of shared interests/destiny' slogan thus communicates the idea that China can construct and lead regional groupings of nations which do not depend on the United States or the West for their funding or organization. Such slogans represent a major shift from the cautiousness of the Deng era in terms of their vision of an active global role for China.

Xi is also known for promoting a new confidence and assertiveness for China represented by the slogan 'great changes unseen in a century'.[19] Rush Doshi, who works as Director for China in the US National Security Council under the Biden administration, claims that the 'great changes' slogan is a reaction to what Chinese experts justifiably believe to be the ongoing decline of US power.[20] In this interpretation, endorsed by some influential Chinese scholars, the slogan suggests that an inflexion point in global affairs has been reached.[21] From this point on, China is destined to take over from the United States as the predominant global power. Li Jie, a colonel in the PLA Navy's Military Academy, puts it like this:

> The volatility of the international situation has increased, and instability, uncertainty, and unpredictability have become the norm … In the face of great changes, contradictions within the Western camp … are developing. There is a sharp contrast between the rule of China and the chaos in the world.[22]

The 'great changes' and 'actively accomplish something' slogans are therefore intended to convey the message that China is ready to displace the failing United States and become the leader of a new international order.

However, there is another aspect to the 'great changes unseen in a century' slogan, beyond just a transfer of power from one hegemon to another: the idea that a momentous transformation in global affairs is occurring. Politically and economically a transition is in progress because of the rise of Asian countries and the relative decline of the West – but there is also a need to plan for drastic environmental shifts such as climate change and global warming. While the slogan 'great changes unseen in a century' recalls the political state of the world one hundred years ago when the First World War shook the international order, and the United States was forced to emerge from its international isolation to take a leading role, it also refers to the need to address the emerging environmental and economic crises. As in 1919, there will be a need for a new vision for international political structures – but this time also environmental sustainability and the global economy. There will be shifts in the global balance of power, the structure of international trade and commerce, as well as inevitable further impacts from global warming and climate change. Changes will also emerge from the historical shift of the global centre of gravity from the West to the East – from Europe and the United States to Asia.

The 'great changes unseen in a century' slogan, in addition to indicating a new assertiveness, is thus meant to point out that China is better equipped to take advantage of complex global shifts than the West due to its geographical position in Asia and supposedly unique Chinese characteristics which the West simply does not possess. Accordingly, the 'great changes' slogan *does* refer to China displacing the United States; but it *also* indicates China's readiness to shoulder the responsibility of giving shape to the future of world history. In Xi's vision, the emerging global transformation demands a new, Chinese-led approach to world affairs since the existing Western-created international order does not appear to be flexible enough to cope with the emerging shifts.

In short, Xi's 'great changes unseen in a century' slogan addresses the idea that China is intending to take charge of world affairs. It implies that China believes that the United States is in decline as the dominant global power and that it is China's destiny to replace it. However, it also addresses the need for a new approach which takes account of the complex interaction of a range of emerging problems which are going to affect the whole world. In the coming two sections, we will examine the interlocking web of issues facing humanity and the characteristics China possesses which may allow it to address the contradictions and complexity of our era of global transition better than the United States or the EU. In the chapter's final section, I argue that even if China is unable to direct the path of the coming global juggernaut of change (in truth, which single country could?), it will still be the driving force of transition due to its pivotal role in twenty-first-century international affairs.

China: master of contradiction?

In classical Western (European) logic, contradiction is a problem. Western thinking tends to focus on binaries: if one thing is true, the opposite cannot also be the case. In fact, the principle of binary exclusion is a very powerful analytical tool which has allowed scientists, since the time of Aristotle, to categorize by evaluating what a thing is and is not through comparison with another thing. Using this approach has generated some of the greatest innovations of Western science. Not least among them is modern computing with its use of the simple binary digits '0' and '1' to generate calculations of huge complexity and life-like simulations containing extraordinary levels of detail.[23]

At the same time, using classical logic we tend to assume that if one situation pertains, another situation with very different – even opposed – characteristics cannot simultaneously exist. Finding evidence for situation 'a' disproves the possibility of 'b'. If independent variable 'x' is the direct cause of event 'y', then independent variable 'z' cannot also be a contributing factor. If a light particle is in one place, it cannot be in another. If a cat is black, it cannot also be white. So far, so straightforward.

Unfortunately, scientists have discovered that binary exclusion does not always accurately describe physical states in the material world – or immaterial states inherent in human affairs. In the natural sciences, quantum physics has demonstrated that apparently contradictory situations turn out to be not necessarily true. According to experimental results, light can apparently be both a particle and a wave and a single particle can appear in two places at the same time. Quantum uncertainty is a principle which shows that it is a fundamental characteristic of the universe that we cannot predict outcomes from the precise measuring of initial conditions. These findings, which have been used in the development of real-world technologies such as nuclear fission, are difficult for us to grasp because our brains do not like uncertainty and tend towards the binary exclusion principle which neatly packages information into 'yes' and 'no' categories.[24]

In an important sense the Western focus on logical contradiction limits our thinking by persuading us that two apparently contradictory situations cannot exist at the same time. This is a useful limitation for the purposes of scientific research. However, it tends to blind us to the complexity inherent in human social affairs. Interestingly, while contradiction is problematic for the standard Aristotelian logic which has dominated Western thinking since the Middle Ages, it is accepted and encompassed within Marxism and traditional Chinese philosophy. Marxist dialectics – derived from the work of Hegel – is based on the idea that two opposed ideas – a thesis and antithesis – can be reconciled and synthesized. It focuses on relations between ideas rather than the semantics of a single isolated proposition. In this, there are similarities between Marxist dialectics and the traditional Chinese concept of *yin-yang*, which focuses on contradictions between contrary forces.[25] Conceiving of phenomena as having *yin* (dark) and *yang* (light) properties means that apparently oppositional forces can be understood as complementary, interconnected and interdependent. In Chinese thought, there can be relational links between contradictory states or entities which transcend their discrete properties. Indeed, the Chinese scholar Qin Yaqing has demonstrated that Chinese thought about dialectics and relationships can bring a very different perspective to bear on international relations (IR) than those familiar to Westerners.[26]

While it is certainly not the case that Chinese people are all skilled logicians conversant in the nuances of Marxist dialectics and traditional Chinese philosophy, a casual familiarity with the idea of potential relational harmony between opposites generates a very different approach to the natural and social worlds than that in Aristotelian logic or Cartesian reasoning.[27] For Descartes, the assumption of dualism led to the separation of body and mind. In Descartes's most famous thought experiment, he concluded that 'body' and 'mind' are discrete entities. This means that they can exist independently of each other. The mind is not dependent on the body and is separate from it, as asserted in the proposition 'I think, therefore I am', which identifies human identity with thoughts and omits to mention the body. The problem with Cartesian dualism is that modern neuroscience has established beyond reasonable doubt that in humans the functioning of body and mind is intertwined and interdependent.[28] For instance, the thoughts and emotions of the human brain are influenced by complex physical processes within the body arising from entities such as hormones, sugars and even gut bacteria.[29] Thus, like Aristotelian logic, Cartesian dualism is incompatible with the findings of modern science concerning the complex intertwining of mental and physical processes. This leads us to the conclusion that the tendency to binary exclusion inherent in traditional Western logic and reasoning is not satisfactory or sufficient for understanding apparent contradictions in phenomena.[30]

Marxist dialectics and *yin-yang* theory, whatever deficiencies they may have, do at the very least present alternative methods for approaching contradiction which are not necessarily at odds with modern science. Chinese Communist Party (CCP) elites are familiar with both traditional Chinese thought and Marxist dialectics, having received education in both.[31] The supposed hard-line Communist Mao famously read classics of Chinese and Western philosophy in his youth and was influenced by both.[32] Significantly, Mao constantly repeated that 'the world would not remain static; contradiction and disequilibrium were a law of nature.'[33]

While Chinese leaders probably do not consciously combine Marxism and the *yin-yang* concept, the simple fact that they do not view the world through Aristotelian or Cartesian binary logic based on contradiction, exclusion and discreteness means that they are more flexible than Westerners when it comes to reconciling and combining apparently opposed ideas and information.[34] For instance, for many economists and political scientists versed in Western logic, capitalism and communism appear mutually irreconcilable, leading to the expectation that they cannot co-exist; yet a version of capitalist economics has been applied in China since the 1980s while the political system has remained stubbornly authoritarian under the leadership of the CCP. For David Shambaugh this is 'atrophy and adaptation', while for Minxin Pei it is a 'trapped transition': the expectation is that the contradiction must eventually resolve through the collapse of either CCP rule or China's economic model.[35] Yet although supposedly fragile due to internal contradiction, China's model of 'red capitalism' has endured – and flourished – for four decades so far without signs of imminent internal disintegration.[36] In no small part this is due to the refusal of Chinese leaders to accept the Western teaching that Leninist authoritarianism cannot co-exist with a modified form of state-backed capitalism.

Similarly, Xi Jinping's 'China dream' slogan is an attempt to reconcile contradictory tendencies in Chinese society. In a capitalist market economy – even one in which the state intervenes often, as in China – the individual is encouraged above all to strive for personal wealth. The selfish goal of making oneself rich provides the energy that drives the model. Unfortunately, this self-interest inherent in capitalism clashes with the idea of collective good promoted by communism. It also undermines the idea of patriotic support for the nation: if an individual is focused on generating personal income, they are not thinking about the national interest. Even if it is not wholly convincing, Xi's 'China dream' rhetoric is an attempt to solve the contradiction between self-interest and the collective, between accumulating personal wealth and nation-building. The China dream is a conscious attempt to create a dialectical synthesis between the opposed thesis and antithesis of selfish gain and the collective good.

Chinese approaches to policymaking since the Deng era demonstrate both pragmatism and an ability to utilize concepts eclectically from theories or schools of thought which are usually considered to be in contradiction with one another.[37] There are many factors forcing them to do so as they strive to consolidate political control over a country of 1.4 billion people. They aim to generate continued economic growth while maintaining political and social stability ('harmony'). They need to balance ever-increasing demands for energy production with the need to mitigate or reduce environmental deterioration. They must ensure that top-down control does not impede the necessary delegation of on-the-spot decision-making to provincial administrators and company directors. They seek to expand China's influence abroad while minimizing the risk of involvement in regional conflicts. They try to introduce elements drawn from the Chinese experience to the organization of global affairs without this being interpreted as an attempt to overthrow the existing international system based on Western ideas. Domestically, they have been trying to square the circle of ensuring continued economic growth while gradually deflating the bubble in house prices which has blown up over several decades.[38]

It may surprise those who assume that the CCP's autocratic political structure is inflexible and slow to adapt that, despite frequent missteps, China's communist elites have frequently demonstrated the capacity to react decisively to changing circumstances by adjusting policy to match the demands of specific situations. The altogether unexpected switch from a command to a capitalist economy during the 1980s was something which took Western observers by surprise, but which has so far worked out to China's advantage. The decision was based on Deng Xiaoping's conclusion that the application of capitalist economics to China would produce better results than Marxist economics, even though such reasoning stood in direct contradiction to the teachings of Karl Marx. Taking the decision to introduce capitalist market economics to the CCP-led People's Republic of China demonstrates a willingness to meet contradiction head on and to try to resolve it for the benefit of national development, even at the expense of what Westerners would regard as standard logic and consistency.[39]

As we saw in the previous chapter, another contradiction emerges from Chinese understandings of China as both a historically great empire and as a victim of humiliation at the hands of foreigners. In his book *China: The Pessoptimist Nation*, William Callahan analyses the CCP's use of China's 'century of humiliation' to motivate people to work towards the national goal of restoring national glory.[40] Chinese people's interpretation of their national destiny emerges from the contradiction of simultaneously experienced inferiority and superiority complexes: inferiority to the victorious West, and superiority to all foreigners. This contradiction can only be resolved when China returns to its 'rightful' place at the head of the global table. Nevertheless, by using a narrative of humiliation and restoration of status, the CCP has rather cleverly managed to resolve a dialectical contradiction by using it to motivate people in the service of national growth goals.

Like other great powers, China also struggles to deal with numerous contradictions in its foreign policy. Sometimes Beijing falls short of navigating such contradictions convincingly. For instance, China's expansionist island-building and the use of coastguard vessels to bully other actors into compliance in the South China Sea contradict the long-term declared policies of 'peaceful development' and 'harmonious' relations with neighbouring countries. The use of coastguards to expand and defend territory creates a 'grey zone', 'blurring the line between military and nonmilitary actions and the attribution of events'.[41] Still, even amid such apparent contradiction, China's officials have made a conscious effort to reconcile what would seem to be irreconcilable. The official Chinese military strategy – according to a 2015 defence white paper – is 'active defence'. The white paper states that 'We will not attack unless we are attacked, but we will surely counterattack if attacked.'[42] The policy of 'active defence' is another clear attempt to generate dialectical synthesis from a contradiction.

In the South China Sea, 'active defence' consists of the Chinese People's Liberation Army Navy (PLAN) constantly pushing to the limits of international law. The PLAN seeks to expand Chinese territory without provoking outright war, using pressure to the maximum extent it can get away with. This strategy, dubbed 'salami slicing' or the 'grey zone' in the West, is known as a 'cabbage strategy' in China: wrapping islands in cabbage-like layers, beginning at the closest point with fishing boats, behind which are coastguard ships, and finally naval vessels.[43] Since a deadly clash with Vietnam in 1988 over Johnson South Reef, which China won, the People's Liberation Army Navy (PLAN) admirals have been careful to ensure that they do not cross the line into outright invasion of another country's occupied territory.[44] During the first two decades of the twenty-first century, the PLAN has managed not to overstep an imaginary line which would permit territorial disputes in the South China Sea to escalate into full-blown crisis. The contradiction between military assertiveness and peaceful development is not exactly resolved, but it is contained within barely legal limits of international sovereignty law that are sustainable – at least as far as China is concerned.

In contrast, the United States tends to lack pragmatic and rhetorical strategies for working round contradictions in its foreign policy. America also lacks self-awareness about the contradictions between what it says it is going to do and what it actually does. For instance, the United States sees itself as a standard-bearer for democracy. Yet there are well-known historical cases where US operatives have actively sought to overthrow governments – some of them democratically elected – if their policies did not suit US interests, most notably in Latin America.[45] The United States also continues to support an autocratic regime in Saudi Arabia with no substantive attempt to promote democratization in the country. Attempts to establish fledgling democracies in Afghanistan and Iraq have been half-hearted, with little attempt to build sustainable institutions. Claims to be the defender of the 'liberal international order' and 'freedom' ring hollow when American national interests are clearly being prioritized. Even if some see through the hypocritical veneer to the hard kernel of cynical self-interest beneath,[46] the inherent contradiction between what is said and what is done in US foreign policy remains publicly unacknowledged and unjustified.

Another important contradiction in US foreign policy relates to China itself. In 1972, Nixon surprisingly visited China to exploit the divide – the so-called Sino-Soviet split – that had appeared between the PRC and the Soviet Union. The aim of Nixon's meeting with Mao was to build better relations between the United States and China, in the process reducing the possibility of a rapprochement between the Chinese and the Soviets. This step was intended, in part at least, to weaken the spread of world communism. Meanwhile, the United Nations voted to hand the Chinese seat on the Security Council (UNSC), which from 1949 to 1971 had been filled by Taiwan, to the PRC.[47] Taiwan was not only kicked off the UNSC but was excluded from the UN altogether. Henceforth, the 'One China' policy officially accepted by the United States and the UN stated that Taiwan was a part of China and not an independent state.[48] Hence, since it did not have official status as a nation state, it could not participate in the proceedings of the UN as an ordinary member. In one fell swoop, Taiwan had been removed from the UNSC and the UN, as well as being effectively sold down the river by the United States in favour of a budding alliance with the PRC designed to avert the spread of communism.

The decision in 1971–2 by the Nixon administration to cut a deal with Mao and the PRC and undercut its erstwhile ally Taiwan represents a powerful contradiction in US foreign policy over the last half-century. Like his predecessors, President Biden officially endorses the 'One China' policy – which proclaims that China is a single sovereign state including the PRC and Taiwan with one seat in the United Nations – while continuing to defend the autonomous status of democratic Taiwan.[49] When US leaders and officials express disapproval of what they term Chinese aggression in the Taiwan Straits, they know that Nixon's 1972 rapprochement and its ongoing repercussions undermine their arguments. Even if US officials believe that the elected government of Taiwan is the rightful government of China rather than the CCP, they cannot state this publicly due to their need to maintain relatively amicable relations with Beijing. As the authors of a 2020 paper on US policy towards Taiwan point out, 'the US "One China" policy is ambiguous at best and indecipherable at worst'.[50] The contradiction inherent in US policy on Taiwan and China, evident in the logical contortions into which they have to twist their public utterances, represents an underlying problem in US policy towards China which remains unresolved to this day.

One more example is the US-China trade war initiated by President Donald Trump in 2018. Placing tariffs on Chinese exports to 'teach them a lesson' about free trade might seem like a good idea until one understands that China is a vital manufacturing base for a plethora of US companies. China also holds just under $1 trillion of US treasury bonds.[51] This is money China has lent to the United States to sustain – at least to an extent – the ever-mushrooming US national debt. The intertwining and interdependence of the American and Chinese economies undercut all arguments about 'not doing business with China'. It also represents a logical contradiction in Trump's China policy which has not yet been acknowledged or resolved by the Biden administration.

The EU also struggles with at least one important contradiction in presenting policy concerning the global South: the fact that Europe's history of colonialism and imperialism formed the basis for its present-day wealth and prestige. Europe became rich by exploiting Africa, Asia and Latin America. It left them in a disadvantaged position which persists in the early twenty-first century. The fact of European colonial exploitation, centre-periphery differences between global North and South, structural violence and continuing privilege undercuts European claims to be a 'normative power' promoting democracy, decency and human rights.[52] This underacknowledged contradiction remains as a thorn in the side of the EU's relations with the developing nations of the global South – a point to be covered in more depth in Chapter 3. Importantly, China does not have this kind of baggage as it engages with developing nations.

Although China is beset with contradictions in its domestic and foreign policy, its people have been forced to cope with them due to bitter historical experience and rapid change. The last two centuries of disruption and upheaval have given the Chinese direct experience of all manner of contradictions, be they political, economic or social. In addition, Marxist dialectics and traditional Chinese thought – even if not always consciously formulated – serve as mental tools for Chinese leaders to resolve contradiction in ways that standard Western thinking based on Aristotelian and Cartesian logic cannot. Such approaches arguably give the Chinese – most notably the governing elites, who undergo years of training, selection and practical experience before reaching the top – an ideational advantage over the West. Thinking in a holistic, eclectic way encourages pragmatism rather than dogmatism in dealing with contradiction, circumventing the logical blockages that often impede Westerners as they attempt to make sense of the world. We will see how this translates into the planning and implementation of the BRI in the developing world in subsequent chapters.

China: master of complexity?

In the social sciences, where fuzziness is an occupational hazard, it is notoriously difficult to prove linear causality – the idea that a single independent variable (the cause) brings about a single dependent variable (the result).[53] However much we would like it not to be the case, where human beings are concerned there is generally a range of factors which intersect and interact to generate outcomes – many of them unexpected, messy and hard to pin down. It is difficult to prove that an event has a single cause to the exclusion of all other possible factors. If the physical world is based on uncertainties at the quantum level, is there any chance that social phenomena can be easily predictable and monocausal?[54] Common sense suggests not.

In a complex system full of many moving parts – such as an ecosystem, a human society or a global economic system – outcomes can be difficult to predict. This is because the system has characteristics which emerge from the interaction of the components; however, the emergent characteristics are not present in the components when examined individually.[55] It is also difficult to identify and quantify all the initial conditions in an emerging systemic phenomenon, which makes the path to the future unpredictable. Yet at the same time the path to the future is dependent on those initial conditions.[56] Accordingly, in a complex system it is certainly not the case that there is a single independent variable producing a single outcome. Instead, there are multiple intersecting variables producing a range of hard-to-predict outcomes. In the language of complexity theory, this means that we should expect nonlinear rather than linear outcomes: wobbly rather than straight lines.[57]

As the political scientist Robert Jervis has demonstrated, it is necessary to account for complexity and uncertainty in political and social affairs as much as in other fields.[58] Ben Ramalingam has demonstrated that aid and development programmes in what used to be called the 'third world' also need to account for complexity, uncertainty, risk and multiple interlocking factors.[59] We need to learn to live with uncertainty and risk. We should also allow for the possibility of 'black swans' and 'grey rhinos': game-changing outcomes which may be improbable to one degree or another, but which will eventually inevitably occur. These can be unexpected events like natural disasters, pandemics, stock market crashes, rapid climate change or wars. The essential difference between them is that while black swans are unlikely and unpredictable, grey rhinos are eminently foreseeable events to which observers pay insufficient attention[60]

Although it is not the case that Chinese leaders are experts in complexity theory, their public utterances and publications sometimes contain elements of it. For instance, Xi Jinping and Chinese state media have spoken of the need to plan for black swans and grey rhinos.[61] Such references reveal the awareness among Chinese opinion-forming elites that there is a need to prepare for complex political, economic and environmental risks in both the domestic and international arenas.[62] Henry Kissinger's first-hand experience of listening to Mao reveals that he 'never tired of stressing' the need for policymakers to plan for shifting circumstances, contradictions and disequilibrium in the world.[63] In short, Chinese leaders' discourse reveals a consciousness of the complexity of intersecting and interacting phenomena. And they know that they must get ready for unexpected shifts in the global landscape by planning for uncertainty and unexpected change.

Over the first two decades of the twenty-first century, Chinese strategic planning has incorporated complexity thinking (CT) far more coherently than US foreign policy.[64] Partly this has to do with inevitable shifts from one US administration to another with a wildly different style, such as the Trump administration. But it also emerges from Chinese long-term planning for uncertainty and risk. For instance, the Chinese multifaceted approach to important regions such as Central Asia and the Middle East – both vital sources of energy imports for China – contrasts sharply with the linear US approach to these regions after 9/11. As later chapters will reveal, the Chinese approach incorporates diplomacy, economic statecraft, energy security, institution building and infrastructure investment; the US approach has included none of these things in any particularly coherent fashion, but instead relies heavily on military clout.

Most specifically, US strategy in Iraq and Afghanistan after 9/11 took the form of 'invade, change the regime, introduce democracy, and everything will soon be fine'. By 2021 – or arguably much earlier – this simplistic approach had clearly failed. It failed because the Americans did not see the need to build strong institutions or to establish ties with local actors across the spectrum rather than just favoured groups. Instead of understanding the complexity and nonlinearity of engaging with fractured societies containing many different interest groups, US foreign policy reduced these countries to the simple problem of a failed regime which needed replacing with a democratically elected one. The problem was supposed to be instantly soluble via the use of military force and the replacement of the failed regime with one endorsed by the Americans. Of course, as we now know, there was no way it was going to be so easy to 'solve' Iraq and Afghanistan. The problem was compounded because the American solution apparently did not include any institution building or economic planning. The failure of US policy in the period 2001–21 in this regard is surprising given the success of the Marshall Plan in Europe and the rebuilding of Japan after the Second World War using a strategy of economic and political statecraft – as well as institution building through NATO and other mechanisms – which took full account of the complexity of the post-war situation.[65]

Instead of the failed US approach, the Chinese have taken a more comprehensive approach to their relations with energy-producing regional actors which takes account of both sides' interests. First, they build connections with heads of state and business leaders. This generates trust and influence at the top, paving the way for bilateral deals to be negotiated. In all cases, they work with the existing regime rather than supporting opposition groups. At the same time, they offer infrastructure projects, financed by Chinese state banks, and carried out by Chinese construction companies. These create business opportunities for Chinese companies and provide roads, railways, power plants and ports for partner countries. Finally, they prioritize energy imports from the partner country. Doing so guarantees the partner country some export income and enhances China's energy security. The Chinese approach also incorporates attempts at building regional cooperation mechanisms such as the Shanghai Cooperation Organisation (SCO), the Forum on China-Africa Cooperation (FOCAC) and the China-Arab States Cooperation Forum (CASCF).[66]

Thus, Chinese planning incorporates politics, economics and energy security in a complex web of strategic planning which Chinese leaders call 'comprehensive national security' or 'comprehensive national power'.[67] As American scholar William Norris has shown, Chinese economic statecraft involves the use by the state of Chinese commercial actors to attain national goals as well as benefitting the companies themselves.[68] Chinese companies have been directed to 'go global' (*zou chuqu*) to alleviate industrial overcapacity at home and open up new opportunities in emerging markets.[69] Planning in this way allows the Chinese to develop an integrated approach which links together the various aspects of foreign policy instead of addressing them as discrete elements. Even when apparent contradictions arise – such as the ousting of a sitting government or the inability of the partner country to repay money owed – the Chinese are thus able to take such obstacles relatively in stride (despite obvious difficulties) through a down-to-earth, pragmatic approach which does not get bogged down in abstract logic or fixed ideology but instead adjusts flexibly to the reality on the ground.

Of course, this is not to suggest that the Chinese approach is without its own inherent problems brought on by having so many irons in the fire in so many partner countries. The Chinese are not fond of commissioning feasibility or environmental sustainability studies, meaning that an essential part of the planning process has seemingly been bypassed in many cases. As a result, rather than forestalling black swans or grey rhinos, some Chinese-built infrastructure projects end up as white elephants, standing unused, unneeded and abandoned: for instance, the almost-unused Mattala Rajapaksa international airport in Sri Lanka.[70] The question of heavy debt loads in cash-poor developing countries looms over the future of BRI projects in countries such as Pakistan, Laos and Montenegro.[71] The general lack of transparency about cash flows and interest payments does not inspire confidence in the financial sustainability of Chinese projects. Arguably, it is this lack of transparency which has led to the popular perception that China is guilty of 'debt trap diplomacy': the idea that China is (allegedly) deliberately indebting partner governments in order to exert influence and obtain territorial assets such as ports.[72]

Further complexity emerges from what has been called 'fragmented authoritarianism': the idea that the central government in practice has to delegate decision-making about regional matters to provincial governments and other actors such as businessmen, thereby creating a situation in which many cooks boil – or spoil – the broth.[73] The result is a principal-agent problem whereby the motives and actions of Chinese agents – such as commercial actors – sometimes clash with those of the state they are supposedly representing. An example of this occurred when the company CEFC failed to pay instalments on its ill-conceived investments in the Czech Republic, thereby tarnishing China's image and necessitating the takeover of the investments by the state-owned company CITIC.[74]

Without doubt, the complexity inherent in international interactions is going to cause China problems just as it does all other countries. Terrorism, wars, piracy, blockades, political tensions, pandemics and economic downturns can all hit China' fortunes hard no matter how prepared Chinese leaders believe themselves to be. This is precisely why the Chinese have taken measures to hedge against such black swans by spreading their investments rather than putting all their eggs in one basket. For example, Beijing has cultivated relations with both Saudi Arabia and Iran, despite the competition between the two Persian Gulf rivals for regional supremacy. China's policy of 'strategic hedging' means that if its supplies of oil from one partner are cut off for some reason, for example due to sanctions or a blockade, it will still have access to imports from the other.[75]

In short, Chinese leaders are forced to take account of complexity in foreign and domestic policy on a daily basis. Their strategic equations include such factors as the need to keep the Chinese economy growing to maintain the legitimacy of the regime, the 'good problem' of rising salaries reducing China's competitive edge in global markets and the 'demographic timebomb' arising from an aging population and low fertility rate. Other problems include energy output versus pollution, energy imports versus energy security, investment versus debt, house construction versus housing bubbles: the Chinese leadership is constantly juggling armfuls of inherently contradictory policy balls at home and abroad. They cannot stop juggling or all the balls will fall to earth. The miracle is that they have managed to keep most of the balls in the air for four decades now – and, so far, there is no sign that they are getting tired.

China: agent of change

Every government has to deal with complexity and contradiction in its approach to both domestic and foreign policy. Few manage it well. Despite what I have written in the previous two sections, it is possible to argue that there are problems with China's approach to global complexity. For instance, it has been argued that China's foreign policy under the umbrella of the BRI is fragmented rather than coherent, since the interests and actions of a range of commercial and regional actors undercut the Chinese government's ability to 'control' what happens. Such arguments point to a conclusion that China is not a 'master' of anything, least of all complexity or contradiction. This is because 'China' – as a unitary actor – does not exist.[76]

At the same time, even if one accepts that the Chinese government is not able to exert direct control over the course of international affairs, the rise of China will still be the driving force of complex and contradictory global changes in the twenty-first century. There are five characteristics of China's rise which generate an emergent – and urgent – energy which drives transition. They give China's development a momentum which makes it the single most vital player in twenty-first-century processes of global change, even if one argues that China is not in full control of its destiny.

First, as discussed in Chapter 1, there is China's sheer size: 1.4 billion people represent roughly one fifth of the world's population. Only India has a similar population size, and no other country is anywhere close. Although size is not everything in international relations, it definitely matters: larger countries have more heft, more ability to affect affairs, more mass drawing others into their orbit. In particular, the size and growth of China's economy mean that it is now second only to the United States: most remarkably, in 2009 China's GDP was still smaller than Japan's, while in 2020 it was three times larger.[77] Allied with ongoing economic growth, China has acquired an economic gravity like no other country on earth. Even though it is true that there are huge inequalities in China and that despite lifting 400 million out of poverty there are still many more who remain poor, China's size means that its collective economic gravity is enormous compared to other countries. It is simply not possible to ignore the effects of China's ever-growing economic heft.

Second, there is the relative homogeneity of its people: 90 per cent identify as Han Chinese. China is more homogeneous than either the United States or Europe, giving it a vast swathe of population who view China's present and future role in the world in roughly similar terms. Although obviously all Han Chinese are not the same, it is arguably fair to say that their worldviews converge more than those of the diverse ethnic and linguistic groups living in the United States or Europe. This characteristic gives China a higher degree of internal unity based on shared values and culture than either the United States or the EU. For instance, despite clear signs of dissidence from sections of the Chinese population, there is evidence that over 70 per cent of the population supports the direction chosen for China by its leadership. In general, Han Chinese in particular are satisfied that their standard of living has improved in recent decades and proud that China's global status is on an upwards trajectory.[78]

Third, there is the fact that Asia is now the key regional driver of global economic growth. It is not just China whose economy has been growing. Japan hit the big time first, followed by the tiger economies: South Korea, Singapore and Taiwan. Asia has now overtaken the West as the centre of world economic activity. In 2022, Asia's gross domestic product (GDP) made up almost half of the total for the whole world. It was far ahead of the totals for Europe or North America.[79] There is no evidence that this shift of economic gravity to Asia will go into reverse in the future.

Fourth, there is the fact that China has become the single biggest centre of global manufacturing, vital to industrial output and value chains: almost every other country's economic well-being is now closely linked to China's. During the Trump administration, many in the United States began to discuss the desirability of 'decoupling' from China.[80] It was assumed that it would be possible to sever US economic ties with China, that policymakers would somehow be able to separate the two economies like a surgical operation on conjoined twins. In fact, in conditions of contemporary economic interdependence, decoupling is an unachievable aim. So many economic processes are linked to China. China is present in many global value chains: systems of production and trade of goods. Many US firms rely on China for their industrial production. Chinese companies are becoming increasingly influential in the United States and worldwide: Huawei, Lenovo and Xiaomi in electronics, Tencent in computer gaming, Alibaba in e-commerce, TikTok in internet videos. These companies' fortunes are tied up with those of their export markets. It is simply not possible to sever the ties between what economic historian Niall Ferguson calls the 'Chimerica' twins at this advanced stage in their development.[81]

And fifth, through the BRI and other measures, China is portraying itself – rather effectively for the most part – as the leader of the developing world. By investing in infrastructure and creating new markets in Asia, Africa, Latin America and the Middle East, China has filled a gap left by Europe and ignored by the United States after decolonization. China has exploited the North-South global development divide to present itself as the propagator of an alternative order. This is an order with Chinese characteristics, yet which appeals to developing countries through its focus on alleviating their disadvantages vis-à-vis the dominant West. China, because of its growing economic clout, has become the de facto leader of the global South – and this, despite numerous problems of project implementation along the route of the BRI, gives strength to the Chinese vision of the future.

Of course, the Covid-19 pandemic disrupted the progress of the global 'China dream' represented by the BRI. China's image suffered: unfavourable views of China, which were anyway increasing, have reached record levels in the developed societies of the global North. Of seventeen countries surveyed by the Pew Research Center in 2021, only in Singapore and Greece did more people have a favourable than unfavourable view of China.[82] China's authoritarianism and lack of interest in individual freedoms represent the opposite of the Western-shaped idea of a 'responsible' global leader.

Still, in the early 2020s none of this matters. This is so because the West is no longer where the growth opportunities are. As an ever-growing economic powerhouse, Beijing can afford to ignore the strictures of the West because of its economic strength and growing political influence in the global South. For instance, as Chapter 6 will demonstrate, China has a leading share of energy exports from countries such as Brazil, Angola and Saudi Arabia. In Africa, Chinese mobile phone companies are developing markets which their higher-priced Western rivals cannot reach.[83] Chinese companies dominate the world production of cobalt – an essential component in electric vehicle batteries – since they control 70 per cent of cobalt mining in the Democratic Republic of Congo.[84] China is therefore fast becoming the leading player in the crucial growth market of electric cars. Chapters 4, 5 and 6 will demonstrate in more depth and detail how China's economic expansion and influence-building is taking place across the developing world, both in China's backyard (Chapter 5) and further afield (Chapter 6).

Thus, even if one can argue that the Chinese leadership is not in full control of the policy ship due to its inherent complexity, the course it is charting is changing perceptions of what a non-Western power is capable of offering. Whatever route China plots, everybody else will have to follow. There is no getting away from the notion that before long – perhaps already – the West is going to be tagging along in the slipstream of the Chinese super-tanker as it picks a course through the waves of history; and, like the rest of the world, Westerners will be picking up scraps tossed from the deck like a pack of hungry gulls.

Chapter 3

CHINA'S COMPARATIVE ADVANTAGE

For people who have lived in only one country, it can be difficult to imagine what life is like elsewhere. We may not realize it, but there is a tendency to assume that everybody thinks and behaves in much the same way as we do. Or that of course people from other countries think and behave differently – just not *that* much differently. Human beings are essentially the same everywhere. They have families, houses, jobs just as we do. Everybody has similar problems: how to make money, how to find a partner, how to feed the children. Especially in the UK or the United States, talking about differences in culture or historical development is generally interpreted as mere stereotyping. It should be avoided at all costs. Unfortunately, however, this well-intentioned tendency – which arises from the desire to learn from the two countries' histories of slavery and colonialism – generates a certain degree of blindness about important differences in the ways people from very different parts of the world think about their lives, especially among those who have never lived anywhere else.

This brings to mind the parable of the frog in the well. The story is included in the *Zhuangzi*, a Chinese philosophical or mystical text dating to around the fourth century BCE. Its protagonist is a frog who has lived in a well his whole life and so believes that the interior of the well and the circle of sky at its top are all that exists. His lack of experience misleads him into the ignorant assumption that he knows everything about the world when all he really knows about is his little corner of it. When a sea turtle appears at the top of the well, telling him of the vast expanse of the ocean, he is dumbfounded. He had thought that all he saw in front of his eyes was all that existed.[1]

For this and other reasons, there is a need to qualify the assumption that societal, cultural and historical differences do not matter because people are all essentially the same. While of course people everywhere are biologically the same, it is not the case that they are automatically exactly the same in terms of thinking, attitudes and behaviour. Making such an assumption indicates a lack of understanding of difference. It stems from the erroneous idea that people everywhere think and behave in the same ways as people in one's own country. This error can generate serious consequences when made by politicians or diplomats, whose decisions directly affect world affairs. When differences between nations – such as population size, resources or geography – are omitted from the analytical frameworks of international relations (IR) scholars, it generates the mistaken assumption that all countries approach their foreign affairs in the same way and under precisely the same conditions.[2]

Of course, it is important to avoid cultural stereotyping. It is unsafe to assume that everybody in a country thinks and acts in precisely the same way. Yet at the same time, it is uncontroversial to state that most of the people who live inside a fixed geographical territory possess a shared language and practices which allow them to understand and communicate with each other. Inevitably, their shared understandings will have characteristics which are not necessarily shared by peoples of other countries – or sometimes even with ethnic minorities within their country. Han Chinese people – who constitute over 90 per cent of the PRC's population – will therefore tend to approach their relations with each other, with foreigners and with minorities living within their borders in a very different way than Americans or Europeans do.[3]

I have lived and worked for extended periods in six countries: two in East Asia (South Korea and China), two in continental Europe (Italy and the Czech Republic) and two with a dominant Anglo-Protestant heritage (the United States of America and the UK). While obviously this does not give me the right to declare that I know everything about these countries, it does at least give me a degree of insight into the differences between the lived conditions, historical circumstances and thinking of the people who live there. My experiences have convinced me that while many aspects of life in these countries are similar, there are definable patterns of difference which impact the interactions between people in those countries and in the countries' approach to foreign relations. These differences affect behaviours and practices to the extent that each country has acquired a distinct attitudinal heritage which affects its internal development and relations with the peoples of other nations.

In this chapter I will conduct a comparative analysis of the history, politics, economics, practices, culture and attitudinal heritages of the United States, the EU and China which influence their approaches to international relations. The comparison is not conducted lightly; it is intended to demonstrate that modern China has some specific characteristics which give it certain distinct long-term advantages over the United States and the EU. While bearing in mind the dangers of 'flattening' or over-generalizing about countries and actors, the aim, as in the whole book, is to reveal the areas where the West is struggling to compete with China and which Westerners would be well advised to understand. A better grasp of China's rise is needed in order to begin the Sisyphean task of picking away at the PRC's advantage.

I want to be clear that I am not arguing that China holds all the aces. Instead, my argument is that the PRC has specific strengths which the West lacks, and which it has learned to use to its advantage. The quotation at the beginning of this chapter is indicative of how China went through a process of learning from its weakness vis-à-vis the West: my argument is that it is now time for the West to do the same vis-à-vis China. This chapter is an attempt to draw out the specific areas where the West now needs to learn some lessons from China's rise. I will start with the United States and the EU before returning to China.

The United States: the implications of history

The land on which the United States of America is now established was occupied by other peoples before European settlers arrived. However, the characteristics of the modern US state are largely the product of European colonization. As much as some Americans might not be comfortable acknowledging the fact, the United States has a historical heritage which emerged from European settlement and eradication of the natives. Above all, as the political scientist Samuel Huntington points out, the culture, institutions and practices of the United States emerged from the values imparted by white Anglo-Saxon protestant settlers in the northeast of the country.[4] Over time, immigrants from Europe were assimilated into these values, then those from other parts of the world. The English language was chosen as the nation's lingua franca. Until recently, with the influx of large numbers of Spanish speaking migrants from Latin America, English had largely eliminated the use of other languages. Through gradual processes of assimilation – whether Americans were aware of the fact or not – Anglo-Protestant values and heritage came to dominate the internal development of the American state.

The Anglo-Protestant colonists' struggle to establish their fledgling state in the face of opposition from outside (Britain) and inside (native Americans, the Spanish and the Confederates in the south) has defined the American approach to nation-building and Americans' relations with each other. Above all, the white settlers imposed their will by force of arms. The indigenous peoples were all but annihilated, and the small numbers that remained were corralled into reservations in remote parts of the landscape that were of no use to the settlers. In the South, slaves from Africa were imported to work on cotton and tobacco plantations. When they resisted or escaped, they would be brought back into line through physical force. White Europeans spread across the continental mass of the emerging United States, from sea to shining sea, imposing their will upon native Americans, African slaves, Mexicans, animals and each other through the violent use of modern weaponry.

Enshrined in the constitution as the right to bear arms, this bloody history has bequeathed contemporary America a tendency to see the use of physical force as a default method for addressing conflicts both domestically and in the international arena. Under the veneer of American democratic values lies an unacknowledged belief that violence is a decisive tool for problem-solving. This has become entrenched deep in the American psyche due to its historical success in enabling the white settlers to subdue the lands they occupied.[5] At the same time, America remains reluctant to acknowledge what philosopher and political activist Cornel West calls 'the nightside of its own history'. As he puts it:

> The American democratic experiment is unique in human history not because we are God's chosen people to lead the world, nor because we are always a force for good in the world, but because of our refusal to acknowledge the deeply racist and imperial roots of our democratic project. We are exceptional because of our denial of the antidemocratic foundation stones of American democracy. No other democratic nation revels so blatantly in such self-deceptive innocence.[6]

In the United States, as in the UK, the development of a capitalist economy in the nineteenth century occurred alongside the creation of democratic institutions. The growth of democracy was a necessary adjustment to a new era of industrialization and large-scale capitalist production of goods. The era was defined by the conflictual relations of production – between capitalist elites and their workers – which had emerged from industrialization and the dislocation of peasants from villages to cities. The new urban working class, thousands of whom were necessarily thrown together in one place to labour in factories, demanded recognition of their rights and better working conditions. In practice, democracy evolved as a by-product of capitalist economics rather than originating in a noble belief in the right of all men to have freedom.[7]

Like the nation itself, American freedoms have also been born of confrontation, competition and conflict. The Anglo-Protestant northern states had to fight a war against the slave-owning South. The descendants of the slaves freed after the Civil War were forced to struggle for equity with the whites.[8] Nowadays, libertarians and other right-wing groups define their freedoms in terms of the rights of individuals to defend themselves against the state and other people, including by use of arms. In a non-physical form of conflict, Americans spend more money – roughly $310 billion per year, or 2.2 per cent of GDP – fighting lawsuits against each other than any other people on earth.[9]

Psychologist Alain Ehrenberg goes so far as to suggest that conflict is an inherent characteristic of liberal democracy:

> The institutionalization of conflict allows the free confrontation of contradictory interests and the achievement of acceptable compromise. It is the very condition of democracy insofar as it allows the representation of social division within a political arena. Equally as important, mental conflicts are the counterpart of the self-creation that defines modern individuality. The notion of conflict is what maintains the gap between what is possible and what is allowed … From the political to the private, conflict is the normative centre of democratic life.[10]

During the nineteenth century, as the white settlers expanded westwards towards the Pacific and territorial wars were fought, the United States did not involve itself much with the affairs of Europe and Asia. Busy with its internal development and uninterested in problems across the oceans, the United States mostly stayed out of foreign entanglements until it was dragged into the First World War in 1917 by the sinking of the Lusitania. Even then, the United States avoided any commitment to solving problems on the Eurasian 'heartland'[11] until once again forced to join the Allied effort by the Japanese attack on Pearl Harbor in 1941. Influenced by the nation's geography, the tendency to isolationism has long been a powerful force in American politics, implying a certain psychological detachment from world affairs.[12]

Since being dragged into the Second World War, the United States has assumed an originally unwanted role as the leading global power. However, American understandings of this role have, to a great extent, revolved around the use of force in attempts to shape the world according to American interests. Since the Second World War, and especially since the start of the Cold War with the Soviet Union, the United States has fought five major wars as a leading protagonist: in Korea, Vietnam, Iraq (twice) and Afghanistan. It has also intervened militarily in conflicts in Laos, Lebanon, Cuba, the Dominican Republic, Cambodia, Grenada, Panama, Haiti, Libya, Bosnia, Kosovo, Yemen, Somalia, Pakistan and Syria. Many of these interventions have involved an active intent to change the regime in the targeted country; most of these attempts have failed or ended inconclusively. One only need recall the outcomes of the wars in Korea (North Korea remains Communist), Vietnam (the Communists took power after defeating the United States), Iraq (democratic but unstable) and Afghanistan (returned to Taliban control after US withdrawal) to understand the low success rate of US interventions.

The United States has overseas military bases in over fifty countries. It has intervened militarily in at least nineteen countries since the Second World War. The projection of US power and influence since 1945 has thus – when national interests are at stake – tended to focus on military solutions rather than the promotion of democratization and liberal values in the developing world. This has happened repeatedly even as US leaders claim to be promoting democracy and human rights agendas around the world. As I will argue in the next section, the focus on military strength to enforce America's will constitutes a key strategic shortcoming. It is a product of black-and-white linear thinking that fails to take account of the world's complexities.[13] The United States will need a radical readjustment of strategic focus if it is to retain its preeminent position in the world – or, indeed, if the United States aims even to remain roughly level with China in the medium- to long-term.

American shortcomings

Clearly the United States has been the dominant global power of the last hundred years for a reason. Primarily, its dominance is due to the strength of its economy and the size of the military which its financial and other resources have allowed it to fund. However, the US economic advantage over China has been *shrinking* year by year as China's GDP has grown at a much faster rate since the 1990s (see Figure 3.1). While the United States remains far ahead of China in terms of military spending (see Figure 3.2) and military technology, there are many reasons why this hard power advantage is less significant than it seems in terms of maintaining global influence – and, in fact, is likely to constitute a disadvantage in the long run.

First and foremost, as the historical record analysed in the previous section revealed, most US military interventionism since the Second World War – especially from the Vietnam War onwards – has not worked. This is because the focus has been overwhelmingly on winning wars rather than post-conflict reconstruction. American leaders have tended to be guilty of believing that defeating the enemy's army and toppling the incumbent regime fulfils their mission, whereas in fact it leaves the job at most half done. They have not understood the difficulties and

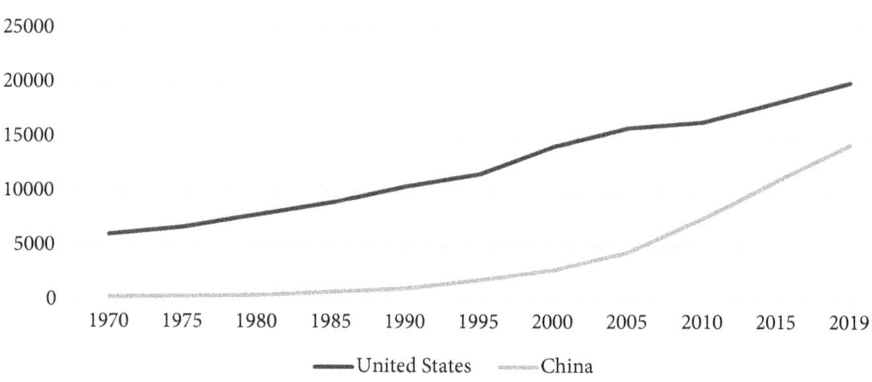

Figure 3.1 Gross domestic product (constant 2015 prices), $ million

Source: author, based on data from United Nations database (UNdata)

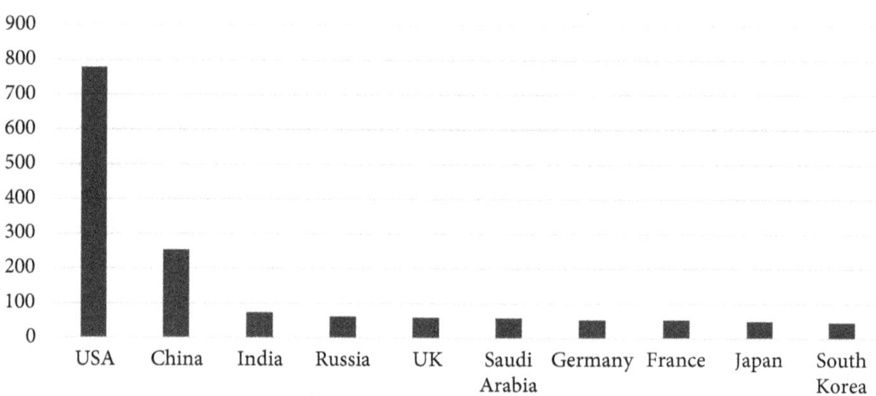

Figure 3.2 Military expenditure by nation, top 10, $ billion (2020)

Source: author, based on data from SIPRI Military Expenditure Database

costs inherent in rebuilding a cash-poor country which lacks functioning political, financial and legal institutions. The most obvious example of this tendency to underestimate post-conflict reconstruction is President George W. Bush, who said during a presidential debate in 2000:

> I don't think our troops ought to be used for what's called nation-building.
> I think our troops ought to be used to fight and win war.[14]

As a result, after ordering US troops to invade Afghanistan in October 2001, Bush stated that he would pressure the United Nations to 'take over the so-called nation-building'.[15] Ultimately it fell to the occupying US-led coalition forces to do the nation-building, a task at which they proved remarkably unsuccessful over the next two decades. When US forces left Afghanistan in August 2021, the erstwhile government of Afghanistan collapsed, the Taliban reclaimed control of the country only ten days after initiating its offensive and the erstwhile president, Ashraf Ghani, fled to Uzbekistan.[16] Accusations of corruption had dogged Ghani for years and followed him on his flight out of the country, with accusations that he had stolen millions of dollars.[17]

In addition to the depressing record of military occupations in which the United States has been involved, the use of hard power has been counterproductive because it has negatively impacted American soft power. Soft power is defined by the US scholar Joseph Nye as the ability to exert influence through attraction rather than force.[18] US military adventurism – which has included the use of indiscriminate bombing, 'collateral damage' in the form of civilian deaths, and sometimes, as in Guantanamo, torture – has undermined the image of the United States as a promoter and defender of freedom and human rights. Overall, in the last twenty years the American use of its hard power advantage – as the prominent IR scholar Stephen Walt points out – has been poorly planned and poorly executed.[19] It has also impacted the capacity of the United States to maintain and extend its ideational influence – its soft power – in the global South. As a result, according to survey data obtained by Pew Global Research, the image of the United States declined in Europe, Australia, Japan and Canada from 2010 onwards.[20] Support for US views about democracy also deteriorated between 2012 and 2017 in Africa and Latin America.[21] Of course, China has also struggled to enhance its image, especially since the advent of the Covid-19 pandemic. Nevertheless, the decline in US soft power has allowed Beijing to close the soft power gap, especially in the global South.

The frequent use of interventionism and its failure to promote development in the countries of the global South point to an inherent contradiction in US foreign policy – one which is rarely acknowledged by Americans. While claiming to be promoting democracy and freedom around the world, the United States instead – like other leading powers – prioritizes its national interests. Pursuing self-interest, Stephen Walt demonstrates, is natural for any state; but this fact goes largely unacknowledged in the United States amidst misguided mythologizing about 'American exceptionalism' and the United States being a 'shining city on a hill', setting an example for others to follow.[22] That the American 'example' has included the slaughter of thousands of Iraqi, Afghan, Latin American, Vietnamese, Laotian, Cambodian and Korean civilians using bombs, helicopters, napalm, agent orange and other forms of violence does not figure in the minds of those Americans who insist that the United States is the 'last best hope of earth'. Americans' inability to understand – or even acknowledge – contradictions in US foreign policy such as that between democracy promotion and the tendency to resort to use of military force undermines the nation's claim to be an 'empire of liberty'. As Ipek Burnett points out, the American national myths of exceptionalism and uniqueness 'promote a dualistic outlook in which everything is set up as right or wrong, good or evil, and therefore obstruct an understanding of the complex realities of world affairs'.[23]

An important aspect of the inherent flaw in the 'American exceptionalism' rhetoric is the low level of US commitment to the building of institutions or infrastructure in the countries it invades. After the invasion, a new, democratically elected, US-friendly regime is soon installed; but it is guaranteed to remain in place only for as long as the Americans care to maintain their armed forces in country.

Likewise, infrastructure building in occupied countries has not been well implemented. A *Washington Post* report based on confidential US government interviews with diplomats, military officers and aid workers active in Afghanistan reveals a tale of mismanagement and misuse of funds intended for dams, roads and other projects. Although billions were spent, much of the money went missing, ending up in the pockets of corrupt local officials and contractors.[24] Stephen Hadley, who was the national security advisor in the George W. Bush administration, observed in 2014 that:

> We just don't have a post-conflict stabilization model that works ... Every time we have one of these things it is a pickup game. I don't have any confidence that if we did it again, we would do any better.[25]

The interviewees in the *Washington Post* article also noted the lack of enthusiasm by a series of US administrators for nation-building programmes. In Afghanistan, the Americans were slow to take responsibility for urgently needed post-conflict reconstruction, with predictably lamentable results. Robert Finn, the US ambassador to Afghanistan from 2002 to 2003 commented that:

> This is a systemic problem of our government ... We can't think beyond the next election. When we went to Afghanistan everybody was talking about a year or two, and I said to them that we would be lucky if we were out of here in 20 years.[26]

Other interviewees cited the poor record of nation-building and infrastructure construction from the 1990s onwards after the US military interventions in Iraq, Syria, Libya, Yemen, Haiti and Somalia.

To be fair, the United States is not good at its own infrastructure either. Biden's $1.75 trillion 'Build Back Better' plan for rebuilding America and combatting climate change included nothing about improving US infrastructure in the official documentation.[27] There were some details about investments in clean energy, coastal restoration, forest management and soil conservation, but nothing about upgrading America's inadequate railway network and crumbling road system. Previous administrations stretching back decades also failed to address this issue. Such neglect flies in the face of an assessment based on data from the US Department of Transportation which revealed that:

> Despite the importance of a reliable transportation network, upkeep of critical infrastructure is being neglected across the country as roads, bridges, and

railroads age. Nationwide, 21.8% of roads are in poor condition, 7.6% of bridges are in need of replacement or repair, and there have been 4.8 derailments for every 100 miles of train track from 2015 to 2019, the most common cause of which are broken rails or welds. In some states, these figures are far worse, indicating a threat to not only the economy, but to public health and safety as well.[28]

Indeed, on 28 January 2022, just hours before President Biden was due to speak about his plans for US infrastructure in Pittsburgh, a bridge collapsed in the city, revealing starkly the dire state of US transport infrastructure.[29] Although in 2022 $1.25 trillion was allocated by Congress to infrastructure investments, it remained unclear in early 2023 how exactly the funds were going to be used: many complications loomed as contractors sought to understand how to gain access to a portion of the budget.[30]

My own visits to the United States – I have been there three times and made two extensive trips through more than twenty states – have revealed to me the inadequacy of America's public transport infrastructure. The United States and Canada are the only countries out of more than fifty I have visited in which it is essential to travel by private car almost everywhere (with the notable exceptions of New York and San Francisco) because of the lack of rail and bus access. The Greyhound buses on which I journeyed from state to state were not bad; but their routes cover only intercity travel. Trying to reach less populated destinations without a car is virtually impossible. This is not the case in the EU or China, where one can reach most towns and villages by bus. When the United States is so poor at its own transport infrastructure, how likely is it that it would be good at constructing roads and railways in other countries that lack them?

It should be noted that it has not always been the case that the United States has been poor at nation-building and post-conflict reconstruction. The Marshall Plan was an economic reconstruction programme for Europe after the Second World War which was relatively well planned and implemented.[31] Western Europe was financially assisted and rapidly incorporated into the US sphere of influence through NATO. US-occupied Japan was also effectively reconstructed. Research into Japanese culture conducted by the anthropologist Ruth Benedict and published in her book *The Chrysanthemum and the Sword* was effectively used as a basis for understanding how to rebuild (rather than punish) Japan after the US occupation in 1945.[32] In contrast, it seems – for whatever reason – that the need to understand the traditions, history, politics and economic circumstances of the people whose country one is occupying has not been prioritized by US administrations from the Korean War onwards.[33]

In short, American strategic thinking of the last seventy years tends to be linear and zero-sum in its reliance on hard power to solve problems: invade a country, defeat the evildoers (in George W. Bush's memorable usage), replace the regime and everything will be fine. Thinking like this ignores the fact that everything is not fine because the reality on the ground is messier than the linear language of dependent and independent variables would indicate.[34] Overall, the US approach can be characterized as failing to plan sufficiently for uncertainty and complexity.[35]

Rather than identifying grey rhinos on the horizon, American thinking tends to view the world in black and white.

The American reluctance to systematically plan, implement and commit to nation-building investment programmes is the Achilles heel of US engagement with the global South. It is difficult to find cases where a US military occupation has benefitted an economically developing country. At the present time, until Biden's B3W takes shape (if it does), there is no coordinated programme of US investment in impoverished nations. The United States would need to shift its focus from short-term military solutions to long-term economic ones in order to rebuild its image as a global benefactor, and to counter and compete with China through the rest of the twenty-first century.

The European Union: history and implications

Europeans like to think of themselves as cultivated, ethical people. Modern Europe is a peaceful place, full of beautiful architecture, courteous manners and highly developed social welfare systems. Yet Europe has a history of vicious conflict which lies metaphorically buried beneath its elegant palaces, boulevards and coffee shops. Down the centuries, through innumerable wars, Europe has been the site of some of the bloodiest violence in human history. Europeans exported their violence to the rest of the world through colonialism. This legacy of brutality, which continued up to the middle of the twentieth century, is important because it impacts European claims to be a 'normative power' through the promotion of human rights and democracy worldwide.[36] Europe's violent colonial past affects the EU's relations with the developing nations of the global South in Africa, Latin America, the Middle East and Asia. Arguably, they are still affected by 'structural violence' today through unequal trade deals and other measures which the EU uses to protect its interests and ensure the continued flow of natural resources.[37] For instance, ever-hardening EU policy towards migrants from Africa, Asia and the Middle East is suggestive of a 'fortress Europe' mentality rather than an ethical, inclusive approach.[38] Similarly, there is evidence to show that Europe's 'ethical foreign policy' is nothing more than 'organized hypocrisy': Europeans sell just as many arms to autocratic countries with records of human rights abuses as they do to nations which support democracy.[39]

Throughout European history, armies regularly swept across the continent, ravaging everything in their path. The Romans conquered much of the continent, as well as areas of north Africa and the Middle East, before being overrun by barbarian hordes. There then followed roughly one thousand years of power struggles known as the Middle Ages. The Thirty Years War of 1618–48 was one of the most destructive and exhausting conflicts ever seen, laying waste to large tracts of central Europe. Similarly, the Napoleonic Wars swept hither and thither across the continent in the late eighteenth and early nineteenth centuries. Europe was relatively peaceful from 1815 to 1914, after the fall of Napoleon. However, elsewhere it was a different story, as Europeans exported violence to their newly established colonies. Later, in the twentieth century, even those horrors were eventually eclipsed by two World Wars, the second of which included the Nazi Holocaust. Concentration camps are a European invention, originating with the Spanish in Cuba, continuing through the British internment of Dutch settlers in South Africa during the Boer War and culminating in Hitler's use of them to eradicate the Jews.[40] Warfare and violence, one might say, constituted the dark side of European history right up to the end of the Second World War.

The industrial revolution which took place in Europe from the late eighteenth century onwards produced, among other things, the machinery of modern warfare such as machine guns, planes and tanks. It also produced capitalism and modern democratic institutions. Capitalist economics was based on industrial production in factories and created conditions of conflict through the class divide between factory owners and employees. This conflict eventually produced democratization as workers grouped together and fought for their rights. The industrial revolution also brought capitalism and violence to the rest of the world as European countries expanded by sea. They established colonies designed to obtain natural resources for industrial production and became wealthy in large part through the exploitation of Asia, Africa and the Americas. Millions of people in what became the global South were exploited, enslaved or killed at the behest of their European colonial masters.

The idea of founding the European Union emerged from the ashes of the First and Second World Wars. It was decided that the best way to keep the major European powers such as Germany and France from going to war with each other was to make them economically interdependent on each other by binding them together through complex trade deals and bureaucratic entanglements. This approach to European regional integration, based on the work of Ernst B. Haas, came to be called neofunctionalism.[41] In the formation of the European Union, the idea of integrating nations through supranational market regimes – in a process called spillover – was implemented by Jean Monnet.[42] The process began in 1952 with the establishment of the European Coal and Steel Community (ECSC).[43] This transformed into the European Economic Community (EEC) and eventually, in 1993, the European Union (EU). However, a plan for political integration via a European constitution met with resistance in the 2000s and was dropped.

By binding its member states together, the EU has prevented further wars between them since the Second World War. This is a remarkable achievement. However, the EU has some significant structural weaknesses which severely reduce its potential for effective international action. These weaknesses contribute to the EU's inability to create transformational policies for the development of the global South. They will be examined in the next section.

European shortcomings

There are two obvious weaknesses of the EU as an actor on the global stage. The first, despite the successes noted above, is the bloc's tendency to disunity. The second is its weak international power projection. The first weakness stems from

Europe's history as an arena for warfare between nations with different cultures and languages. Despite the efforts at unification since the Second World War, the EU still contains twenty-seven distinct polities, each with its own political, legal and taxation system. To be clear: the EU has been remarkably successful in damping down rivalries between its members; but divisions remain, most notably between the Eastern and Western halves of the continent. Some Central and Eastern European countries – most notably Hungary and Poland – have proved reluctant to bow to Brussels's will on accepting refugees or sticking to EU norms and laws on human rights and democracy.[44] Disintegrative impulses in the east have tugged at the EU's already fragile unity.

The second weakness – the EU's relatively weak international power projection – arises from the fact that there is no European army. European countries are dependent for their security on the US-led North Atlantic Treaty Organization (NATO) or powerful individual members (such as France). There have been half-hearted proposals for a European army – for instance by President Macron of France in 2018 – but no steps have so far been taken to implement them.[45] Individually, even the strongest European powers have only limited power projection beyond the European sphere; this has been further impacted by the departure of Britain from the EU. In combination, the two weaknesses mean that the EU is not able to establish a strong presence in other regions, particularly in distant ones such as Asia and the Americas.

The inability to project power is exacerbated by two further shortcomings relating to the development of policy. First, there is the fact that, alongside the lack of progress towards an EU army, the proposal for a common EU foreign and security policy (CFSP) has remained more-or-less on the drawing board. Individual countries still form their foreign policies unilaterally. Second, there is the absence of a clear overall vision for the EU's approach to the global South. In 2021 came the first signs of a reaction to China's BRI with the proposal for coordinated investment in an international development initiative to be called the 'Global Gateway'.[46] However, despite the presentation of a funding plan in late 2021, the initiative remained vague, without a clear plan for how the money was to be invested.[47] In addition, much of the 315 billion euros of finance presented in the proposal was based on existing funds rather than new resources in a 'repackaging of existing financial commitments from the 2021–2027 budget'.[48] In 2022–3, as the EU became understandably fixated on dealing with the fallout from Russia's invasion of Ukraine, it remained unclear how and to what extent the Global Gateway would be implemented, if at all.

At any rate, Europe's colonialist past acts as an impediment to whatever strategy for investing in the global South might eventually be formed. African, Latin American and Asian countries can hardly be expected to embrace the EU's vision for them while they still recall their hard-won struggles to free themselves of their white masters during the twentieth century. The past may feel like a far-off, discarded part of history to Europeans; but it is still very vivid in the memories of the peoples who were colonized. As the Brussels-based commentator Shada Islam puts it, 'Racism, xenophobia and Europe's colonial legacies are increasingly acute obstacles to EU efforts to open a new chapter in relations with Africa.'[49] Deep-rooted mistrust of European intentions should not be discounted as an obstacle to the implementation of the Global Gateway initiative, and to whatever activity the EU proposes in former European colonies – which make up much of the global South.

There are other problems too. Where the United States can be said to have a hubristic, holier-than-thou 'city on the hill' mentality containing undertones of self-deception, the EU's philosophy arguably smacks of 'fortress Europe': a knee-jerk instinct to protect the continent from hostile invading forces.[50] As a result, the refugee crisis goes unsolved because simply protecting borders does not make the waves of migrants go away. The reason for their presence at Europe's borders remains unaddressed: fundamentally, it is the discrepancy between Europe's prosperous peace and the war-torn poverty of the refugees' home countries. To stop the flow of migrants it would be desirable to motivate them to stay at home. Most people do not move themselves and their families thousands of kilometres unless they feel that economic and security conditions are so desperate that they have no opportunity to improve their lives unless they leave.

Ameliorating this situation from the EU's perspective would require a coordinated approach to investing in economic development in the global South; but Europeans have been slow to understand that a large-scale investment programme is needed. Shada Islam identifies the source of the problem thus: 'EU leaders may live in a well-insulated parallel universe where domestic and external issues are unconnected.'[51] Now that the Global Gateway has been proposed as an idea, there will likely be another delay while the EU works out how to implement it. While it does so, the refugees will keep coming because they continue to lack economic opportunities and a secure living environment in their home countries.

Delays and slowness are built into the EU's DNA. As a report in Deutsche Press-Agentur puts it, 'decision-making in the European Union is notoriously slow and forging consensus can be painstaking.'[52] The neo-functionalist logic of tying economies together inevitably generates large amounts of red tape. Complex bureaucratic processes are rarely conducive to the speedy resolution of problems, least of all when those problems are themselves the result of complex processes of change due to disruption in the global environment. If bureaucracy is prioritized above all else – as it often seems to be in Brussels's cumbersome administrative structures and institutions – the result is an inability to move rapidly to adjust appropriately to change.

Difficulty planning and implementing large-scale transport and energy projects also reveals the slowness inherent in the EU. For instance, the idea of establishing an integrated European transport network is one that Brussels has ostensibly prioritized. Yet, despite initiating the Trans-European Transport Network (TEN-T) in 1996, progress on implementation has been slow. The European Commission's official 2021 report concludes that the TEN-T's core network will not be completed by 2030 due to construction delays, funding issues and the non-compliance of member states.[53] Cross-border train travel in the EU remains generally inefficient, expensive and slow, as anybody who has attempted to book rail tickets from Prague to Brussels (as I have) will know only too well: unfortunately for the environment, flying is far the better option. In other words, TEN-T once again demonstrates the difficulty of getting member states to work together efficiently and to prioritize EU-level goals over national ones. The same applies to energy: in April 2022, the director of the EU Agency for the Cooperation of Energy Regulators (ACER) complained that member states' lack of implementation of agreements 'decided years ago' was introducing 'significant delays' to the integration of energy supplies, 'impeding enhanced power trade'.[54] The decades trickle by and the EU still cannot do international transport and energy connectivity with efficiency.

In short, the EU's relative lack of flexibility emerges from its plodding internal processes and nations prioritizing their own interests over those of the group. Inflexibility is exacerbated by the difficulty Brussels has in coordinating action at the macro-level. When responses are required in a crisis, they tend to come out half-cocked and ill-conceived, at least until the dust has settled. Discrepancies arise across national borders as policy is made on the hoof by individual governments. The second decade of the twenty-first century bore witness to discombobulated reactions to the refugee crisis – which reached a tipping point in 2015 – and the Covid-19 pandemic. These two black swans – or, rather, grey rhinos – revealed the ineffectiveness and lack of flexibility of EU structures, as well as a lack of overall forward planning for dealing with crises.

Another unanticipated event which has afflicted the EU since 2016 is Britain's departure from the bloc. Predictably, the process of extracting the UK from the EU has been tortuous and protracted. Although not Brussels's fault, Brexit has added to the administrative burden by creating a new set of bureaucratic and diplomatic problems to solve. With the Covid-19 pandemic hitting Europe not long after the official leaving date, the EU's already ponderous policy implementation processes have been slowed further still. Bickering between Britain and France about fishing quotas and who should be responsible for the safety of refugees crossing the English Channel also demonstrate the extent to which the European focus tends to be distracted from addressing problems further afield – for instance, in the developing world.

Overall, problems connected to difficulties with integration and generating unified policy impede the EU's capacity to project influence and present a coordinated vision of investment in the global South's development. As we will see in the following section, these are problems that China has also experienced; but which – due to the innate advantages examined in the preceding two chapters – China is arguably better placed to transcend.

China's comparative advantages

We have already examined some important aspects of China's history and development in the first two chapters. However, the discussion needs to be extended here in order to draw out the comparison with the United States and the EU.

As Chapter 1 demonstrated, a succession of Communist Party leaders – including Xi Jinping – have used so-called 'patriotic education' to exploit the collective remembrance of the 'century of humiliation'. Connected to this is the notion of what Martin Jacques calls China's 'Middle Kingdom' mentality: the idea, originating in the imperial era, that China was the centre of Asia and the centre of the world.[55] The rest of the world was less civilized and lay on the 'outside'. In Chinese, the word for 'China' – *zhongguo* (中国) – literally means 'centre country' (or 'Middle Kingdom', in its standard English rendering), while the word for 'foreign' – *waiguo* (外国) – literally means 'outside country'.

By exploiting the 'century of humiliation' and the Chinese people's 'Middle Kingdom mentality' to generate nationalist sentiments, China's communist leaders have persuaded them they have a mission: to put China back where it rightfully belongs. The energy at the heart of China's rise comes from the Han Chinese belief that by their combined efforts they are restoring China's former glory. This drive to action – the modern China dream – gives China's leaders an important advantage over their Western counterparts: they can mobilize the Chinese population to collective action in ways that are barely imaginable in the West. For example, it seems incredible to Americans or Europeans that it would be possible to shut down an entire city, to lock everybody in their homes, to contain a pandemic; yet this is exactly what the Chinese did repeatedly during the Covid-19 outbreak. Quarantine may seem like a case of restriction rather than action. Nevertheless, the fact that tens of millions of people were – without widespread protests until almost three years into the pandemic – strictly confined to their homes, keeping the rate of infection at remarkably low rates (or eliminating the spread altogether), is evidence of an instilled collective discipline (of course, enforced by authoritarian rule) at which the West could only stare in disbelief.

Here we need to address the question of what psychologist Michele Gelfand calls 'loose' versus 'tight' cultures. In a ground-breaking study based on a survey of 7,000 people in thirty-three countries, Gelfand classified countries along a spectrum from loose to tight: the United States comes in at the loose end of the spectrum, while China is among the tightest nations.[56] Loose societies have weak social norms and a high tolerance for nonconformity (like the United States), while tight societies expect people to conform and have strong enforcement of social norms (like China). While this distinction is not exactly the same as the collectivist/individualist divide previously identified by the Dutch social psychologist Geert Hofstede, there are similarities.[57] At any rate, the peer-reviewed paper upon which Gelfand's book is based reveals that the difference between American 'looseness' and Chinese 'tightness' is measurable and statistically significant.[58] The implications are clear: the Chinese government's ability to enforce rules and mobilize a huge population – as observation, anecdote and the Covid-19 pandemic all suggest – is far greater than in the United States or most Western countries. The Chinese government's capacity, through networks of party members nestled within the internal structures of companies, universities and village councils alike, to roughly coordinate the activity of its 1.4 billion population without significant levels of outright physical resistance is nothing short of extraordinary. Although one can attribute this to the authoritarian nature of the regime, it is also, to a significant extent, due to China's social cohesion and conformity, which are far greater than in Western countries.

Of course, there are also disadvantages to being a 'tight' culture, just as there are clear advantages to having a 'loose' culture. Looseness encourages freedom of expression and creativity, while tightness tends to demand conformity and adherence to rules. In a tight community, stepping out of line is frowned upon, which may discourage original thought and invention. There are concerns that entrepreneurship in China may be stifled by the need to stick to official (or semi-official) guidelines. Actors may be unwilling to take the risks necessary to innovate scientifically or to build a new business. Nevertheless, the fact remains that having a relatively high degree of tightness is an asset for a political unit of immense size, such as China, because it enables the government to mobilize the population in support of national drives. Chinese leaders are therefore able to implement policy relatively efficiently and swiftly.

Contrary to Western expectations, since the crushing of the pro-democracy student demonstration in Beijing in 1989, the Chinese population has tended not to oppose decisions imposed from on high. Surprisingly, as a study by the US professor of political science Bruce Dickson demonstrates, the Party garners broad public support – around 70 per cent – for its broad policy goals.[59] CCP leaders manage to do this without the degree of transparency required in Western democracies. In fact, keeping decision-making processes non-transparent may very well constitute part of the secret to their success. The philosopher Byung-Chul Han has noted the necessity in politics for leaders to present a clear vision, to strike out ahead of the public on the path into the future, to show them the way forward. However, he laments that, in democratic countries in the internet era, the urge to make everything public, including decision-making processes, leads to a culture of immediacy which undermines long-term strategic planning:

> The future, as the time of the political, is disappearing ... As strategic action, politics demands power of information – sovereignty over its production and distribution. Accordingly, it cannot do without closed spaces where information is held back on purpose. The political – in other words, strategic communication – calls for confidentiality. If everything is made public at once, politics necessarily grows short of breath and becomes short-term; issues thin out into idle talk. Total transparency imposes a temporality on political communication that makes slow, long-term planning impossible. It becomes impossible to let things ripen.[60]

Whatever one would wish to say about China's authoritarianism, human rights record and lack of the individual freedoms taken for granted in the West, Han's observation (however it may be intended) points to a clear practical advantage for China over liberal democracies. The ability to be non-transparent about decision-making and long-term goals gives China's leaders a tremendous advantage in terms of their capacity to plan and implement strategy without the need to present decision-making processes to the public. China specialist David Shambaugh points out that Chinese leaders are well aware of the advantages of keeping their discussions top secret.[61] In an era of instant digital communication, not having to reveal information gives the Chinese leadership the ability to push through long-term, large-scale policy initiatives such as the Belt and Road Initiative, even in the face of numerous difficulties – and failures – along the way.

Meanwhile, American and EU leaders have no such luxury. Constitutional processes – checks and balances – require transparency. In the United States, large-scale initiatives involving huge budgets require rubber-stamping by the Senate and Congress. As a result, the end of 2021 saw an attempt by the US oil lobby to use a Democrat senator to block President Joe Biden's $1.75 trillion 'Build Back Better' (BBB) initiative for improved infrastructure and a switch to renewable energy.[62] With Biden's infrastructure initiative finally passing through Congress but facing difficulties with finance and implementation,[63], the chances that the international version – 'Build Back Better World', or B3W – can be successfully implemented seem minimal. B3W is supposed to compete with China's BRI, but so far lacks detail beyond a vague vision of investment in developing countries. Its inevitably slow progress is also endangered by the fact that Biden – unlike Xi Jinping – is forced to seek re-election before the end of a four-year term. If he loses, his successor may choose to undo any progress made on BBB and B3W, just as Trump revoked Obama's commitment to the 2015 Paris Agreement on climate change. Undesirable as reforms may seem to many Americans, the United States will need to conduct a radical rethink of its political decision-making, strategic planning and nation-building programmes if it wants to compete with China on the international stage as a long-term provider of assistance to the global South. Much the same can be said of the EU. Global Gateway seems to be just a vague promise to the developing world containing cash mostly reallocated from existing funds, even if the aim is to use these funds more efficiently and strategically.[64]

In contrast to Western dithering, China's Belt and Road Initiative is already in progress – and has been for years already. China's policy of sending its construction companies out originated in the 1990s with Jiang Zemin's introduction of the 'Going Global' (*zou chuqu*, 走出去) policy.[65] Xi Jinping's introduction of the BRI in 2013 added a new umbrella term to replace 'Going Global'; it also provided incentives in the form of a coordinated state-backed funding programme. As Chapters 5 and 6 will show, China has supplied loans and construction expertise to countries from Southeast Asia to Africa to Latin America. Admittedly, the BRI has its problems: white elephants, lack of transparency, so-called 'debt traps', the lack of feasibility and sustainability studies and so on (see Table 3.1). However, as we shall see in the next three chapters, despite all these shortcomings (and more), the BRI is at least *in progress*, more than can be said for B3W and the Global Gateway (see Tables 3.2 and 3.3).

From a Western point of view, the negatives of China's expansion, whether under the label 'BRI' or not, outweigh the positives by a huge margin. Increased Chinese influence in the global South, debt burdens, support for autocratic regimes and environmental damage are severely problematic for the West. On

Table 3.1 Belt and Road Initiative

	'Positives'	'Negatives'
1	Investment	Debt/sustainability
2	Infrastructure building	White elephants
3	Funding and construction coordinated	Money circulates back to Chinese hands
4	Soft power charm offensive	Influence building
5	Elite level cooperation/coordination	Support for autocratic regimes
6	Increased energy production	Environmental damage
7	Top-down oversight	Fragmentation/principal-agent problem
8	Fast results	Lack of feasibility and sustainability studies

Source: author

Table 3.2 The liberal international order (LIO, led by the United States)

'Positives'	'Negatives'
Functional international institutions (World Bank/IMF/United Nations)	Lack of coordinated support for institution- and infrastructure-building in the global South
Functional global economic system (market capitalism)	Economic inequalities/lack of coordinated investment in global South
Strong US support (dollar/military)	Frequent inconsistency and bias in favour of US interests

Source: author

Table 3.3 The European Union

'Positives'	'Negatives'
Normative power (human rights, democracy)	Lack of global reach
Neo-functionalist logic: economic integration processes	Fortress Europe mentality: exclusion of developing countries
Relatively strong institutions	Little attempt to support institution- or infrastructure-building in global South
Successful record of preventing military conflicts between EU members since the Second World War	Common Foreign and Security Policy (CFSP) is not functional – each country has its own foreign policy

Source: author

the other hand, from a Chinese perspective, the positives may outweigh the negatives. As we will see in Chapters 5 and 6, among other things, the BRI is giving opportunities to Chinese construction companies, creating new markets, giving China access to resource supplies and generating Chinese political influence across the global South.

From a global perspective, if we ask questions such as 'Is the BRI having an impact on the circumstances of developing countries?', 'Is the BRI changing how we think about development?', 'Is the BRI generating change in the global South?', the answer is yes in each case. Whether the changes are positive or negative, whether projects have succeeded or failed in specific countries, there is little doubt that the BRI has produced changes which emerged from China rather than the West. It is not the case that the BRI has not produced any changes or has completely failed. This is true even if there have been notable failures or significant problems with high debt loads or white elephants, as in Sri Lanka and Montenegro. By introducing the BRI and attempting to implement it through an investment and infrastructure construction program utilizing Chinese commercial actors, Beijing has created a new model for development which had not previously been envisaged. Recognition of this fact comes in the fact that the United States and the EU have been forced to come up with their own schemes to rival the BRI.[66]

The question of debt in emerging economies is a difficult one to resolve. It has been the source of much criticism of the Chinese and the BRI. It is also one which the West has been trying to address since the middle of the last century, through mechanisms such as the Paris Club and the International Monetary Fund (IMF). However, such mechanisms, while striving to alleviate third world debt, have failed to give agency to the countries of the global South. Paris Club negotiations and debt restructuring are run by official representatives of Western creditors. While the meetings conducted under the Paris Club label have been effective as far as creditors are concerned, they lack both transparency and sufficient input from the debtor nations. At any rate, over the course of decades the IMF and Paris Club 'strategies have not been very successful at reducing the debt levels of developing countries'.[67] Given this track record, it is not clear that BRI loans have been worse for the global South's debt struggles than the frameworks the West has offered since the Second World War.

There is another problem for the United States and the EU: they are not competitive with China in infrastructure building either at home or overseas. Expertise and cost effectiveness in infrastructure construction are the key to whatever success the BRI has enjoyed so far. Through many of the more than sixty countries included in the initiative, there has been an overwhelming focus on the construction of energy and transport infrastructure by Chinese companies: dams, ports, railways, roads, airports and power plants. This is because China has what is termed 'industrial overcapacity' in these areas. Put simply, the Chinese domestic market is over-saturated with competing construction companies. It therefore suits China to export this overcapacity overseas in the service of foreign policy goals.[68] This is a luxury that is not enjoyed by the United States, which reportedly has difficulty finding a sufficient number of skilled workers for domestic infrastructure projects even once funding has been allocated.[69]

Meanwhile, the EU so far seems unable to coordinate a large-scale push by its construction companies into foreign markets, or even to get close to completing an integrated pan-European transport network. The EU's inability to get TEN-T off the ground since the 1990s compares extremely unfavourably with China's progress in constructing a high-speed rail (HSR) network: in China, more than 40,000 kilometres of track were constructed and put into operation between 2007 and 2021.[70] Anyone who has attempted to cross Europe by train knows that trans-European high-speed rail remains a distant dream. France launched its Paris-Lyon TGV line in 1981, but further construction of high-speed lines across Europe has been limited or non-existent.[71] International rail connections in the EU often require multiple changes and environmentally unfriendly air travel often remains the best option. Arguments about China abusing human rights by forcing people off their land to build rail connections miss the main point: whether one approves of the methods or not, China is getting transport infrastructure done rapidly, while the EU is not. The United States is even worse off, with only one line – Amtrak's North East Corridor – which can be said to qualify for HSR status with maximum speeds of up to 240 kilometres per hour.[72]

Despite China's image in the West as a producer of shoddy, low-quality goods (which is often deserved), China's HSR overall has an exemplary safety record. It is true that there was a deadly crash at Wenzhou in 2011: forty people were killed and 191 injured in a collision between two trains when lightning struck the line, causing the electronic system to send faulty signals. An investigation by the Chinese authorities into the Wenzhou crash resulted in a review of HSR safety procedures, the punishment of fifty-four officials judged to have been negligent and a reduction in maximum speed.[73] As a result, since 2011, there have been no other deadly HSR crashes in China. Given that by late 2020 there were over 9,600 high-speed trains travelling per day in China, the safety record of Chinese HSR since 2011 is, in fact, remarkably solid.[74]

Massive hydropower projects such as the Three Gorges Dam are another sign of China's ability to install new infrastructure of gigantic proportions. Of course, completing the Three Gorges project required more than one million people to be displaced from their homes.[75] Yet this is a sign of the advantage in mobilization power enjoyed by the Chinese state. It is almost unimaginable that a project planned in the West would involve displacing such a large number of people.

China has also steadily generated a competitive advantage in internet technology and infrastructure. This was an area in which the West – and especially the United States – held an enormous lead in the 1990s. Yet by the 2010s the advantage had been frittered away. For instance, Jonathan Hillman explains that the reason why the Chinese company Huawei dominates 5G internet infrastructure is because the West decided not to invest in it. Western companies had already handed Huawei and other Chinese companies the keys to the internet infrastructure sector by assisting their development from the 1990s onwards. They did this because they wanted to profit from penetrating the Chinese market and did not foresee Chinese companies moving swiftly to bridge the expertise gap. In doing so, Western internet firms created their own future competition and enabled Chinese companies to catch up, overtake and become market leaders in some sectors.[76]

China also has comparative economic advantages over the West. First, there is its geographical position at the heart of Asia. Asia contains around 60 per cent of the world's population. According to the International Monetary Fund (IMF), the Asia-Pacific region has the world's largest regional economy by GDP.[77] Since the 1970s, the Asia-Pacific has been the world's fastest growing region economically. Between 1971 and 1992, the Asia-Pacific economies grew at a collective rate of 7.7 per cent compared to a world average 2.9 per cent.[78] It remains the fastest growing region today.[79] With its own economy having grown at annual rates of between 5 and 10 per cent since the late 1970s, China is, and will continue to be, central to Asia's economic rise. While it is true that China's competitive advantage is in relative decline due to rising salaries, huge industrial hubs such as the one in Guangdong province (next to Hong Kong) still give the Middle Kingdom a good hand of cards. China remains a key player in world trade due to its established centres of production. This situation is not likely to change soon since it is not clear which countries might mount a serious challenge to Chinese dominance of regional and global markets.

Another comparative advantage for China arises from its so-called 'non-interference' policy. China's non-interference principle dictates that no state shall interfere in the internal affairs of another state. It is based on the idea, enshrined in the UN Charter, of respect for member states' national sovereignty. The Chinese leadership interprets the principle by strictly dealing only with the ruling government of a state, whatever its political persuasion. China, keenly aware of the need to maintain its internal cohesion, never offers support to opposition movements in other countries, particularly those which advocate separatism. By striking deals with national regimes regardless of whether they are democratic or authoritarian, China essentially supports those regimes. As a result, Chinese companies are able to gain access to individual countries' markets in a way that firms from principled Western nations with democratic normative agendas are not. The economic advantage of this is clear: Chinese companies garner contracts in countries – some of which are resource-rich, such as Sudan, Iran or Turkmenistan – that Western companies cannot touch with a bargepole. A relationship of mutual support between the Chinese and the partner country's regime develops which favours Chinese economic interests in the country – and allows BRI projects to be implemented. Whether this is at the cost of the human rights of individuals in those countries – undoubtedly that is the case – is extraneous to the main point as far as Beijing is concerned: China is gaining influence and promoting its economic and political interests in developing countries by establishing relationships with their incumbent regimes. This gives China a clear advantage over the United States and the EU, which, for the most part, do not engage with regimes in countries they regard as 'rogue states'.

This brings us to another advantage China has over the United States and the EU: its pragmatism in foreign policy. China is pragmatic in that it places economic and political goals ahead of ideals. China's pragmatism, as already discussed in Chapter 1, is embodied by Deng Xiaoping's maxim that 'it doesn't matter if a cat is black or white as long as it catches mice'. Pragmatism accounts for China's meshing of capitalism with communism and lack of interest in the political orientation of regimes in partner countries. It also accounts for China's strategy of strategic hedging: dealing equally with regional rivals (such as Saudi Arabia and Iran) rather than putting all its eggs in one basket.[80] Interestingly, pragmatism was once a watchword for the United States, most notably in the rebuilding of Japan and Germany after the Second World War, and when Henry Kissinger arranged in 1971 for Richard Nixon to go to Beijing and strike a deal with communist China in a successful attempt to counter the Soviet Union. However, as already discussed, US foreign policy has not been noted for its pragmatism since 9/11 and the poorly planned interventions in Afghanistan and Iraq.

Allied to China's pragmatism is its long-term consistency in foreign policy. Despite frequent Western claims of inconsistency, in fact Chinese foreign policy does not undergo tectonic shifts like the changes in US foreign policy seen after presidential elections. China sticks rigidly to some core diplomatic principles, most notably non-interference in the internal affairs of sovereign states and the One China policy. Leaders change; new leaders introduce new slogans; policy aims gradually shift and evolve; but China's core goal has remained consistent over the last several decades: to build up China's economic power, political influence and international status. It does this by mobilizing the population in the service of national goals and establishing strategic partnerships with developing countries, even those which the West ignores or shuns.

This brings us to China's final advantage. This is the fact that China has not used large-scale military interventions to solve international problems since its ill-fated invasion of Vietnam in 1979. Despite China's reputation in the West for military aggression, the historical record since 1979 reveals that Chinese forces have fought only relatively minor skirmishes – for instance on the border with India or with Vietnam in the South China Sea – and have not been involved in any wars. This is in marked contrast to the United States, which has participated in numerous conflicts over the last four decades, often as the aggressor. China's non-use of military solutions gives it two advantages over the United States in particular: first, it does not waste resources on military interventions; and second, it generates a reputation with most countries in the global South as a country which will not resort to military means to enforce its will. This does not negate the fact that China enforces its will through economic means; but it does mean that most countries – with obvious exceptions such as India and Vietnam – expect to be able to sustain relatively peaceful and economically orientated relations with China.

This does not mean that China will never use military force. The People's Liberation Army (PLA) is under the direct control of the Chinese Communist Party. However, its guiding principle is 'active defence' rather than the principles of regime change and pre-emptive strikes prevalent in the US military since the 1990s.[81] According to the PLA, 'active defence' means that 'We will not attack unless we are attacked, but we will surely counterattack if attacked.'[82] This sentence is a warning to would-be assailants formulated in the 1960s by Mao Zedong.[83] Under this principle, part of Chinese military policy is to expand territorial claims if possible where there is no clarity about sovereignty in international law (as in the South China Sea) and then make assertive noises in defence of those territories. Thus, the PLA and the Communist Party are united in standing firm against those who even slightly challenge what they regard as their sovereign claims vital to the defensive integrity of China. This explains why they protest about US freedom of navigation operations (FONOPs) in the South and East China Seas, and why they constantly push back against Indian activity on the border with Tibet. However, it is worth repeating that the Chinese have not launched any large-scale force into action beyond what they regard as a disputed border since the ill-fated 1979 invasion of north Vietnam.

Although it may seem a cliché to some, there is no doubt that the Chinese leadership and the PLA are well versed in the 'Art of War' style strategizing advocated by Sun-Tzu. This influences their strategic hedging style of international diplomacy mentioned earlier. Essentially, 'Art of War' strategy means weighing up your opponent's relative strength, position and preparedness before making any move against them. An intelligent military strategist only acts when sure of a victory which will lead to permanent gains. Such chess-like strategic thinking is an area in which the Americans have become increasingly fallible in recent decades, for instance in failing to consider the possibility of not being able to eradicate the Taliban and create a strong new regime in Afghanistan after the 2001 invasion. In contrast, the Chinese quietly learnt the lessons of their failed 1979 incursion into Vietnam and decided not to repeat it. Chinese leaders are surely also aware of the relatively untested character of their forces and know that committing them to fighting a conflict in large numbers would be a huge gamble, especially against enemy forces possessing equivalent or superior technology (such as the United States).

Conclusion

The discussion in this chapter reveals that contemporary China has numerous advantages over the United States and the EU. First, there is its cohesion, its 'tightness'. It is relatively easier for Chinese leaders to mobilize large swathes of the population in the service of national goals than for Western leaders to do so – as the Covid-19 pandemic, with its high rates of infections in the West and low rates in China, has demonstrated. The ability to incentivize the people to work for the nation in a relatively coordinated fashion gives China an enormous advantage over the West. There are also the Chinese advantages in infrastructure expertise, pragmatism and gaining access to resource-rich countries in the global South, some of which are shunned by the West. The strategically hedged Chinese engagement with a multitude of states – whatever their political persuasions and rivalries – will produce further results if the race for natural resources heats up over the course of the twenty-first century.

On the other hand, the main Western candidates that might be able to outdo or contain China's rise – the United States and the EU – have numerous disadvantages in the contemporary era. Above all comes their relative 'looseness' – relative lack of cohesion and unity. Lack of long-term consistency in planning and implementation of foreign policy also undermines their ability to counter China's rise. They do not conceive foreign policy as pragmatic strategic hedging, instead putting their eggs into certain baskets, such as the uncompromising promotion of Western norms. They do not tend to employ Art of War style thinking, preferring to fall back on normative agendas based on proselytizing about human rights and democracy – even if the record shows that ideals go out of the window when self-interested security is at stake (as in the refugee crisis in the EU).

In the end, whatever one thinks of China – and it is certainly possible to be concerned or appalled by many aspects of Chinese approaches to domestic and foreign policy – its advantages over the United States and the EU are numerous. One area, as we have noted, in which China has surged ahead of the West is in developing a relatively coordinated approach to infrastructure investment in the global South. In part, it has done this via the framework of Xi Jinping's Belt and Road Initiative. However, it is certainly not the case that the BRI is all plain sailing. There are various problems associated with the BRI, such as lack of transparency, environmental impacts, white elephant projects and debt loads for partner countries. At the same time, whatever its long-term impacts, Chinese BRI investment projects have changed the ground rules for investment by large economies in the global South. By 'Going Global' through the BRI, China has become an agent of change in the global South by altering perceptions of what is possible and desirable. In an era of disruption, one thing is for sure: in true complexity theory style, the outcomes of the BRI will not necessarily be linear or predictable. In the next chapter we turn to examining the details of the BRI's implementation – including both its successes and failures – to show how Xi Jinping's flagship foreign policy is changing the global South – and with it, the world.

Chapter 4

THE BELT AND ROAD INITIATIVE

The date was 7 September 2013, the location a lecture theatre at Nazarbayev University in Astana, the capital of Kazakhstan. As the audience settled, a besuited, middle-aged Chinese man waited patiently at the lectern for his time to speak. As silence fell on the room, President Xi Jinping began to talk about his vision for improved connectivity between Asia and Europe via Central Asia. He gave his vision a name: the 'Silk Road Economic Belt'.[1]

A month later, he made another speech in Indonesia explaining how China was going to build a 'twenty first-century Maritime Silk Road' to enhance cooperation in southeast Asia and beyond.[2] Few guessed at that time that what the Chinese president was unleashing upon an unsuspecting world in these two speeches would alter the landscape of international development over the course of the next decade.

To give you a flavour of what Xi said, here is an excerpt from his Nazarbayev University speech:

> To forge closer economic ties, deepen cooperation and expand development space in the Eurasian region, we should take an innovative approach and jointly build an economic belt along the Silk Road. This will be a great undertaking benefitting the people of all countries along the route. To turn this vision into reality, we may start in specific areas and connect them over time to cover the whole region.[3]

When I visited Nazarbayev University in Kazakhstan's capital city Astana five years later, I was struck by how small and unassuming the venue for the speech was. It took place in a standard-sized lecture theatre with a capacity for perhaps 200–300 people. While elegantly furnished, this was no grand ceremonial chamber such as the one used for the annual conventions of the Chinese Communist Party, attended by thousands of delegates. Yet Xi's speech, attended by a hand-selected group of spectators, continues to have global repercussions beyond its relatively modest setting.[4]

Xi probably did not have a clear conception of how his plan would be received. In the wake of the speech, even his acolytes seemed at first to be unsure exactly what he meant. Arriving at an official interpretation of the speeches took some time – and presumably much behind-the-scenes consultation. It was only in March 2015 that an official document presenting the goals of the BRI – entitled *Vision and actions on jointly building Belt and Road* – was finally published.[5] The document outlined six 'economic corridors' along which Xi's vision for trade and investment connectivity would be implemented. The implication was that Chinese-funded development would be concentrated in developing these chiefly Asian regions, as well as connecting them over land and sea to Europe. It had taken over a year to transform the speech into a policy programme – albeit one painted in broad brushstrokes.

After the appearance of the *Vision and Actions* formal declaration of intent, the rush to jump on the BRI bandwagon gathered pace. Chinese state media talked up the initiative. Unofficial maps of the 'route' of the BRI through Central Asia to Europe were published. Since almost all the countries included in *Vision and Actions* were economically developing ones, it seemed clear that the main focus of the BRI was on developing trade, investment and connectivity between China and the nations of the global South. Chinese companies fell over each other in their haste to secure fully endorsed state funding for overseas projects under the BRI umbrella. Data concerning Chinese overseas investments reveal a spike in outlay on the part of Chinese state financial institutions and corporations during 2014 to 2017.[6] During this period, there was a gold rush as Chinese firms stampeded into designated Belt and Road countries chasing a trail of fluttering banknotes.

Yet almost a decade later, the BRI was generally still not well understood either in the West – or even in China. European commentators frequently described it as 'vague' and 'over-ambitious', especially in its early days.[7] The Chinese themselves have not exactly helped the outside world to understand what the BRI means: public relations campaigns have been half-baked and unconvincing. Getting multi-ethnic children or rappers to sing sappy songs on YouTube in praise of the BRI has not been a good look for a state-led economic initiative with political undertones.[8] The result is that Xi Jinping's flagship foreign policy initiative has tended to acquire different characteristics depending on the eye of the beholder. These run along a spectrum from a sinister bid for global domination to an attempt to build win-win friendships based on mutual respect.[9] Of course, the reality lies somewhere between these two extremes. However, there can be little doubt that the BRI enables China to garner influence in the developing world despite initial claims that the initiative was devoid of political content.[10] It is also certain that the initiative is intended to promote China's long-term goal of securing supplies of raw materials, creating new opportunities for Chinese firms and generally spreading risk by putting eggs in as many baskets as possible.[11]

To me, the BRI's vision of connectivity and integration from Asia to Europe initially made sense. I had travelled widely in Asia and Eastern Europe for two decades and knew that many countries lacked good transport and other infrastructure. For instance, different gauges meant that trains had to be refitted at China's border with Kazakhstan, resulting in substantial delays. In Mongolia, I had witnessed how the road simply ran out once we had left the vicinity of Ulan Bataar: our intercity bus started bouncing over the grasslands and weaving between trees in the forest. Once, when the bus got stuck in mud in the middle of the night, we had to get out so that all the passengers could help get the wheels free by piling stones under them and pushing. In Himachal Pradesh, our bus had traversed precarious unpaved ledges along mountainsides and even driven along a riverbed piled high with boulders. In Laos, the main road to the border crossing with Vietnam was a muddy track. The road leading out of Cambodia to the Thai border was full of potholes. All these countries urgently needed radical upgrades to their transport networks.

Thus, in the eyes of optimistic observers – including me – it was logical for China to build improved connections to help develop trade and economic ties across the Eurasian landmass.[12] Yet those initial impressions were naive: the BRI would turn out to be about much more than just transport infrastructure. An important part of China's motivation for 'Going Global' has always been to protect and sustain what it calls its 'comprehensive national power' – which includes its economic, energy and resource security.[13] In 2014, Xi Jinping introduced the idea of a 'holistic security concept', which included energy and economic security as key components.[14]

There are three aspects to the BRI which go beyond the obvious investment and infrastructure component. First, Beijing seeks to secure its energy supplies by negotiating deals and gaining influence in resource-rich countries. Second, it tries to maintain China's economic growth by developing untapped markets. Third, China seeks to gain more political and economic influence in nations of the global South which feel neglected by the West. As observers came to understand these concealed aspects of the BRI, some of them began to challenge the connectivity vision, raising questions about issues such as Chinese political influence, economic coercion, white elephant infrastructure projects and alleged 'debt traps'.[15] Soon there could be little doubt that there was much more to the BRI than just roads and railways. Like any emergent phenomena in conditions of complexity, outcomes would be hard to predict – and hard to control.

There were also important lessons to be learnt about how China was reshaping regional orders in its own image, altering the (often Western-based) norms of interaction between target countries.[16] It was clear that China's engagement with the outside world via the BRI was complex and multifaceted, containing intertwined ideational and material aspects – even if the former were not emphasized as much as the latter in official and media narratives.[17] As we will see in the remainder of this chapter, and as Lina Benabdallah demonstrates in her book about China-Africa relations, China's ideational influence-building and norm-setting are at least as important in the implementation and outcomes of the initiative as physical infrastructure and economic development.[18]

There are already plenty of volumes examining many aspects of the BRI.[19] Rather than simply synthesizing or critiquing existing accounts, in this chapter I set out to focus specifically on the extent to which the BRI has transformed the complex ideational and material landscape in which regional and global interactions are situated. For China as an agent of change – a revisionist or reformist power, in the parlance of academic international relations[20] – the BRI is (at least as long as Xi Jinping remains president) the primary framework through which Beijing attempts to alter conceptions of international development.[21] Therefore, to assess the significance of the BRI, we need to examine evidence concerning its implementation and how it has impacted international and regional relations. The most important point is to reveal the extent to which the introduction of the BRI into Chinese foreign policy has altered the landscape in which global affairs take place.

The remainder of this chapter will explore the broad characteristics and implementation of the BRI to evaluate its impacts and potential. I begin by comparing the official presentation of the BRI with the on-the-ground reality of its implementation from several aspects: the use of 'economic corridors', regionalization and the use of loans to fund projects. In each case, as I did in my first two books about the BRI and CPEC, I interrogate an aspect of the initiative by comparing expectation with implementation.[22] I do this to establish the extent to which mediated representations of the BRI (in official documents, the media or academic publications) and its real-world impacts correlate. Unsurprisingly, often they do not. The following is intended to show the extent to which expectations do or do not match reality, in order to reveal the level of real-world impact that the BRI has had – in both material and ideational terms.

Economic 'corridors': connecting what with where?

In 2015 and 2016, the BRI appeared to consist mainly of announcements of massive infrastructure construction projects in upwards of sixty mostly developing countries which had been included by China in the initiative. It should be noted that in its early phase, the BRI was not focused on the global North. It arguably still is not, despite ongoing adjustments to the *Vision and Actions* manifesto such as the addition of a 'Polar Silk Road' between China and Western Europe.[23] The *Vision and Actions* document mentioned six 'economic corridors' involving Asian and European regions: Central Asia, Southeast Asia, South Asia, the Middle East (called 'West Asia' by the Chinese) and Central and Eastern Europe (CEE). Unofficial maps of the BRI's route or routes across Asia towards Europe were published by media outlets and think tanks.[24]

Thus, in the initiative's early years it appeared that the BRI focused on economic development of selected Asian and Central and East European countries classified as belonging to the global South. Ostensibly, economic development was to be achieved through infrastructure construction funded by Chinese banks and built by Chinese companies. The BRI seemed to be an economic project focused on connectivity, trade, investment and transport links. In other words, it had the appearance of a highly ambitious infrastructure construction megaproject with strictly material goals and specific target regions.

In terms of the overseas expansion of commercial activity by Chinese enterprises, Xi's announcement of the BRI was not as revolutionary as it seemed. To an extent, the BRI is a new label on an old tin. Chinese companies have been encouraged to 'go global' since the Jiang Zemin era in the 1990s.[25] Sinologist David Shambaugh points out that it was Xi's predecessor as Chinese president, Hu Jintao, who put more focus on the importance of developing the global South (rather than just emphasizing developed countries and major power diplomacy).[26] Long before that, in the era of Chairman Mao, China had built infrastructure in the global South, such as a railway between Tanzania and Zambia, construction of which began in 1970.[27] The Karakoram Highway connecting China to Pakistan across the Himalayas was completed in 1979.[28] On the other hand, these and other investments were somewhat piecemeal and unsystematically applied: for instance, the Tanzania railway fell into disrepair in the decades after its completion. The lack of systematic overseas investment is not surprising given the turmoil in China under Mao and the fact that China was still building its domestic economy through the Deng, Jiang and Hu eras (1978–2012). China's Mao-era investments in the global South did not have the weight of a global economic superpower behind them. Thus, while the BRI shares some characteristics with Jiang Zemin's 'Going Global' strategy, Mao's 'Third World' solidarity and Hu's focus on building a 'harmonious world', it is on a completely different level in terms of scale and investment.

On the map at least, the BRI's six 'corridors' stretch to all corners of Asia like a vast cobweb made of roads and railways. However, it should be noted that almost a decade after Xi proposed the BRI, the 'economic corridors' exist more as ideas than as completed physical realities. The first corridor is the New Eurasian Land Bridge, which is essentially another name for what Xi called the 'Silk Road Economic Belt' in his 2013 speech. It is intended to connect China with Central and Eastern Europe via Central Asia and Russia. The second is the China-Central Asia-West Asia Corridor (CCAWEC), which is supposed to connect China to Europe via Central Asia, Iran and Turkey. The third is the China-Pakistan Economic Corridor (CPEC), which is supposed to connect Xinjiang in northwest China with the Indian Ocean and beyond via Pakistani territory. The other three corridors are the Bangladesh-China-India-Myanmar Corridor (BCIM), the China-Mongolia-Russia Corridor and the China-Indochina Peninsula Corridor. In all six cases, proposed, new or pre-existing railways appear to be the main proposed transport connections linking China with the outside world.

Of the six corridors, two contain existing rail routes through Russia to Europe: the New Eurasian Land Bridge and the China-Mongolia-Russia Corridor. The railways through these routes appear to have been improved to some extent since 2013, but they are not new links. The other four contain some railways, including ones recently constructed by Chinese companies. However, along these four 'corridors' so far there is no complete connection with the supposed endpoint. A case in point is CPEC, where there has been some work on railways *within* Pakistan (most notably, the new ML-1 link from Karachi to Peshawar). However, as of 2022 there is no plan for a cross-border rail link to China.[29] Hence, the 'corridor' label can largely only be applied to intra-Pakistan connectivity since the only cross-border connection is the pre-existing (and problematic) Karakoram Highway built in the 1970s.[30] Similarly, there is no complete connection via BCIM: it does not appear likely that there will be given India's refusal to participate in the BRI. India has also apparently pressured Bangladesh not to accept Chinese construction projects such as the one at Sonadia port. The main international connection consists of two pipelines, one for oil and one for natural gas, from Kunming in China's Yunnan province to Kyaukpyu port in Myanmar. As far as CCAWEC is concerned, a rail connection has been established from Beijing to Iran, but it does not yet extend through Turkey. Lastly, regarding the China-Indochina Peninsula Corridor, a new railway was completed in December 2021 from Boten on the Chinese border to Vientiane, the capital of Laos; but this has not yet been connected to the Thai rail system, and Thai rail does not yet cross the border into Malaysia.[31] Therefore, the China-Indochina Peninsula Corridor remains in a development phase, especially since Chinese companies do not appear to be working on an international road network in any systematic way so far (more details in Chapter 5).

The 'economic corridor' concept is thus a problematic one. Generally, as I showed in my previous book about the China-Pakistan Economic Corridor, it has not been very clearly explained either by the Chinese government or by scholars.[32] For instance, Siegfried Wolf makes mighty efforts to clarify the concept; but since he ends up including no fewer than eighteen 'key indicators', his definition is too diffuse to be useful as a concise mental aid.[33] In contrast, Hans-Peter Brunner's more concise suggestions that 'economic corridors connect economic agents along a defined geography', and that 'they have to be analysed as part of integrated economic networks' present a framework which is rather broad and vague. Brunner's assertion that economic corridors 'are not mere transport connections along which people and goods move' is also somewhat undermined by the emphasis of the Chinese government's *Vision and Actions* document on enhancing transport connections and the heavy focus on transport infrastructure among BRI projects.[34]

One would assume that the primary intention of an economic corridor would be to enhance both intra-regional and international trade connectivity. After all, a corridor, by definition, is a route connecting two or more points in space. However, in the cases of the six corridors included in the *Vision and Actions* publication, there does not appear to be much (if any) progress in creating free trade zones in the style of the EU. Bilateral trade agreements still govern relations between China and specific countries, with no serious attempt to introduce wider regional trade agreements.[35]

Consequently, at many points on the route of the BRI, cross-border trade remains inefficient and prone to corruption. For instance, Kyrgyz researchers found that goods worth tens of billions of dollars were smuggled from Xinjiang province in northwest China into Kyrgyzstan and Kazakhstan between 2001 and 2020.[36] In January 2022, Kazakhstan's President Tokayev pointed to smuggling on the China-Kazakhstan border as a serious problem that had been affecting national revenues for years. He promised to address the problem by boosting transparency and dismantling the corrupt oligopoly which controlled Kazakhstan's economy under his predecessor President Nazarbayev: time will tell if his words are transformed into actions.[37]

Another example of cross-border inefficiency is the Khunjerab Pass, the only point at which Pakistan and China are connected overland via the Karakoram Highway at a height of 4500 metres above sea level: the pass is closed for four months of the year due to heavy snowfall.[38] Even when open, the passage of goods between the two countries is tightly controlled by China. The border was closed to goods trade for almost the whole of 2020, meaning that Pakistani traders reliant on cross-border commerce were severely affected.[39] The closure occurred ostensibly because of the Covid-19 pandemic. However, it was also certainly related to security issues relating to China's need to prevent cross-border support for separatists in Xinjiang.[40]

Thus, in an important sense the six 'economic corridors' remain abstract concepts or public relations slogans rather than fully implemented trade zones in any meaningful sense. Even so, by reshaping public conceptions of what might be possible, China's promotion of the economic corridor concept has introduced a new normative element into the public sphere: the idea that it may be possible to reshape regional economic relations by enhancing trade and transport connectivity between neighbouring countries. Since 'economic corridors' are conceptually part of the overarching BRI, participants have been led to believe that China intends to assist them into a more economically developed future in which they are part of a regional trading bloc. This expectation, even against the backdrop of criticisms and the BRI's inherent problems, has of itself altered the ideational (if not necessarily the material) landscape in which economic development in the global South takes place. This normative shift has shifted the development narrative to one in which China is viewed as the potential purveyor of economic and societal transformation on a regional and global scale – rather than the West.

BRI regions: what's their value to China?

In its original conception, the BRI was directed towards five regions: Central Asia, Southeast Asia, South Asia, the Middle East (which the Chinese call 'West Asia', or *xiya*, 西亚) and Central and Eastern Europe (CEE). The number of regions increased once Africa, Latin America, Western Europe and the Arctic were included. However, as I showed in a previous book, there are some good reasons to believe that the core focus of the BRI is on the Eurasian landmass and the original five regions (even though one should not discount Chinese investments in Africa and Latin America).[41]

Obviously, geography plays an important role in global affairs, and this includes Chinese foreign policy. Like any nation state, China generally puts more focus on developing relations with countries and regions in its immediate vicinity than those that are geographically distant. China has land borders with more neighbouring countries (fourteen) than any other country on Earth except Russia (also fourteen). An important part of the Beijing government's foreign policy – at least in the minds of leaders – is to avoid being 'encircled' by hostile neighbours, probably at the instigation of the United States.[42] For this reason, the Chinese government feels that it cannot allow its global rivals – most notably the United States – to gain more influence in neighbouring countries.[43] Beijing therefore tries to steadily develop what one might term a neighbourhood influence network in order to keep the United States at arm's length and to make sure its neighbours are either somewhat friendly or neutral. This, for instance, is one of the reasons why China founded the Shanghai Cooperation Organization (SCO): to manage and coordinate China and Russia's security relations with Central Asian states. In a region regarded in the nineteenth and early twentieth centuries as the site of a 'great game' for territorial control between Britain and Russia, the SCO has facilitated reasonably amicable cooperation instead of Sino-Russian power competition.[44]

Feeling pressured by the United States from the east, especially since the Obama administration's supposed 'pivot to Asia' after 2010, it was a natural decision for China to try to develop its relations with countries immediately to the south and west, especially those in which American influence was relatively weak. There is not much that China can do about US influence in Japan or South Korea, since the Americans have long-standing ties and military bases there; but Beijing has a relatively free hand in countries such as Myanmar, Laos, Cambodia, Pakistan and Kyrgyzstan, since the United States has either neglected relations with these countries or has decided to leave them to their own devices. It is also relatively easier to develop trade with countries which are on one's doorstep than those which are far away. One might therefore expect China's economic activity to be more intense in its backyard. Exceptions to this principle would be countries that have substantial reserves of fossil fuels or other natural resources which China may wish to tap, such as certain countries in Africa (e.g., Angola, Sudan, Nigeria) or Latin America (Brazil, Venezuela).

Based on proximity alone, the most important regions for BRI investments might thus be expected to be Central Asia, Southeast Asia and South Asia, which are situated immediately to the west and south of China. However, investment data obtained from the AEI's China Global Investment Tracker (see Table 4.1) reveal that the Middle East also figures highly in China's outbound foreign direct investment (OFDI) between 2013 and 2021 (the BRI era). Clearly, the Middle East is a key region for China because of its oil and natural gas reserves. Persian Gulf countries supply more than half of China's imported oil, so it is natural for China to focus investment there, especially in the energy sector.[45] While total investment in Central Asia appears lower than might be predicted in comparison to other regions, of course one must acknowledge the fact that there are only five Central Asian states. Central Asia also has a much lower total population than the other regions: comparing total investment to total population reveals that China's OFDI in the region is relatively high. The relative size of China's investments in Central Asian countries is revealed by dividing OFDI by regional population: this calculation demonstrates that China has focused more investment per capita in Central Asia than in any of the other four regions. The Middle East is in second place. South Asia trails in a distant last when accounting for its vast population.

It is probable that Central Asia and the Middle East have received comparatively larger volumes of Chinese investments because of their known fossil fuel reserves.

Table 4.1 BRI investments

Region	Population in millions (2020)	Number of countries	Total BRI investment (OFDI), 2013–21, US$ billion	OFDI divided by population
Central Asia	74.3	5	35.58	0.48
Southeast Asia	768.6	11	203.55	0.26
South Asia	1856.4	8	114.25	0.06
Middle East (West Asia)	448.8	17	157.51	0.35
Central and Eastern Europe	187.2	20	38.1	0.20

Source: author, based on data from AEI China Global Investment Tracker, UN population statistics

Some Southeast Asian countries such as Indonesia, Malaysia and Brunei also have sizeable oil and natural gas reserves, while others (Cambodia, Myanmar) are in the process of being developed. This makes Southeast Asia the third most attractive region for Chinese investment. In contrast, Central and Eastern Europe (CEE) and South Asia are not obviously rich in fossil fuels or other natural resources which would assist China's economic growth. This means that there is less obvious motivation for China to invest in these two regions. When compounded with the fact that they lag behind the West in terms of high-tech industries and other assets which are attractive to Chinese companies and investors, the reason for relatively lower levels of Chinese OFDI becomes clear. An additional point is that South Asia includes India, which has refused to participate in the BRI. India sees the BRI (and its 'flagship project', the China-Pakistan Economic Corridor, which obviously involves India's nuclear rival Pakistan) as an attempt to establish Chinese hegemony in the region at India's expense. These factors help to explain the remarkably low per capita levels of BRI investment in South Asia.

Beijing has been keen to develop what it calls 'regional cooperation frameworks' as part of the BRI. In all five regions except South Asia, cooperation frameworks including China already existed before the BRI. The SCO, an expansion of the Shanghai Five mutual security agreement created in 1996, was set up in 2003. China became a 'dialogue partner' of the Association of Southeast Asian Nations (ASEAN) in 1996: annual summits have been held ever since.[46] In the Middle East, taking account of regional tensions, China set up the China-Arab States Cooperation Forum in 2004. In CEE, a framework called the '16+1' to encourage cooperation between sixteen selected countries and China was set up in 2012. There is no China-South Asia cooperation framework due to tensions between Pakistan and India (and between China and India). In lieu of formal regional cooperation in South Asia, India and Pakistan joined the SCO in 2017.

However, working within these regional cooperation frameworks has been far from plain sailing for Beijing in many cases. For instance, the 16+1 (relabelled '17+1' after the admission of Greece in 2019) failed to establish functioning regional cooperation in the CEE region during its first decade.[47] By 2019, Poland, the Czech Republic, Romania and the three Baltic states were in the process of disengaging themselves from the framework.[48] In 2021, Lithuania went so far as to withdraw itself from the framework formally.[49] In August 2022, Estonia and Latvia also pulled out.[50] An additional problem is that the Chinese did not include Belarus, Moldova and Ukraine in the 16/17+1, presumably as a sign of respect for Russian influence (or intention to increase influence) in those countries, making the arrangement an odd one in regional terms. Russia's invasion of Ukraine in February 2022 reveals the rationale behind China's decision not to include these three countries in a hypothetical Chinese 'sphere of influence'.

In South Asia, India's suspicion of China's intentions along its northern border and in the Indian Ocean has resulted in its refusal to participate in the BRI and the China-Pakistan Economic Corridor (CPEC). Regional cooperation remains impossible, with India suspicious of Chinese port-building projects in Sri Lanka, Pakistan, Myanmar and Bangladesh (where a Chinese project was rejected, presumably at the behest of India).[51] For these and similar reasons, China has pragmatically tended to emphasize bilateral 'strategic partnerships' in building working relationships with individual partners.

What the above analysis reveals is that while the 'economic corridor' concept may be used mainly for rhetorical purposes, and regional cooperation frameworks have not worked as well as Beijing surely hoped, Chinese OFDI in individual countries within the five key regions identified in the *Vision and Actions* document has still been substantial. There are significant investments in the energy sectors of the resource-rich countries of Central Asia and the Middle East, as well as in some countries in Southeast Asia. Although from the regionalization angle China's expansion into the five regions seems underwhelming, from the viewpoint of investment activity in energy – mining, power plants, oil pipelines and so on – China's development programme has had some important impacts in individual countries. The next section (and the next chapter) will go into more detail on these.

BRI investments and infrastructure: good for what, good for whom?

At the level of detail, investments under the BRI label are somewhat difficult to evaluate for two reasons. The first is that amounts pledged may not be equal to amounts really invested. There is a tendency in some cases for actual funds disbursed to lag behind promises. For instance, seventeen agreements for over 8 billion euros of Chinese investments in the Czech Republic were signed during Xi Jinping's visit to Prague in 2016.[52] However, by 2020 cumulative Chinese investments in the Czech Republic (including some made between 2000 and 2016) amounted to only around 1.2 billion euros.[53] Similarly, repeated media reports of a $400 billion Chinese investment programme in Iran[54] have so far turned out to be wholly exaggerated. Chinese overseas foreign direct investment (OFDI) in Iran amounted to only $12.24 billion between 2014 and 2019, with no signs of any larger inflows by 2022.[55] Outcomes like these mean that care must be taken to evaluate realized investment totals rather than pledges. Fortunately, the American Enterprise Institute's (AEI) China Global Investment Tracker is a relatively good guide to the realities of Chinese OFDI.[56]

The second difficulty in evaluating BRI investments is their general lack of transparency due to reliance on bilateral trade deals signed between heads of state behind closed doors. While it is true that investments coordinated by China's Asian Infrastructure Investment Bank (AIIB) are fully transparent since the accounts are accessible on the AIIB website, these constitute only a fraction of the total of BRI investments. By the end of 2020, the AIIB had a little over $32 billion in total assets, funded by contributions from 105 member countries, among which China is the largest shareholder.[57] According to the AEI's China Global Investment Tracker, total cumulative Belt and Road investments amounted to $332.6 billion in early 2022.[58] The difference between the two numbers – the second figure is more than ten times the first – reveals that most Chinese OFDI is being delivered non-transparently outside the totally transparent AIIB. Although the AIIB was founded by China in 2015 to coordinate member states' investments in the developing world, the data demonstrate that most Chinese investment does not go through this bank. In fact, the much-trumpeted AIIB appears to be a highly publicized distraction from the real business of the BRI, which is mostly conducted behind closed doors. Investment funds are mostly disbursed directly from Chinese state banks to individual countries for specific projects in which Chinese companies obtain the contract. They are allocated via agreements signed at the leadership level for which details are not usually supplied. The difference between AIIB and BRI investments is even more striking when BRI construction projects are added to investments to make a total of $838 billion.[59] This impressive sum is indicative of a global investment and infrastructure construction drive with important impacts for the countries in which projects are taking place.

What is less certain is the quality of the impacts. The most important question is whether Chinese-funded energy and transport infrastructure projects – according to the AEI's investment tracker the most prevalent in BRI countries – are really transforming the relevant sectors of the target countries' economies. How many of them are more likely to be white elephants resulting in useless hunks of concrete sitting in places where they are not needed? Are they generating unsustainable levels of debt in vulnerable countries, as some analysts believe?[60] Or are allegations of 'debt-trap diplomacy' exaggerated, as another group of analysts insist?[61] What are the environmental impacts of infrastructure megaprojects such as dams, power plants and ports? On the other hand, even if not all emerging outcomes are the ones originally intended or desired (as complexity theory predicts), any changes – even negative ones – would indicate a transformative impact from China's involvement in the investment and infrastructure environment in partner nations.

In developing countries, BRI projects are mainly focused on energy and transport infrastructure. For instance, this is the case in Pakistan under the label of the China-Pakistan Economic Corridor (CPEC): forty-four out of sixty-three projects concern energy and transport infrastructure directly, while eight more are connected to the development of Gwadar port.[62] Energy and transport are fields in which Chinese companies can deliver since they can utilize expertise obtained domestically. Where relevant, the projects are backed by low-interest loans from Chinese state banks in exchange for preferential access to natural resources. One might call this the 'Angola model': since 2002, China has been constructing infrastructure such as roads and hospitals in Angola in exchange for oil at cut-price rates.[63] The exchange benefits both sides. Similarly, China is gaining access to cobalt – a rare earth needed for electric vehicle batteries – in the Democratic Republic of Congo (DRC) in exchange for roads, railways and power plants. China now controls fifteen out of nineteen cobalt mines in the DRC.[64] In the Xi Jinping era, the model of Chinese state-backed loans for energy and transport infrastructure in exchange for natural resource exports has also been applied in Central Asian countries such as Kazakhstan and Uzbekistan under the BRI banner.

In contrast, the loans plus infrastructure for natural resources model have not been applied in the global North, where acquiring existing assets rather than developing greenfield sites has largely been the preferred approach. For comparison, fifty-two of seventy-four major Chinese investments in Pakistan between 2013 and 2021 were construction projects, while this classification applies to only one out of sixty-four Chinese projects in Germany, and only one out of thirty-seven Chinese investments in France.[65] Clearly, and understandably, the Chinese strategy towards developed economies is on an entirely different track to that in the developing world. In the global South, China overwhelmingly creates new assets using state-backed loans and construction companies, while in the global North it attempts to acquire existing assets. This is a dual-track pattern which apparently seems natural to the Chinese, but which has not been systematically applied by Western countries in the contemporary era.

The question then is whether one should be concerned about China's seemingly systematic acquisition of assets in the global North and loan-backed construction projects in the global South. Does it constitute a deliberate strategy of extracting advanced technologies and blueprints for use in Chinese research and development alongside a programme of infrastructure- and influence-building in the developing world? In other words, does the BRI's investment and infrastructure strategy constitute a plan for global domination by Chinese companies under the guidance of the Chinese Communist Party? Or is it possible to take at face value China's assertion that the BRI is intended to establish a 'community of shared destiny' which can generate mutually beneficial outcomes?[66] These questions drive the next two sections.

State-backed loans: development tool or debt trap?

There are two schools of thought on Chinese loan-backed investment and infrastructure projects. The first school claims that they constitute a long-term strategy for the neo-colonialist exploitation of developing countries.[67] The idea is that by deliberately getting partner countries into debt acquired to pay for infrastructure construction by Chinese companies, China aims for debt-equity swaps that allow it to obtain long-term control over some of the assets it has built. As part of the deal, China can also gain access to cut-price natural resources such as oil and natural gas, which it obtains at reduced cost in exchange for investments. At the same time, as a by-product of ill-conceived projects, infrastructure of poor quality or which is superfluous to requirements – white elephants or so-called 'ghost cities' – are bequeathed on the partner country. The resulting package of advantages for China – and disadvantages for the partner – based on state-backed loans to cash-poor countries has commonly been labelled 'debt-trap diplomacy'. Since 2017, the phrase has gained broad traction, especially in international media. Although one prominent China scholar has labelled it a 'meme' based on media spin which lacks a factual basis,[68] the debt-trap diplomacy hypothesis needs to be taken seriously due to the precarious finances of many developing countries. The hypothesis therefore demands careful analysis using data concerning debt, investment and trade.

The alternative hypothesis is that China has filled a development gap left by the West and offers new economic opportunities to the countries concerned. In this version, BRI loans do not load partners with excessive debt burdens and the new infrastructure can be genuinely transformational for developing economies. Rather than neo-colonialist exploitation, China is offering leadership and investment, creating 'win-win' outcomes for both partner countries and China.[69] As both a member and the self-appointed leader of the global South, China is constructing a new order. This is different from the imperialist expansion of European powers who colonized most of the nations which are now included in the BRI.[70] In this interpretation, China's New Silk Road offers an alternative to the ongoing exploitation – via structural power and the logic of capitalist relations of production – of the global South by the nations of the global North.[71]

So which of the two versions is correct? The reality is that while each interpretation presents some useful analysis of certain aspects of the issue, neither provides a full explanation. The reason is that both perspectives focus primarily on economic relations and take little account of non-material factors such as questions of political influence and the power to shape new norms upon which interactions will be based. A full picture of Chinese investments under the label of the BRI would need to account for China's emerging normative power and influence attempts as well as the economics. Nevertheless, before diving into an analysis of the BRI's ideational aspects in the next section, it is necessary to examine the question of 'debt-trap diplomacy' versus 'mutual benefit' with reference to economic data.

Scholars have done some groundwork on this question. In an important study published in 2018, Hurley et al examined BRI debt in sixty-eight countries. Their study revealed that while in most cases there were not likely to be severe problems with debt, eight countries were at high risk of debt distress. The countries identified were Montenegro, Mongolia, Pakistan, the Maldives, Djibouti, Laos, Kyrgyzstan and Tajikistan.[72] The authors note the need for greater transparency, multilateral standards, channelling funds through international institutions such as the International Monetary Fund (IMF) and a systematic rather than ad hoc approach to lending on the part of China. They point out that interest rates on loans have tended to be higher than claimed in some cases, for instance in Pakistan, where rates have reached 5 per cent.[73] They also note that interest rates have varied from interest-free loans to fully commercial rates (in the case of the Ethiopia-Djibouti railway).[74] At the same time, they acknowledge that the Chinese government is aware of the need for more regulation. In November 2017, the China Banking Regulatory Commission introduced increased risk controls for overseas lending by Chinese state banks such as Exim Bank.[75] Overall, Hurley et al's study suggests a mixed, complex picture for Chinese lending to BRI countries rather than a sophisticated, coordinated scheme of debt-trap diplomacy.

Similarly, Deborah Bräutigam demonstrates that the media portrayal of the BRI as a vehicle for debt-trap diplomacy is misleading. She points out, through case studies of Sri Lanka, Venezuela, Djibouti and Angola, that 'Chinese lending is far more complicated, interesting and potentially developmental than it is currently portrayed'.[76] For instance, in Angola an apparent 'ghost city' was empty in the first few years after its construction. However, it filled up with people once prices went down and the city was connected to sewage and water systems.[77] Venezuela, the largest recipient of Chinese overseas finance, was supposed to supply China with cut-price oil in return for loans. However, when Venezuela's economic situation deteriorated, China was unable to secure either the total promised oil imports or a return on its loans. The Chinese demonstrated 'little interest in accumulating Venezuelan assets, even when Venezuela was unable to resume repayment'.[78] China, lacking any leverage to get its money back, became more unwilling to risk any deeper involvement with a country it began to assess as an economic failure. In this case, China's supposed 'debt-trap diplomacy' ended up looking like more of a trap for China than Venezuela. Bräutigam also shows that the governments of Sri Lanka and Djibouti are as much responsible for their debts as China since they actively sought out Chinese loans.[79] The same can be said of Pakistan, whose structural economic problems and circular debt due to elite corruption date back to long before the advent of the China-Pakistan Economic Corridor.[80]

Lee Jones and Shahar Hameiri agree that it is wrong to assign all the blame for excessive debt to China.[81] Debtor governments should assume responsibility for the repayment of the loans they request. They should also do more to ensure the sustainability of the projects financed by the loans. Using the examples of Sri Lanka and Malaysia, they concur with Bräutigam in showing that debtor countries co-construct the conditions of their loans and infrastructure projects with China. Accordingly, both China and countries receiving loans should do more to ensure debt sustainability and the viability of the projects being financed under the BRI label. Like Bräutigam, Jones and Hameiri conclude that 'debt-trap diplomacy' is a myth since it often suits recipient governments 'to serve their own domestic agendas' such as sustaining economic growth.[82] Meanwhile, they did not discern much in the way of benefits for China in the cases of Sri Lanka and Malaysia, with mismanagement and inadequate assessment of risk on both sides.[83]

Beyond these studies, since 2017 there are signs of China's awareness of the need to manage risk. The Chinese government is far from foolish and wants a return on its money. It also does not want to be perceived by its domestic audience as throwing money away. The Chinese public finds it difficult to understand why China is investing billions overseas when so many parts of China still lack development. For these reasons, the flow of Chinese investment capital slowed after the peak years of 2016 and 2017 when the irrational exuberance of enthusiasm for the BRI was at its height. For instance, after reaching a peak in 2016, the flow of Chinese investments to Pakistan and Iran slowed down.[84] This supports the assertion that the debt-trap diplomacy hypothesis is not fully representative of the BRI story. Rather than China trapping recipient countries, it appears that it is now China that is trying to avoid falling into a debt trap where it does not recoup its investments. At the same time, 'win-win cooperation' is also falling apart in cases – such as Malaysia – where both sides are having doubts about the wisdom of continuing as projects founder and trust dissipates.

There is also the question of why Chinese investments are viewed with general suspicion when funds provided by other countries or Western institutions are not. For instance, bailouts from the International Monetary Fund (IMF) are not seen as a debt trap. Yet this is certainly how they were perceived in South Korea after the Asian currency crisis of 1997: I know because I lived there between 1998 and 2004. At that time, Koreans were surprisingly bitter about being forced to borrow from the IMF and submit to conditions imposed by the institution. As part of the bailout package, Korea was required to radically restructure its economy and consult economic decisions with the IMF. The Korean government decided to pay the money back as quickly as possible and managed to mobilize citizens in support of this decision. To escape from what Koreans called the 'IMF Crisis', Koreans made huge sacrifices for their country, most notably melting down over $2 billion of family gold and contributing it to the national coffers.[85] As a result, the debt was repaid remarkably quickly: just four years later the last repayment was made. A foreign ministry spokesman commented: 'We've retaken our economic sovereignty … From now on, we no longer need prior consultations with the IMF in planning and executing our economic policies.'[86]

Nevertheless, despite the Korean reaction, IMF loans are not generally perceived – in the West at least – as a 'debt trap'. Rather, they are seen as aid. BRI loans are placed in a different category, even though they fund the construction of much-needed infrastructure rather than as bailouts to bankrupt economies. They also generally consist of relatively smaller amounts than the $58 billion 1997 IMF loan to South Korea, although of course such calculations must be weighed against the ability of the debtor country to repay based on its cash reserves (or lack of them). Be all this as it may, it is evident that negative perceptions of BRI loans tend to originate in suspicions of Chinese intentions rather than hard economic data. This returns us to questions of Chinese influence and global expansion, as well as Western perceptions of Chinese long-term strategy. Such questions can be difficult to answer since we do not have access to discussions at the highest level of the Chinese Communist Party and we cannot be sure that Western perceptions are not skewed by a fear of being pushed aside by the Chinese juggernaut.

What can we say for sure? Well, it is certainly safe to say that there is a range of well-documented problems with BRI investments. These include lack of transparency, lack of sustainability studies and lack of unrestricted access to Chinese markets for partner countries. China's preference for bilateral trade deals with individual countries rather than free market economics tends to support the accusation that China is prioritizing its own needs over the needs of the global or regional collective. However, as we have seen, the hypothesis of debt-trap diplomacy does not appear logical from China's point of view. This leads to the double-edged conclusion that debt-trap diplomacy is not proven, but that win-win cooperation is not proven either. This conclusion leaves us looking for a more nuanced alternative that takes better account of the data and situational evidence.

Offensive mercantilism and economic statecraft: a Chinese takeover?

A plausible alternative to debt-trap diplomacy is what Jonathan Holslag calls 'offensive mercantilism'. In Holslag's interpretation, Chinese investments are an attempt to exploit economic relations with partner countries to gain advantages for Chinese companies. Being implemented through the BRI, offensive mercantilism has six main goals. The first is to coordinate the activity of Chinese actors such as companies in the service of efficient overseas trade and investment. The second is to increase China's access to energy and raw materials. The third is to boost service exports, most notably in construction and transportation. The fourth is to acquire strategic assets and secure overseas projects. The fifth is to solve the overcapacity problem in the domestic Chinese economy by improving access to overseas markets. The sixth and last goal is to increase political influence via economic means.[87]

There is some support for the offensive mercantilism hypothesis. Timothy Heath demonstrates that since the 1990s Chinese scholars and government officials have been using a strategy of 'economic diplomacy' (*jingji waijiao*) designed to promote China's 'national economic security' (*guojia jingji anquan*).[88] The strategy includes obtaining diversified sources of natural resources to ensure that China's ever-increasing energy needs do not result in energy insecurity. In a similar vein, William Norris concludes, in a book-length study, that China uses its commercial actors in a coordinated program of economic statecraft designed to achieve national objectives.[89] China's strategy, like that of the United States and other countries, includes the use of economic incentives ('carrots') and sanctions ('sticks'). In marked contrast to observers who talk of the fragmentation and decentralization of China's foreign economic policy,[90] Norris assigns the state a high degree of control over Chinese commercial actors such as oil and construction companies. Given that the directors and chairmen of state-owned enterprises are generally Communist Party members and often closely connected to the central government, the idea of coordinated state control over foreign economic policy is not unreasonable.

It is not difficult to identify examples which support the idea of coordinated economic statecraft and state control over companies: we will move on to detailed case studies in the next chapter. At the same time, one needs to bear in mind that control is sometimes lost due to companies diverging from the plan. A case in point is the 2016 Sino-Czech agreement for Chinese investments in the Czech Republic. The private company CEFC Energy was to be the main Chinese commercial actor involved in investments in media, travel and finance companies, as well as a brewery and a football club. However, when CEFC did not make the necessary payments on its investments, the Chinese state was forced to intervene. The state-owned investment group CITIC replaced CEFC in 2018, taking over its investments and paying off the money owed. The head of CEFC was detained in China on unspecified charges. The Czech case shows a loss of control over a private commercial actor by the Chinese state, but then a reassertion of it with the installation of a state-owned actor in its place.[91]

Lithuania presents a clear case of Chinese economic statecraft in Europe. The background to this issue is that in 2021, Lithuania declared that it was withdrawing from the '17+1' cooperation framework between China and CEE countries. The Lithuanian government thereafter made the decision to allow Taiwan to open a Taiwanese Representative Office in Vilnius.[92] These actions were a clear snub to China and in contravention of its 'One China' policy which has been officially recognized by the United States and most other nations. The One China policy states that Taiwan is inalienably part of China, does not have the status of a nation-state, and the name 'Taipei' rather than 'Taiwan' should be used for Taiwan's overseas offices. In retaliation against Lithuania's actions, the Chinese government instructed its companies to cut their ties with Lithuania. The German car manufacturer Continental was also pressured not to use Lithuania-made parts in its vehicles.[93] Although the outcomes of such pressure are not entirely clear, this was definitely a state-led campaign of economic coercion. As such, it supports the notion of China using economic statecraft as a government-led instrument in support of its national interests overseas.

Thus, it is clearly the case that China is attempting to generate international influence and leverage through BRI investments and other economic instruments. Whether one labels this influence and leverage 'economic statecraft', 'debt-trap diplomacy' or 'offensive mercantilism' is a moot point: whatever one calls it, this is a government-led, top-down attempt to influence international affairs through the coordinated use of economic instruments. Observers who suggest that the authority of the Chinese state is significantly fragmented because multiple interested actors are competing for pieces of the economic pie would do well to rethink their conclusions in the light of the evidence.[94] Although of course it is true that China is huge and has a multitude of competing actors bargaining for funds, this does not mean that the ability of the Chinese state to impose decisions from above has somehow been drastically eroded. Rather, as William Norris demonstrates, Chinese state control over Chinese society and foreign policy remains firm, enabling the state to pursue foreign policy objectives in a strategic and relatively coordinated manner – albeit one which whose goals and methods are shifting over time.[95]

Norms, influence and leverage: the true face of the BRI?

There is another way of looking at the question of China's economic foreign policy under the label of the BRI. It can be seen as having two non-economic aims: first, to introduce Chinese *norms* into China's relations with developing countries; and second, to increase China's economic and political *influence* in those countries. In other words, one needs to examine the non-material aspects of the BRI in addition to its material (economic) ones. This means acknowledging the fact that China is pursuing a campaign of promoting its *ideational* power through the BRI in order to gain influence in the global South.

Scholars have identified ideational power using a variety of labels. Of these, Joseph Nye's conception of soft power is the best known. The main characteristic of soft power, as it is most often formulated, is that it focuses primarily on attraction based on culture, values, commerce or other means.[96] Essentially, soft power is the ability to 'get others to admire your ideals and to want what you want'.[97] At the same time, Nye sees soft power as 'co-optive'.[98] It is the mirror image of hard power in that it 'is simply a form of power, one way of getting desired outcomes'.[99] This means that soft power is, in Nye's conception, 'a descriptive, rather than a normative, concept'.[100] In other words, soft power does not aim to change a partner country's values or behaviour. Rather, it draws the partner onto its side by persuading it to believe that the powerful country is one whose leadership it should follow.

The soft power attraction model is one which the United States has used effectively since the Second World War. Over the last three-quarters of a century, the United States has used its movie, music and fast-food industries to promote American interests overseas. Due to the global spread of Hollywood, American TV series, rock, rap, McDonalds and other cultural artefacts, the United States has been able to attract generations of young people to its national brand. In addition, since the 1980s and 1990s, information technology firms such as Apple, Microsoft and Google have been added to the US roster of national champions, allowing America to cast its web of enchantment over almost every country in the world. However, there are signs that in the last two decades America's power of attraction has slowed down: it has been impacted by negative perceptions of the 'war on terror' which included the failed occupations of Afghanistan and Iraq, as well as the poor international reaction to the Trump administration and the US mishandling of the Covid-19 pandemic. Public opinion surveys conducted at intervals by the Pew Research Center between 2000 and 2020 indicate that views of the United States have become markedly more unfavourable. In the UK, France, Germany, Japan, Canada and Australia, well over half of respondents expressed a favourable opinion of the United States in 2000. However, by 2020 the figure had declined far below 50 per cent. Across thirteen countries surveyed, the median percentage of respondents who had a favourable view of the United States was only 34 per cent in 2020, while 64 per cent had an unfavourable impression.[101]

Nonetheless, US soft power remains a more significant factor in global affairs than China's. Despite a focus on promoting its soft power since the mid-2000s, China has failed to make as much of a dent in the US lead as it might have. Pew Research Center data reveal that the percentage of respondents who have a favourable impression of China is even lower than for the United States. Across fourteen countries, the median percentage of respondents with a favourable impression was only 24 per cent in 2020, with 73 per cent having an unfavourable view of China. Thus, despite perceptions of the United States reaching historic lows, impressions of China are even more negative and in decline in many countries in the global North. In the mid-2000s, over 50 per cent of respondents had a favourable perception of China in countries such as the UK, South Korea, France and Canada. By 2020, these figures had fallen below 30 per cent in all four countries. China has therefore failed so far to close the soft power gap to the United States.[102]

There are at least four reasons for the decline in Chinese soft power. First, Chinese movies, music and other cultural outputs have not gained much traction in the global entertainment marketplace. Chinese traditional culture and food have been attractive for a long time; but this inherent advantage has been whittled away due to the perceived unattractiveness of contemporary China with its pollution, high rises, low-quality exports and communism. Second, China's political system based on authoritarianism and its heavy-handed approach to human rights are not attractive in many parts of the world, especially the West. China's suppression of separatist or democratic movements in Tibet, Xinjiang and Hong Kong, alongside the PRC's perceived threat to Taiwan and expansion into the South China Sea, have not endeared it to those who believe in liberal democracy. Third, since 2018, some Chinese officials and commentators have compounded the damage by resorting to what has been labelled 'wolf warrior diplomacy': aggressively shouting down criticisms of China and attacking the West.[103] Fourth, Western companies also complain about their inability to gain access to Chinese markets despite Chinese promises of 'unimpeded trade'.[104] In the context of such significant downsides, slogans such as 'harmonious world', 'peaceful rise' (promoted during the Hu presidency from 2002 to 2012) and 'community of shared interests/destiny' (promoted during the Xi presidency) have not exactly caught on with the public, in the developed world in particular. In short: there is a contradiction between China's official BRI rhetoric of 'win-win cooperation' and perceptions that it is aggressive, irresponsible or uncooperative.

On the other hand, the advent of wolf warrior diplomacy demonstrates not only China's new-found confidence but also its realization that it does not need to dominate the soft power race with the United States to come out on top in the long run. This is because, in contrast to soft power, the connected concept of normative power frames ideational power as the ability to shape interactions rather than the ability to win the friendship of partner states. Logically, diffusing norms does not necessarily have to be connected to strong cultural attraction (although if the norm-diffuser is attractive it certainly helps). In some cases – as with China – it could be enough for the country to be seen as economically powerful and rapidly rising. For instance, China can gain influence by offering economic opportunities to the partner country that are not being supplied by other leading powers. Thereafter, by negotiating bilateral trade agreements and establishing regional cooperation frameworks, China gradually normalizes shared practices at the elite level based on the Chinese approach to social and industrial development. In this way, China gains normative power – influence over *how* interactions take place – without necessarily having much in the way of soft power attractiveness as far as the general population is concerned.

As a concept, normative power was first applied to the European Union. In a seminal paper, Ian Manners suggested that the EU, lacking any kind of hard power projection, was a different kind of power: a *normative* power. By this he meant that the EU was attempting to shape the values of other international actors through the diffusion of norms – chiefly those based on the Western conception of human rights and democracy.[105] This distinguished it from nation-states which project hard power through their militaries. Manners's analysis was eventually developed further by other scholars. These include Thomas Diez, who shows that normative power is connected to questions of national interests, influence and hegemony, and Emilian Kavalski, who demonstrates that there is no logical reason to restrict the concept of normative power to Europe alone.[106] Kavalski connects normative power directly to China, so it is his framing of the concept that is of most interest here.

According to Manners's account, normative power is 'the ability to define what passes for "normal" in world politics'.[107] Kavalski argues convincingly that on this basis, China – and other major powers such as the United States – can also be classified as normative powers to the extent that they attempt to shape norms of interaction in the international arena. He uses the example of China's 'socialization' of Central Asia by means of the Shanghai Cooperation Organization (SCO) to illustrate China's ability to introduce new norms of cooperation into regional settings.[108] Kavalski's analysis of normative power is directly relevant to the BRI. He shows that by introducing Chinese norms of regional and economic cooperation, China has altered the ideational landscape in which international affairs take place. Through the BRI, regional cooperation mechanisms such as the SCO, and other economic instruments such as the Asian Infrastructure Investment Bank (AIIB), Beijing has created an alternative to the usual Western-led way of conducting international affairs. On this point, in her magisterial book *China's Rise in the Global South*, Dawn Murphy emphasizes the need to acknowledge China's 'normative interactions with the Global South [to] better understand the degree to which norms of interaction are developing among those states through socialization with China'.[109]

The Western-led system is often labelled the 'liberal international order' (LIO). The LIO includes institutions such as the World Trade Organization (WTO), the IMF and the World Bank. It assumes the use of free market (capitalist) economics, as well as the promotion of Western norms of human rights and democracy.[110] By introducing an alternative set of institutions and norms to the global South (and other countries not standardly included among Western nations, such as CEE countries), China has issued a challenge to the LIO.[111] The evidence of the challenge came with a Western counter-response in 2021: the United States introduced its 'B3W' global investment framework, and the EU introduced its 'Global Gateway'. They are direct reactions to the BRI, demonstrating that China's initiative has changed thinking about how international development should take place.

China's alternative order presents a challenge which is particularly strong in parts of Asia, Africa and Latin America due to China's establishment of new norms of interaction, as well as its political influence and economic leverage. Of course, these are all parts of the world that were colonized by European powers: Britain, Spain, France, Portugal, the Netherlands and others. Parts of China – Hong Kong and Macao – were also colonized. Thus, China can portray itself as a victim of Europeans alongside its partners in the global South. This is a point that appears to be missed by modern Europeans with their talk of the EU as a 'normative power': Europe lacks credibility in the global South because of its colonial past, including exploitation of people (through slavery) and resources. China has no such baggage – although of course it has other notable baggage such as its political system and authoritarian approach to human rights. Be this as it may, the fact that China was not previously a colonial power means that Beijing can gain influence in places where Europe's leverage is impeded by perceptions of its past record.

A different point can be made about the United States. When Hilary Clinton announced in 2011 a US 'pivot to Asia', everybody expected a realignment of American foreign policy from the Middle East to East Asia.[112] That nothing specific consequently happened was a surprise. Yet there is little doubt that the Chinese took the 'pivot' very seriously. The BRI is evidence of this: a Chinese pivot towards its southern and western neighbours to build China's influence there at the expense of the United States.[113] Where the Obama administration's 'pivot to Asia' amounted to little more than rhetoric, the Chinese pivot to the global South was backed by money and construction companies as well as a public relations campaign. Where the United States failed to match its words with actions, China filled the gap by putting its money where its mouth was.

There are two ways to interpret and react to China's strategy of norms promotion via the BRI. The first is to take Chinese talk of 'win-win cooperation' and a 'community of shared interests/destiny' at face value.[114] The second is to see the BRI as advancing an authoritarian model of governance which acts to oppose the LIO and replace the Western-led international order. To a degree, distinguishing between these two options is in the eye of the beholder. In fact, as Dawn Murphy points out, China is pragmatically and eclectically utilizing a mix of its own norms and Western ones as needs demand.[115]

Be this as it may, there is no doubt that through a complex package of political and economic activities, China is increasing its influence and leverage in the developing world. Ultimately, this may well prove the most significant outcome of the BRI. In addition, there is little doubt that China has changed the rules of interaction between a large power and developing countries. It is an interaction which therefore needs to be clearly analysed and understood by the United States and the EU if they are to organize a counter-model. They also need to be much better coordinated in their approach to counter it. Preferably, they would coordinate their approaches with each other. However, a pan-Western integrated approach to influence and investment in the global South does not seem to be on the horizon – even in the face of the obvious challenge presented by China and its energy-rich Russian ally.

In the end, while the material impacts of Chinese investments and infrastructure construction are variable and debatable, the BRI's *ideational* (non-material) impacts reverberate beyond the investment data and construction projects. When push comes to shove, there are three connected conclusions one can draw about the ideational impacts of the BRI. First, Chinese norms are being diffused into developing countries and regions of the global South where Western norms are often weakly diffused or not present.[116] This is altering the landscape of possibility concerning development funding and infrastructure building, challenging the ability of the West to set the terms of how development should take place. In other words, China is setting itself up to replace the West as the perceived benefactor or leader of the global South. Second, China is increasing its political influence in developing countries and regions through its BRI investment, construction and norm diffusion campaign. This challenges the United States' capacity to maintain its global geopolitical hegemony. Third, China is gradually filling the developmental and normative void left by the West. The United States and the EU have simply not been paying attention to being perceived as consistent and meaningful partners of countries in the global South. Whether justifiably or not, the narrative they have generated of being the main providers of aid (and charity) to the developing world is being challenged by China. Consequently, Beijing's influence in developing and mid-level economies is increasing. In the next two chapters, we will examine the extent to which the spread of China's BRI across the regions and continents of the global South is having transformative impacts on local and global affairs.

Chapter 5

CHINA'S RELATIONS WITH ITS NEIGHBOURS

China is the largest and most populated country in Asia. Its only competition for this title is India, which is fast catching up in terms of population, but still lags far behind in economic development. Whatever happens in China, whatever emanates from China, has repercussions elsewhere in Asia. Asia cannot ignore China: the future of the continent is bound up with China's. At the same time, the West should not ignore China's interactions with other Asian countries because these are shaping not only the continent but also the future of the world. As of 2022, Asia is the world's leading continent in terms of gross domestic product (GDP). In fact, from 2020 onwards, Asia's annual GDP has been larger than that of the rest of the world *combined*.[1] As the retired diplomat and former United Nations Security Council President Kishore Mahbubani puts it:

> [W]e are reaching the end of the era of Western domination of world history ... without a shadow of doubt, we will soon be sailing full steam ahead into the Asian twenty-first century.[2]

It is therefore vitally important for everybody – in the East, West or wherever – to gain a clear understanding of the spread of Chinese economic and political influence through Asia's regions under the BRI label. Yet, in fact, Westerners generally do not pay enough attention to the detail of China's interactions and entanglements with its Asian neighbours such as those in Southeast Asia.[3] This is understandable, given geographical, cultural and linguistic distance, as well as the difficulty of keeping up with the ever-evolving complexities of intra-regional relations. It is understandable because we all tend to pay most attention to what is going on in our own backyard and shut out all the noise coming from elsewhere. All the same, it will be a mistake of epic proportions if the West does not make more effort to understand what is happening in Asia, increasingly at the behest of China, because it is changing the world.

I can understand the Western reluctance to engage with Asia because, in many ways, my attitude to Asia used to be quite typical for a European. Before I visited the continent for the first time it seemed a vast, mysterious and distant zone which had little to do with my life. In all honesty, I had not been much interested in Asia up to that time and had only travelled there due to my wife's enthusiasm for East

Asian culture. Most of what I remember of my first year in South Korea involved being confused, dazzled and culture shocked. The food was weird, the people behaved oddly and society seemed to run by completely different norms (the last part at least was true). I spent much of my time complaining about the conditions and foolishly wondering why Korean people behaved differently to Europeans. At the end of the year, when my work contract expired, I left and swore I would never go back. Yet I ended up returning and spending four more years in South Korea. I have also visited thirteen other Asian countries since then, including three years living in China. Due to my travels in Asia, I realized that understanding what is happening in Asia is vital to understanding the future of humanity. This is one of the main reasons why I decided to engage professionally in the study of China, and Asia. I saw that people in the West (and elsewhere in the world) did not understand China and Asia well and that I could contribute something (however modest) to increasing that understanding.

Since the 1990s, of course, the internet has opened up the world to all of us at the touch of a computer keyboard. We have more access to information about Asia than ever before. Japanese and Korean popular cultures have spread into Western youth consciousness to a degree I would never have imagined possible when I first visited South Korea in the long-ago sultry summer of 1998. Korean and Japanese films have won Oscars, K-pop has taken over the music download charts and Japanese manga comic books can be found occupying shelves in European bookstores and libraries: all unthinkable twenty-five years ago. Yet I believe it is still true that most (not all, but most) Europeans' feelings about Asia resemble mine when I boarded the plane to Seoul all those years ago: they feel little connection to Asia, find it strange and incomprehensible, and have limited interest in finding out more about it. This is not just a pity, but in fact represents a serious problem for Europe and other Western countries in terms of the development of their foreign policy and international relations (IR), because as I found out on my travels, Asia is where the action is in the twenty-first century – not Europe. The world is changing rapidly and in very complex and interconnected ways. And much of that change is – and will continue to be – driven by events in Asia.

This chapter therefore examines the implementation and impacts of China's engagement with its economically developing neighbours. It will evaluate the expansion of Chinese influence in its continental neighbourhood by outlining the BRI's implementation in three key regions that border China: Southeast Asia, South Asia and Central Asia. Within this framework, I will analyse China's relations with individual states in each region. Given limited space, these analyses of bilateral relations in each case will be necessarily concise. However, the aim is to give a clear sense of the general direction of relations in each case while drawing out the implications for the evolution of regional relations at the broader level. At the end of the chapter, I will draw the threads of the chapter together by comparing the implementation and impacts of the BRI across the three regions. The aim is to understand how China is impacting the countries and regions in its neighbourhood, in the process altering the complex, interconnected international development landscape – and changing the world.

China's backyard: Southeast Asia

Southeast Asia has become one of the world's most economically dynamic regions. In 2016, the ten countries in the Association of Southeast Asian Nations (ASEAN) – Vietnam, Laos, Cambodia, Myanmar, Thailand, Malaysia, Singapore, Indonesia, Brunei and the Philippines – had a combined population of 637 million people and a combined GDP of $2.5 trillion. The annual GDP growth of the region outpaced the global average by over 1 per cent.[4] Nevertheless, with the notable exception of Singapore, the ASEAN members are generally classified as belonging to the Global South since they are still relatively poor. Some, such as Myanmar, Laos, Cambodia and the Philippines, have not yet managed entirely to break free of dark histories of war, despotism or colonial dependency.

It is important to note that since about 2010 the South China Sea has become a focus of activity for the navies of both the United States and China. While China has terraformed new islands on uninhabitable reefs and rocks, the Americans have conducted freedom of navigation operations (FONOPs) to try to establish that the South China Sea is international waters and not a Chinese lake.[5] The result has been to make the sea a zone of contention between not only countries such as Vietnam, the Philippines and Malaysia, but also between the world's two biggest economies and largest military spenders. This tussle for dominance in the South China Sea is mirrored by competition between China and the United States for influence across the entire Southeast Asian region.

Among Southeast Asian countries, no one nation is dominant. In addition, ties between countries are not as close as might be expected. ASEAN acts as a forum for resolving issues rather than as a regional integration mechanism in the vein of the EU. Overlapping claims concerning territory in the South China Sea complicate relations between some countries. The lack of a local hegemon, allied with the lack of solid intra-regional alliances, mean that this vibrant, economically growing region is open to outside influence from larger powers. It is for this reason that Southeast Asia's relations with the United States and China – the two main rivals for regional hegemony – have often been classified by scholars as strategic hedging: keeping options open by cultivating relations with both powers at the same time.[6]

In financial markets, hedging refers to the aim of spreading your bets, not putting all your eggs in one basket. The principle of hedging is to protect yourself from risk by making sure you back both the winner and the loser in a two-horse race. For instance, as strange as it may seem, this can be done by betting that markets will go both up and down. In essence, hedging means avoiding a catastrophic loss due to picking the wrong horse and making sure you back the right one. As scholars such as Evelyn Goh and Cheng-Chwee Kuik point out (albeit using more complex conceptual definitions involving concepts derived from IR theory such as bandwagoning and balancing), this is also how hedging should be understood in Southeast Asia.[7] It is a region where China and the United States compete for regional influence. Unable to see the future, most local leaders try to make sure they are on the right side of history by not over-committing to one power or the other.

Yet, as the Chinese scholar Wang Yuzhu points out, in a sense hedging is only a delaying of the inevitable: 'Since the hedger's goal is to side with the winner, this means hedging is in fact a strategy of deferred bandwagoning.'[8] In other words, states keep one foot in each camp so they can quickly hop into the winner's circle once the winner's identity becomes clear. At some point they are forced to come down on one side or the other. Thus, despite the assumption subsumed in the scholarly hedging concept that Southeast Asian states are generally cultivating ties with both China and the United States simultaneously, the reality is that their reluctance to commit is only a way of buying time and delaying the inevitable: namely, that as Beijing steadily gains influence, regional actors will eventually be forced to jump on the China bandwagon. In fact, although he does not make this point in a systematic fashion, this is the implication of David Shambaugh's excellent study comparing US and Chinese influence in Southeast Asia.[9] Nyíri and Tan's multi-authored study of local interactions with China confirms 'that Southeast Asian states are not simply engaged in either balancing or "bandwagoning" with China'.[10] Instead, interactions are complex and involve local reactions to, and renegotiations of, Chinese norm-setting practices.

For this reason, my interpretation of Southeast Asian nations' policy concerning China and the United States differs somewhat from that adopted by scholars such as Goh, Kuik and Shambaugh.[11] In the analysis adopted here, Southeast Asian states can instead be categorized according to the extent to which they have been drawn into the Chinese orbit. In effect, there are two groups of states: *erstwhile hedgers* and *de facto client states* (even if the latter probably do not see themselves in this light). The client state group certainly includes Laos and Cambodia. Myanmar can arguably also be placed in this group even though it is still trying to maintain a degree of independence in the face of increasing reliance on China. The group of erstwhile hedgers contains the other seven countries, each of which is trying to keep the Chinese juggernaut at arms' length with varying degrees of conviction and success.

My dichotomy between erstwhile hedgers and *de facto* client states correlates quite closely with David Shambaugh's placing of the ten countries on a spectrum according to the extent to which they gravitate more towards the United States or China.[12] In his view, only Vietnam, Singapore and the Philippines lean more towards the United States than China – and all three are closer to the central point of the spectrum than to the United States. As Shambaugh points out, of the other seven, Cambodia, Laos and Myanmar have the closest relations with the PRC. In my view, they are *de facto* client states because, as a Chinese scholar points out, all three have become enmeshed in China's economic system.[13] Myanmar and Cambodia are also heavily dependent on China for military equipment and personnel training.[14]

Why are these three countries closer to China than the others? Five factors are significant. First, they are close in a physical sense: Cambodia, Laos and Myanmar all have land borders with China. Second, as Figure 5.1 demonstrates, they are all also very poor. In terms of GDP per capita, they are the three poorest states in Southeast Asia (although Vietnam, the Philippines and Indonesia are not much better off). Third, they all have authoritarian regimes of one sort or another: Laos has a one-party communist system, Myanmar is under the control of the military (after flirting briefly with democracy) and Cambodia, while ostensibly a democracy, is in practice a one-party state.[15] China prefers dealing with authoritarian states than democracies because it is easier to establish influence at the leadership level without having to worry about public opinion and other issues within the partner country. Fourth, the three countries' histories of colonialism and conflict have impeded their development into economically prosperous and stable societies, leaving the door open for China. And fifth, all three countries have been economically neglected by the United States and other Western countries since the end of the Vietnam War in 1975: there has simply been little attention paid to them and essentially no efforts to orchestrate coordinated investment programmes. These five factors render this trio of neighbouring countries highly susceptible to Chinese economic and political influence.

Of course, the same set of factors might be said to apply to next-door Vietnam. However, the key difference is Vietnam's bitter, centuries-long experience of wars with China, which has rendered the Vietnamese automatically sceptical about becoming economically and politically entangled with their far larger neighbour to the north. The most recent full-scale conflict came as recently as 1979, when a Chinese force invaded Vietnam on what was supposed to be a punitive expedition teaching Vietnam a lesson for its 1978 invasion of Cambodia. There have also been negative experiences with China's military in the South China Sea. In 1974, China pushed Vietnam out of the Paracel Islands when it was preoccupied with winning the war against the United States; and in 1988 China seized Johnson South Reef, killing sixty-four Vietnamese marines and sinking three ships.[16]

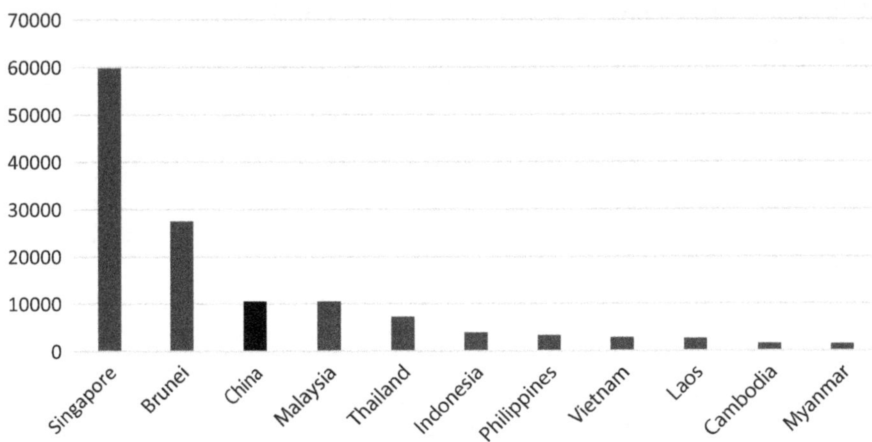

Figure 5.1 GDP per capita (2020 US dollars)

Source: author, based on data from The World Bank (https://data.worldbank.org/indicator/NY.GDP.PCAP.CD?locations=Z4-8S-Z7)

It is little wonder then that informal conversations with Vietnamese people reveal almost universal mistrust of Chinese intentions and a desire to keep China at arm's length.[17] A public opinion survey conducted in mid-2022 supports the conclusion that Vietnamese have more unfavourable views of China than other Southeast Asians. Despite the trauma of the Vietnam War, they also surprisingly have more favourable views of the United States than citizens of other countries in the region.[18] At the same time, Vietnam's economy is becoming increasingly enmeshed with China's. Vietnam is China's eighth largest trading partner and is number one in this category among Southeast Asian nations.[19] This means that it is difficult – and probably impossible – for Hanoi to isolate itself from its neighbour to the north by forming a full-fledged alliance with the United States.

Despite the ostensibly similar levels of per capita GDP, my visits to Vietnam, Laos and Cambodia revealed telling differences, especially in terms of infrastructure. While Vietnamese roads were reasonably well maintained and its cities buzzing with vehicles, Laotian and Cambodian highways were generally in a very poor state, even in and around the capital cities. It was clear that both countries were in dire need of infrastructure investment; and this is exactly what China has provided in recent years, in exchange for business opportunities and increased influence.

The biggest and most controversial Chinese project in Laos is the $6 billion, 414-kilometre Boten-Vientiane railway, which was completed in December 2021.[20] It connects Laos's capital city with the Chinese border, crossing almost the entire country, before connecting with a Chinese rail link to Kunming, the capital of Yunnan province. Although official statistics await confirmation, Laotian media reported that in the first three months of operation the railway transported over one million passengers and half a million tonnes of freight.[21] The next stage in the BRI project will connect Vientiane to Bangkok, and eventually to Kuala Lumpur and Singapore.[22]

There are concerns in some quarters that Laos will end up in severe debt distress due to the railway project since there is a lack of transparency concerning the project's financing.[23] Already by 2014 Laos had a larger Chinese debt load relative to gross national income (9.42 per cent) than any other country on earth.[24] Nevertheless, the jury is still out, since Laos is apparently only required to repay loans covering 30 per cent of the total.[25] In addition, if the reports of passenger and freight volumes are correct, it would seem that the railway is far from being a white elephant and would have the potential to make some impact on Laos's economic fortunes.

However, there are other, even more economically weighty Chinese infrastructure projects in Laos: a cluster of dams costing around $12.5 billion. The government of Laos is hoping these will turn their country into the 'battery of Asia'. Most of the funding for the dams has come from Chinese state banks, meaning that the dams are probably more of a 'debt-trap' concern than the railway. The Chinese loans are a concern given that they are stacked against Laos's relatively modest GDP of $18 billion. The issue was compounded when Laos was forced to hand over control of its electricity grid to China Southern Power Grid Co in 2020 due to its sovereign reserves dwindling to less than $1 billion during the Covid-19 pandemic.[26] As with the railway, the jury is still out concerning the capacity of these hydropower projects to transform Laos into an energy-exporting powerhouse.

Another significant Chinese presence in Laos comes from the Golden Triangle Special Economic Zone (GTSEZ). This is a gambling and tourism enclave in Laos's northwest, close to the border with China, Myanmar and Thailand. In 2007, the Chinese firm Kings Romans Group, led by businessman Zhao Wei, was granted a ninety-nine-year lease and permission to develop the GTSEZ into a casino paradise for gambling-starved Chinese punters (gambling is illegal in China). Zhao became the *de facto* ruler of the enclave, leading to accusations of corruption, money laundering, human and wildlife trafficking and other seedy practices. Zhao is reportedly looking to expand his empire into other border regions, adding to Chinese influence in Laos as he does so.[27]

Similarly, impoverished Cambodia, which was devastated by the brutal Khmer Rouge regime after the end of the Vietnam War – when Cambodia was left to its own devices by the departing United States – has fallen under the spell of Chinese money and influence. From 1994 to 2014, China accounted for around 44 per cent of foreign investments in Cambodia. Between 2000 and 2014, Cambodia received a higher number (132) of Chinese aid-financed projects than any other country in the world.[28] Cambodia's debt to China constitutes more than 25 per cent of the nation's GDP. Funded by Chinese state loans, Chinese companies have built roads and are working on a new airport.[29] Chinese investments in once-sleepy Sihanoukville on the Cambodian coast have reportedly transformed the town into a virtual Chinese enclave full of Chinese businesses, most notably casinos for Chinese tourists.[30] China and Cambodia are now also cooperating closely on military security, having signed a new memorandum of understanding on defence in March 2022.[31] In 2018, China reportedly provided Cambodia with $100 million for defence spending.[32] There were also reports in 2019 of a secret agreement allowing the Chinese navy to use parts of Cambodia's Ream Naval Base. The net result, in the face of US embargos on Cambodia and pressure on China, is to build a zone of economic, political and security influence for China on the Gulf of Thailand.[33]

China has had greater difficulty gaining a foothold in Myanmar. The country formerly known as Burma has, in recent years, flipped from a military dictatorship to a fledgling democracy and back again, bringing uncertainty for the Chinese. China's main long-term investment in Myanmar has a dual aspect: development of the port of Kyaukpyu and the nearby gas fields in the Bay of Bengal, connected to a pipeline transporting the gas across Myanmar to China's Yunnan province. The gas pipeline was completed in 2013, and an oil pipeline was added in 2014. However, both it and the port development have proved controversial with locals, who complain that the Chinese investments have brought them no benefits and are therefore purely exploitative.[34] On the other hand, since Myanmar is perceived in the West as a failed state and a dictatorship, it has had difficulty attracting investments and has little choice but to maintain relations with China.

Beyond these four countries which have land borders with China are six others. Of these, the Philippines and Malaysia have tended to have the most controversial relations with China since around 2010. The Philippines, like Vietnam, disputes the ownership of certain maritime features in the South China Sea with China. This has proved the main sticking point in bilateral relations. Manila even took its claim to an international tribunal in The Hague, which decided in the Philippines's favour in 2016. China refused to acknowledge the legal proceedings or the court's verdict, meaning that the decision was unenforceable. Nothing came of it and China maintained its naval presence in the vicinity of features occupied by the Philippines.[35] These include Scarborough Shoal, where coastguard ships from China and the Philippines constantly manoeuvre, and Thitu Island, which has a runway which is in a poor state and is currently being repaired.[36]

Subsequent to the settlement of the international tribunal, Rodrigo Duterte was elected president, bringing with him further uncertainty in the form of a rather inconsistent approach to China. Initially, he claimed to want to set the maritime disputes on one side and focus on business ties. However, there has been a lack of progress on the specifics of cooperation and the future of China-Philippines relations remains unclear in the context of low levels of Chinese investment.[37] Historically, the perpetually impoverished Philippines has tended to lean more towards the United States, its former colonial power (the United States obtained the Philippines from Spain after victory in the Spanish-American War). As in Vietnam, public opinion in the Philippines favours the United States over China by a wide margin.[38] However, with Chinese vessels still circling features claimed by the Philippines, and with China's obvious economic heft in the region, Manila cannot ignore Beijing. Since the extent of US commitment to intervene on the Philippines's behalf in any future conflict is uncertain, the Philippines's government will probably be forced to engage with China whether it likes it or not.

Malaysia, which also has some territory in the South China Sea, but which is not much involved in maritime disputes with China, appears to be a classic case of hedging between US and Chinese influences. However, the fact that Malaysia and China have been working together on security matters since 1992 indicates a closer relationship with China than might at first sight appear to be the case: defence cooperation agreements were signed in 1999, 2005 and 2014. Although Malaysia's defence cooperation with China still totals less than that with the United States, it is increasing steadily.[39] This fact alone, although not given much attention in the national, regional or global public sphere, is indicative of a stance which, if not fully pro-China, is not exactly anti-China either. Indeed, public opinion survey data reveal very similar perceptions of China and the United States, with China slightly ahead in favourability.[40].

Controversies arose in 2018 concerning China's BRI investments in Malaysia. During his successful election campaign, Prime Minister Mahathir Mohamad criticized Chinese investments, implying that they were debt traps for Malaysia. He suspended and sought to renegotiate $22 billion of projects.[41] However, Mahathir resumed a pro-China approach a few months after the election and the investment projects were mostly reinstated, although three pipeline projects were cancelled. These pipeline projects were linked to the 1MDB corruption scandal associated with Mahathir's predecessor as prime minister, Najib Razak.[42] It might have been expected that 1MDB would have given China a wholly negative image in Malaysia, but the controversy does not appear to have dented the long-term development of Sino-Malaysian relations. In fact, Chinese Foreign Minister Wang Yi suggested in August 2018 that Mahathir 'is a good friend and old friend of the Chinese people' and noted that 'it was during Mahathir's first stint as prime minister that Sino-Malaysian relations gained rapid development'.[43]

The most significant Chinese investments in Malaysia are the building or upgrading of five ports and the East Coast Rail Link, which should eventually connect two of these ports to the Thai border and on towards China through Laos.[44] There are also extensive Chinese investments in Malaysian real estate, agriculture, energy and manufacturing. Two million Chinese tourists visit Malaysia each year. In 2018, the Bank of China and Bank Negara Malaysia signed a $26 billion currency swap arrangement.[45] Malaysia can thus be categorized as an erstwhile hedger: it seeks to cultivate ties with both China and the United States simultaneously while in fact edging closer to China over the long-term.[46]

Thailand, much like Myanmar, is a country which attempts to maintain an independent stance in regional and international affairs despite sharing a border with China. It is one of the few countries in the world which was not colonized by a European power. However, despite American overtures over decades, Thai elites tend to perceive Washington as an unreliable partner which does not place sufficient emphasis on developing relations with Bangkok.[47] In recent years these political elites have instead been cosying up to Beijing.[48] David Shambaugh's conversations with Thai foreign ministry officials reveal that they are leaning increasingly towards China. As one of their numbers put it: 'We can't get out of China's embrace – we just have to make the best of the situation.'[49]

Accordingly, Beijing's influence has been steadily growing in recent years, especially since the 2014 military coup and the subsequent negative US reaction and suspension of aid.[50] Ian Storey notes that 'China has clearly emerged as Thailand's preferred major power partner' after the United States scaled back cooperation.[51] Thailand has a large Chinese diaspora, many of whom 'now occupy the upper echelons of Thai society, business, government, and increasingly the military'.[52] In addition, China is now Thailand's leading trading partner.[53] About 8.8 million Chinese tourists visited Thailand in 2016.[54] Thailand has conducted numerous bilateral military exercises with the PLA since 2005.[55] Imports of military equipment have grown steadily since the 1990s.[56]

The most significant Chinese investment in Thailand is a proposed rail link connecting Bangkok to the border with Laos. This would connect to the already-constructed China-Laos railway. The railway would eventually continue southwards to the border with Malaysia, where it would connect with the East Coast Rail Link and create a continuous railway down the length of the Malay Peninsula from China to Singapore. However, the Thai section of this ambitious BRI project has been repeatedly delayed due to technical, design and financing issues. As in Malaysia, concerns have been raised about the conditions for repayment of Chinese loans. As a result of the delays, the first 200-kilometre section of the railway is not due to come into service until at least 2026.[57] However, given the fact that the Lao section is already in place and work has begun on the Malaysian section, there can be little doubt of China's intention to follow through on its plans, although this will depend on the decision of the Thai government.

Indonesia is an island nation primarily preoccupied with internal matters and hence less invested in international affairs than other nations in the region.[58] It has a sizeable ethnic Chinese minority, but unlike in Thailand, there is a history of intense Sinophobic sentiment among some sections of the population which has periodically broken out into violence.[59] Most notably, in 1965 more than a million ethnic Chinese were slaughtered in an act of retribution against what had come to be seen as Chinese interference in Indonesia's internal affairs via the Indonesian Chinese community and the Indonesian Communist Party.[60] Hence, despite intensification of economic contacts in recent decades and the establishment of a Comprehensive Strategic Partnership, Sino-Indonesian relations have an underlying volatility. This implies that the two countries cannot be expected to reach the levels of closeness seen elsewhere in the region, even if public opinion survey data appear to suggest otherwise, with China and the United States seen as equally favourable.[61]

Nonetheless, China is Indonesia's biggest trading partner and a major investor. There are significant BRI investments in Indonesia, most notably the $6 billion Jakarta-Bandung high-speed railway. By mid-2022, construction was reportedly 80 per cent complete and the railway was due to open to the public in June 2023, cutting journey time from five hours to thirty-six minutes.[62] Chinese companies are also investing in mining, hydropower and the production of solar panels, electric car batteries and industrial silicon in Indonesia. At the same time, Indonesia's debt load in connection with these investments is growing, reaching more than $17 billion by 2021.[63] Thus, there is increasing economic dependence on China. At the same time, Indonesians are generally ambivalent about their partner and have low levels of expertise in China studies.[64]

The two other members of ASEAN are the microstates of Singapore and Brunei. As Figure 5.1 demonstrates, they are also the two wealthiest states in the region. Singapore is a global financial centre, while Brunei's economy is heavily dependent on exports of oil and natural gas. Their prosperity gives them something of a buffer against external forces; but at the same time their small size creates a vulnerability which means, as Singapore's Foreign Minister points out, that they cannot afford to have bad relations with their larger neighbours.[65] As small states, both have tried to steer a course between the Scylla and Charybdis of today's great power politics by maintaining generally cordial relations with both the United States and China. However, as China rises, like other Southeast Asian nations it is difficult for them to avoid being carried by the tide of history towards China.

Since it has wide-ranging trade and investment ties with both the United States and China, Singapore is probably the truest hedger among the ASEAN countries. The United States is the single largest investor in Singapore with $270 billion in direct investments. Bilateral trade totalled $93 billion in 2020. More than 30,000 US citizens live in Singapore.[66] The city-state also hopes that the US military presence in the region continues to act as a stabilizing factor, including serving to restrain China's expansion in the South China Sea and beyond. At the same time, Singapore's ties with China go back centuries, not least because according to a 2010 census about 75 per cent of the city-state's population are of Chinese descent.[67] Close economic cooperation remains in place despite disagreements in 2016 and 2017 about China's role in the South China Sea. Singapore is the world's leading investor in China.[68] Bilateral trade is even larger than that with the United States.[69] As Singapore's founding father Lee Kuan Yew said in 2012: 'China's growing economic sway will be very difficult to fight.'[70] Consequently, public opinion is evenly balanced between the United States and China.[71]

Similarly, tiny Brunei is tossed about in the murky currents of regional relations and great power politics. Like its neighbours Malaysia and the Philippines, Brunei is suspicious of Beijing's intentions in the South China Sea, although it is careful not to make a public show of protest. Nevertheless, there are signs that Chinese economic and political influence are growing, especially since the advent of the BRI in 2013. Chinese investments total $4.1 billion, which includes $3.4 billion for a petrochemical plant. The remaining investments are in transport infrastructure construction projects.[72] In addition, despite some US overtures, there are signs that Brunei's rulers see the writing on the wall and are leaning increasingly towards China. Brunei's Sultan Haji Hassanal Bolkiah has met Xi Jinping on several occasions, including in the Great Hall of the People in Beijing.[73] In an interview with the US scholar David Shambaugh, one senior Bruneian official said: 'We see China as a neighbouring power that is here to stay, which is not so clear with the USA.'[74]

China is also establishing ties with other countries in the Southeast Asian neighbourhood which are not members of ASEAN. Beijing was quick to establish ties with Timor-Leste (East Timor) after it gained its independence from Indonesia in 2002.[75] Chinese companies have sought to exploit the country's oil and gas reserves, albeit without much success so far.[76] Military ties were established in 2007–8, with China supplying equipment and training for the local armed forces.[77] Further east, in April 2022 reports emerged of a security pact between China and the Solomon Islands which might allow the People's Liberation Army Navy (PLAN) to establish a base in the islands.[78] The New Zealand Minister for Foreign Affairs, Nanaia Mahuta, blamed this development on a 'relationship failure' between the Solomons and its larger neighbours New Zealand and Australia.[79] In both these cases, however, the United States and its allies do not appear to have faced up to one of the key reasons why China's influence is spreading: that they have neglected to cultivate relations with economically developing countries in the region. China has stepped in with a viable long-term offer to plug the investment and security gap in these countries.

In short, Southeast Asia is a region where Chinese influence is steadily rising. As Nyíri and Tan's micro-level multi-authored study demonstrates, Chinese norms of bilateral interaction are altering the landscape of economic interaction, even in countries where the image of China is not particularly attractive.[80] BRI investments, although often controversial, are producing some visible results in areas such as transportation and energy. Military cooperation has also been established with several Southeast Asian countries. Meanwhile, the United States has shown itself to be an unreliable, uncommitted partner in recent years, and other Western countries have largely been absent from the scene. Southeast Asian nations can attempt to hedge between China and the United States; but China is on the doorstep and economic ties are growing, so officials in some countries are tending to lean towards increased cooperation with Beijing. Meanwhile, it is not clear what – if anything – the United States and other Western countries are offering. The United States and the West have left a vacuum which China is filling.

India's backyard: South Asia

South Asia as a region has markedly different characteristics to Southeast Asia. This is because it contains a dominant regional power: India. Other states are forced to construct their foreign policies around India's hegemonic status in the region. India is therefore also the predominant influence on Chinese foreign policy in South Asia. Disputed borders and the status of Tibet and Pakistan colour the two behemoths' generally uneasy and antagonistic relations.

South Asia contains seven countries (or eight if Afghanistan is included here rather than in Central Asia). They are (in descending order according to population size): India, Pakistan, Bangladesh, Nepal, Sri Lanka, Bhutan and the Maldives. India, with its massive population of 1.35 billion dwarfs all the others. Although Pakistan (227 million) and Bangladesh (161 million) are large countries, they are reduced in status because of their proximity to India and China, as well as their relative economic weakness. Both were also part of India until they became West and East Pakistan, respectively, in the separation of 1947. Bangladesh declared independence from Pakistan in 1972 after a bloody war in which India acted decisively in its favour. For these and other reasons, regional affairs – even those involving China or the United States – tend to revolve around India.

The problems between China and India date back to 1962. The two countries fought a brief border war which China won. Although not well known in the West, the war is keenly remembered by Indians and the humiliation of defeat dominates much of their thinking about China. To this day, military manoeuvrings continue in the mountains of Kashmir and clashes break out periodically, even though the potential for violence is limited by the fact that soldiers on both sides are not allowed to bear modern weapons. Instead, when skirmishes break out, they pummel each other with sticks and stones. Since Pakistan also disputes some borders with India, Beijing and Islamabad have a mutual need to protect their territorial integrity and counter India. This need is compounded by the existential threat of separatism within each state: in China's case, in Xinjiang and Tibet; and in Pakistan, in Balochistan, Sindh and Gilgit-Baltistan.[81] Three years before the Sino-Indian War, the Dalai Lama fled across the Himalayas to India. He has lived there ever since among the exiled Tibetan community in a ramshackle mountaintop village called McLeod Ganj. Since the Chinese view him as an advocate for an independent Tibet, the fact that India continues to offer him a place of refuge constitutes a perpetual bone of contention. Put simply, the Tibetan issue adds to the lack of trust between China and India.

The intensity of anti-China feeling in India can be seen clearly in public opinion survey data gathered by Morning Consult during 2022. Indian negativity concerning China becomes even more pronounced when contrasted with Indians' broadly positive perception of the United States and the vastly more positive perceptions of China in Pakistan and Bangladesh.[82] The severe contrast between public perceptions of China in India and Pakistan conveys the extent of the entrenched stand-off centred around the relations of these three countries. Analysing what the British scholar Andrew Small calls the 'China-Pakistan Axis' is therefore key to understanding regional dynamics involving China and India.[83]

It is therefore not surprising that India has refused to participate in the BRI due to the perception that the initiative is an attempt by China to establish hegemony in the Indian Ocean region (IOR). Indian analysts fret about China's purported attempt to create a 'string of pearls' based on the Chinese leasing of ports in the IOR such as Hambantota in Sri Lanka and Gwadar in Pakistan.[84] This has led India to invest in the port of Chabahar in Iran, which is about 200 kilometres up the coast. Like Gwadar, the Iranian port remains in a state of development, with India proposing to install modern equipment to load and unload cargo.[85] However, China is also seeking to invest in the port, with Iran seemingly hedging between the two rivals.[86] At the end of 2022, China launched a direct shipping line to Chabahar with the docking of a container ship, suggesting that Iran may intend to favour China over India.[87] Of course, unlike India, Iran and China are united by US activity against them.

In seeking to counter China's evident expansion into the Indian Ocean, India has sought the assistance of the United States. The United States has a naval base at Diego Garcia and has talked up participation in the 'Indo-Pacific' ever since the American 'pivot to Asia' was proposed by Secretary of State Hillary Clinton in 2011.[88] In addition, the so-called 'Quad' (Quadrilateral Security Dialogue) between the United States, India, Japan and Australia has the apparent aim of countering China. However, despite a series of summit meetings, the Quad has not achieved much in practice. India has found it difficult to obtain a firm commitment on regional security cooperation from Washington. India therefore remains relatively isolated in its pushback against China. For its part, China has tried to socialize India into conformity by including it alongside Pakistan in the Shanghai Cooperation Organization (SCO) – but without anything tangible in the way of concrete results so far.

Since India effectively remains resistant to China's influence attempts in the South Asian region, Beijing's diplomatic and investment activity has centred on other countries. Above all, China's most prominent and loyal partner is Pakistan, whose mainly Punjabi ruling elites are keenly aware of threats to the integrity of the state from both within and without.[89] The China-Pakistan Economic Corridor (CPEC) should thus be seen not primarily as an economic 'game changer', as former Prime Minister Nawaz Sharif introduced it, but as a consolidation of long-term cooperation between the two countries, not least on security matters.[90] Pakistan's army remains the dominant force in the nation's politics, and cooperation with the Chinese under the CPEC label is conducted with its consent and involvement at all levels.[91] Although frequently denied or downplayed by both sides, there is little doubt that China has been supplying Pakistan's military with weapons, equipment and know-how over the long-term. This includes the acquisition of nuclear weapons. According to a 2009 US Congressional report, Chinese assistance was vital for the development of Pakistan's nuclear weapons program.[92]

Officially announced in 2015, but with projects in fact beginning two years earlier, CPEC was to be the 'flagship project' of the BRI.[93] It was to be one of six 'economic corridors' boosting regional economic connectivity across the Eurasian landmass. However, it is important to note that CPEC – despite its purported aims – should be seen as internal to Pakistan rather than a regional connectivity megaproject. The reason for claiming this is simple: CPEC investments, as the list of projects on the official CPEC website demonstrates, are almost exclusively focused on the internal development of Pakistan.[94] The only cross-border connectivity project so far is a fibre-optic cable connecting Xinjiang and northern Pakistan.[95] China *has* invested in Pakistan's energy and transport infrastructure under the CPEC label, but at a slower rate than originally anticipated and with less significant results than the government of Pakistan had hoped. For instance, despite progress on expanding Pakistan's energy production and transmission, the country is still dependent on imports of electricity from Iran and other countries and suffers frequent blackouts and brownouts.[96]

In its original conception, the main aim of CPEC was to create a zone – 'corridor' – of economic interaction connecting Gwadar port in Pakistan with China's Xinjiang province. Roads, railways and pipelines carrying oil and gas would cross the Himalayas, enhancing the economies of both countries – and possibly those of Central Asia and other regional actors too. It would also solve China's 'Malacca dilemma': the supposed security risk of relying on energy supplies transported through the narrow Strait of Malacca, which could be easily blockaded.[97] However, the much-trumpeted development of Gwadar port has progressed at a snail's pace, much to the chagrin of Pakistan's government. The harbour has not yet been dredged deep enough to accommodate super-sized oil tankers. The volumes of cargo passing through the port are a fraction of those at Pakistan's main port, Karachi, which also still has excess capacity.[98] Despite CPEC investments in energy infrastructure, Gwadar is not yet self-sufficient in electricity and is dependent on erratic supplies from Iran.[99] Much of the local population in Balochistan is also openly hostile to the Chinese involvement, to the extent that the Balochistan Liberation Army has frequently targeted Chinese workers in terrorist attacks.[100] This has significantly reduced the Chinese appetite for investment.

In the north of the country, the only cross-border connection remains the Karakoram Highway, which was built in the 1970s. However, it is closed for months each winter due to heavy snowfall on the 4,500-metre high Khunjerab Pass, and often in summer too due to landslides, security issues and protests.[101] Despite frequent reports that an oil pipeline is being built to carry oil from Gwadar to Kashgar, the official CPEC website and other official publications reveal no plan for a pipeline.[102] Thus, the idea that the route from Gwadar through the length of Pakistan to the Chinese border could provide a solution to China's 'Malacca dilemma' is simply a myth or a trope. There is plenty of evidence that the Chinese, realizing its impracticality, have quietly dropped the cross-border 'economic corridor' aspect of CPEC.[103]

Terrorist attacks on Chinese workers have evidently convinced Beijing that the security situation in Pakistan – when taken in conjunction with the country's ongoing economic weakness and shortage of cash reserves – is not conducive to continuing to pour large amounts of capital into the country. Instead, Beijing has allowed the flow of BRI investments to slow down and left some proposed projects on the drawing board. Yet there is also no doubt that Chinese influence in Pakistan is strong. As recent survey data reveal, public opinion in Pakistan remains resolutely pro-China.[104] Twenty-eight thousand Pakistani students are studying at universities and colleges in China.[105] Beijing needs to maintain solid relations with its most reliable regional ally to form a wedge against India. At any rate, even if CPEC projects are progressing slower than anticipated, this fact should be set against the almost total withdrawal of US support – both financial and political – for Pakistan which has occurred since the killing of Osama bin Laden on Pakistan's territory by US operatives.[106] In comparison, China remains Pakistan's stalwart ally.

China has made overtures to other countries in the region in the form of BRI investments. Most notable among these are Chinese investments in Sri Lanka. At the forefront of these is the controversial Hambantota port development. An agreement was signed with China under former President and Prime Minister Mahinda Rajapaksa, who was born in Hambantota and solicited the development of the port and other projects in his hometown. The port was constructed using loans from China's state-backed Exim Bank and China Development Bank.[107] When Sri Lanka was unable to service the more than \$1 billion debt for the construction of the port, a ninety-nine-year lease was issued to China Merchant Ports to run Hambantota in exchange for debt forgiveness.[108]

There were fears – especially in India – that Beijing would seek to use the port for military purposes. However, there is no clear evidence so far that China has been developing the port in this way. Indeed, the ninety-nine-year concession agreement states that the Chinese military cannot use the port without the Sri Lankan government's permission.[109] Initially low freight volumes have seen a marked increase since 2020.[110] However, with Sri Lanka entering a debt crisis in the first half of 2022, the status of the port and other BRI investments (such as an almost unused airport at Hambantota) remain controversial. In May 2022, Sri Lanka was reportedly down to its last \$50 million in cash reserves.[111] There were corruption allegations and threats of violence against Rajapaksa. A Chinese state company was found to have handed over \$8 million in cash payments to Rajapaksa's aides.[112] He was forced to resign his post as Prime Minister on 9 May 2022.[113] In the wake of riots in 2022, and in the context of the emerging debt crisis and increasingly negative views of China, China's future role in Sri Lanka is unclear.

In Bangladesh, Chinese companies were also supposed to oversee a deep-sea port development, at Sonadia Island. However, this has been dropped, apparently due to behind-the-scenes pressure from India, possibly backed up by the United States and Japan.[114] Instead, Bangladesh has proposed a Japanese-built port at Matarbari.[115] Bangladesh is also supposed to be a key part of the Bangladesh-China-India-Myanmar (BCIM) Economic Corridor, which was intended to be one of the six key 'economic corridors' of the BRI. Again, however, progress on this has been slow due to Indian reluctance to participate in the BRI.[116] Like CPEC, the BCIM 'corridor' – which looks good on maps – exists only on paper.

Overall, although Beijing's overtures to Dhaka appear to have been blocked by India, the mere fact of proposed Chinese involvement and investment in Bangladesh has altered the environment in which regional relations take place. Bangladesh, forced to make a choice between Beijing and Delhi, has – for the time being – sided with its long-time benefactor and close neighbour India. Nevertheless, opinion poll data demonstrate that Bangladeshis have much more favourable views of China than Indians and view China more favourably than the United States.[117] New Delhi will have to continue monitoring Chinese influence attempts closely if it wishes to keep Bangladesh on India's side.

The situation is similar in the Maldives. These low-lying islands in the Indian Ocean with a population of half a million are dependent on tourism and fishing – not industries which usually generate high cash surpluses. Nevertheless, the Maldives government has pressed ahead with an ambitious public investment program using Chinese loans. China's Exim Bank has provided more than $1 billion for an airport upgrade, a new bridge and a relocation of the country's port. According to a 2018 report, the loans have created a high risk of debt default.[118] Of more concern to India are questions of Chinese influence and the possibility that Beijing may seek to establish a military base in the islands. For this reason, in February 2021 India signed a deal with the Maldives to 'develop, support and maintain' a harbour at Uthuru Thila Falhu naval base – in the process apparently pre-empting the possibility of any similar project by China.[119]

Geographically, Nepal and Bhutan are squeezed between China and India. For this reason, they have no choice but to hedge as best they can between the two giants. Although both have traditionally oriented towards India, Chinese expansionism in the BRI era has created an environment in which they have little choice but to evaluate whether Beijing's offer is superior to New Delhi's. Perhaps unsurprisingly, it is difficult for either to reject Chinese advances given their lack of resources, Chinese pressure and the carrots on offer, even if both appear wary of surrendering their futures to Chinese interests.

Before the Covid-19 pandemic, Nepal-China relations appeared to be on an upwards trajectory. In 2019, agreement was reached on a raft of BRI investments, including a Chinese-built railway connection from Tibet to Kathmandu.[120] The onset of the pandemic brought all this discussion to a standstill. No Chinese investment materialized. China closed the border, inciting protests from Nepalese businessmen who were dependent on cross-border trade.[121] In frustration at the lack of progress, Nepal turned in February 2022 to the United States, signing an agreement for a $500 million grant under the banner of the government-backed Millennium Challenge Corporation.[122] This development immediately pressed China into a burst of renewed activity. Foreign Minister Wang Yi was dispatched to Kathmandu in March and a new nine-point agreement was signed. This included feasibility studies for a cross-border railway and a high-voltage power transmission line. However, a sticking point in the negotiations was the Chinese insistence on using commercial loans rather than grants.[123] Clearly, Nepal's government had been watching the debt servicing problems experienced by other BRI participants such as Sri Lanka and had decided to be careful about following suit. Surprisingly, there was no sign of India at the negotiating table as the Chinese and Americans competed for influence.

The tiny hermetic kingdom of Bhutan – population a little over 700,000 – is unique among China's neighbours in that it does not have full diplomatic relations with Beijing. Large sections of Bhutan's border with China are disputed.[124] For decades, Bhutan has relied on India for its security. In 2017, the Indian army intervened to prevent the Chinese military from building a road on the Doklam plateau, which China claims as its territory.[125] The plateau overlooks the vital Siliguri corridor, a narrow strip of land which connects most of India to its north-eastern states. However, in the face of Chinese occupation of key areas along the border and even within Bhutanese territory, there are signs that Bhutan is losing faith in the ability or willingness of India to defend its interests. A memorandum of understanding was signed in October 2022 which began a process of settling the China-Bhutan border bilaterally. Chinese pressure appears to have resulted in greater influence with Bhutanese elites, who may be eyeing the possible economic benefits of cooperating with China. Meanwhile, according to one Indian commentator, 'New Delhi has chosen to look the other way.'[126]

Afghanistan constitutes a special case in the region for two reasons. First, since it is at the crossroads of South Asia, Central Asia and the Middle East, it is difficult to know in which region to place it. However, since it was not part of the Soviet Union like the other Central Asian states and shares a porous border and some tribal groups with Pakistan, it makes most sense to place it in South Asia. Second, Afghanistan only emerged from two decades of US occupation in 2021, making it a newly independent state with uncertain political and economic characteristics. Its volatile history and rule by the Taliban mean that it is not easy to assess its present and future role in international politics, including Chinese foreign policy.

While the Chinese government has demonstrated a willingness to negotiate with the Taliban, it is not clear that Beijing is intending to commit resources to a country its policymakers regard as 'the graveyard of empires'.[127] For instance, although a Chinese company obtained a $3 billion lease in 2007 to work the Aynak copper mine – potentially the world's second largest – development was stalled during the US occupation. In December 2021, Chinese sources told the state-backed *Global Times* that the situation was still not stable enough to commence work on the mine.[128] Although China and Afghanistan share a narrow border – they are connected through Afghanistan's narrow Wakhan corridor and the Wakhjir pass – the Chinese are not working to develop cross-border connectivity. It is currently being left to the Afghans to build a road to the border without Chinese investment.[129] Thus, while Beijing clearly wants to maintain influence with the Taliban – not least to prevent Uighur separatists from using Afghanistan as a base from which to launch activity in Xinjiang – the Chinese are likely to continue being cautious about large-scale investments, particularly in view of the frequent attacks on Chinese citizens in neighbouring Pakistan.

Overall, across the region, the most significant obstacle to Beijing's attempt to expand Chinese influence in South Asia and the Indian Ocean through BRI investments is India. Just as China-US rivalry generates hedging behaviour in Southeast Asia, the China-India standoff is the backdrop against which all regional interactions occur. At the same time, as the individual country accounts in this section demonstrate, India is not necessarily a consistently committed actor in regional politics. Just as in Southeast Asia, China's attempt to build relations with regional actors is the primary factor driving events in the region. Meanwhile, despite much talk of the 'Indo-Pacific' and Obama's 'pivot to Asia', US influence in the region has declined in recent years with the military withdrawal from Afghanistan, reduced aid to Pakistan and the relative neglect of relations with other regional actors, including India. While the West looks on ineffectively from afar and India dithers, China is actively engaged. Although China is by no means hegemonic in South Asia – that status still belongs to India since it has unfettered access to the Indian Ocean – Beijing's economic diplomacy, whether implemented or merely dangled in front of impoverished partners like a tempting carrot, is the key factor driving the evolution of regional relations. Every decision that the other regional actors make is necessarily driven by calculations concerning Chinese money and expanding influence within a complex and ever-changing political and economic environment.

Russia's backyard: Central Asia

Just as South Asia is dominated by India, Central Asia has long been a zone of Russian hegemony. The five states which constitute the region – Kazakhstan, Uzbekistan, Turkmenistan, Kyrgyzstan and Tajikistan – were all members of the Union of Soviet Socialist Republics (USSR) during the Cold War. They only obtained independence from Russia and established themselves as nation states when the USSR broke up in 1991. This explains why Russia still thinks of the region as its backyard. However, the Russia-centric narrative is being increasingly challenged by China's increasing influence and economic activity via BRI investments, security cooperation with Central Asian states and other means. Questions concerning the extent to which Russia and China can cooperate or compete therefore tend to dominate analysis of regional affairs.

At the same time, Central Asia is not just a potential zone of contention or collaboration between Russia and China. Since independence, the Central Asian nations have struggled to get along with each other. The break-up of the Soviet Union in 1991 and the emergence of new states left a messy legacy of confusing territorial demarcations. Most notably, there are complicated border disputes between Uzbekistan, Tajikistan and Kyrgyzstan. These are focused on the Fergana valley, which is divided between the three countries.[130] There are Uzbek and Tajik exclaves in Kyrgyzstan such as the Uzbek exclave of Sokh: oddly, this is in Kyrgyzstan but populated mainly by Tajiks.[131] The three nations have a history of violent border clashes, often resulting in casualties.[132] While most Central Asians speak Turkic languages, Tajik is more closely related to Persian, further complicating regional affairs. All countries are predominantly Muslim, but as in the Middle East and other Islamic regions, this does not lead to harmonious relations between the states.

Since all five states are not democracies and have varying degrees of political authoritarianism – with Turkmenistan being the most extreme case – there are also internal tensions within countries which sometimes result in riots and disorder. For instance, nationwide riots in Kazakhstan in January 2022 over rising fuel prices resulted in the government inviting Russian troops to intervene.[133] More than one hundred protesters were killed, and thousands reportedly detained before order was restored.[134] Riots against the regional administration in the east of Tajikistan in May 2022 also resulted in at least one death.[135] Thus, there is a sense of underlying volatility amid the apparently smooth relations at the leadership level which affects external actors' relations with the region.

Since the 1990s, one of Beijing's goals in the region has been to socialize the Central Asian states into cooperation with each other and with China and Russia according to Chinese norms of interaction. China's standard approach to building relations with the actors in a region is to establish a cooperation platform with the formula 'n+1', where 'n' stands for the number of states in the region and the '+1' stands for China. For instance, the cooperation platform set up in Central and Eastern Europe is often referred to as the '16+1' or '17+1' cooperation platform. In Africa, China has established the Forum for Cooperation between China and African Countries (FOCAC). In the Middle East, there is the China-Arab States Cooperation Forum (CASCF). These regional platforms provide one of the main conduits through which Beijing attempts to socialize its cooperation partners in a region into 'harmonious' relations with each other and with China. As the Polish scholar Jakub Jakóbowski puts it, these 'comprehensive dialogue mechanisms are based on Chinese-backed norms of non-binding agreements, voluntarism and consensus, derived from the tradition of South-South cooperation'.[136] Each regional cooperation platform provides 'a flexible and loose institutional structure that enables China to combine multilateral and bilateral approaches, creating a highly adaptable blueprint for managing foreign relations on a regional scale'.[137]

The main platform through which the Chinese government has sought to socialize Central Asian states and cultivate common security goals in the region is the Shanghai Cooperation Organization (SCO).[138] The SCO began as the Shanghai Five in 1996, when it included Kazakhstan, Kyrgyzstan and Tajikistan alongside China and Russia. Uzbekistan was added in 2001, when the SCO label was adopted. Reclusive Turkmenistan is not a member state, but officials attend SCO meetings as guests. Despite the border clashes already mentioned, the SCO has been remarkably successful at maintaining relatively peaceful and stable relations between the Central Asian nations – at least as far as their leaders are concerned. It has also ensured that Russia and China do not end up at loggerheads over their goals in the region. On the other hand, citizens of the Central Asian states often have more negative perceptions of Chinese activity. Sinophobia – especially the fear of being 'flooded' by Chinese immigrants – is prevalent in the region. This means that while Beijing has succeeded in obtaining the support of regional leaders, it has much work to do to improve its image and soft power among the general population.[139]

At the same time, as far as the Chinese government is concerned, soft power promotion is lower down the list of priorities than security issues. From China's point of view, keeping its western neighbours aligned with its security agendas is a vital part of the Chinese project of pacifying restive Xinjiang province. By maintaining solid relations with Central Asian leaders, Beijing has secured their cooperation in suppressing support for separatist elements such as the East Turkestan Islamic Movement (ETIM).[140] The counter-terrorist effort, from the Chinese perspective, has been successful so far: the Uighur resistance movement in Xinjiang has evidently been contained, because there have been few reports of violence in recent years. At the state level, China has worked to ensure that its neighbours do not support the foundation of a new state of 'East Turkestan', and that they do not support the Uighurs.[141]

Border surveillance is an important part of China's effort to keep Xinjiang under control. To this end, Tajikistan's government has even allowed China to build military bases on Tajik territory near the border.[142] While officially these are manned only by Tajik personnel, a *Washington Post* reporter in 2019 saw (and even interviewed) Chinese soldiers on the Tajik side of the border.[143] In an interview with the scholar Raffaello Pantucci, unnamed Chinese experts in Beijing confirmed the presence of these troops on Tajik soil.[144] This quiet expansion of China's military across an international border comes, in part, as a long-term consequence of cultivating relations with Central Asian leaders within the framework of the SCO. However, it flies in the face of China's overt insistence on 'non-interference' in the internal affairs of other states.

While the promotion of security cooperation has always been in first place on Beijing's agenda vis-à-vis Central Asia, economic diplomacy has assumed a larger role since the advent of the Belt and Road Initiative in 2013. As outlined earlier in the book, the vision for a 'Silk Road Economic Belt' (SREB) passing through Central Asia and Russia on its way to Europe was first proposed by Xi Jinping while he was visiting Kazakhstan. At least in the initial stages, the idea was for the Central Asian states – especially Kazakhstan – to be a transport corridor and commercial hub for an enhanced trade route between Asia and Europe. Central to this conception was to be the rail link which passes from Xinjiang into Kazakhstan, then travels on through Russia and Belarus to Poland and Western Europe. A special economic zone (SEZ) and logistics centre was built at Khorgos on the China-Kazakhstan border. One reason for establishing Khorgos Gateway was to handle the complications of transferring freight to locally gauged trains (countries which were in the former Soviet Union have a different gauge to that used in China and Europe).[145] Khorgos Gateway was also supposed to be a massive 'dry port' servicing trade and commerce between Asia and Europe.

However, there are problems with Khorgos and the rail route. The unloading and reloading of freight due to different gauges is expensive and an inbuilt inefficiency.[146] Some trains, especially those returning from Europe to China, have reportedly carried empty containers subsidized by the Chinese state.[147] Rail transport generally cannot compete with maritime routes for cost and reliability. The rail transport route still constitutes only a small percentage of freight transport between Asia and Europe. Smuggling, as we saw in the previous chapter, affects tax revenues. Trade volumes at Khorgos are lower than expected due to restriction on how many goods one person can bring across the border.[148]

Thus, there are inherent problems with the idea of Central Asia as a hub or logistics centre for trade between Asia and Europe. As anybody who has travelled across international borders knows, they are rarely vibrant hubs of commercial activity. They tend to be just points which travellers and freight must cross in order to get somewhere else. In effect, the same can be said of any geographical region or country whose function is seen mainly as a transit zone from one commercial hub to another. If Central Asia is defined as the in-between area between Asia and Europe, then it is difficult to see how much profit Central Asian states can draw from merely being the place where goods cross. In fact, it is not even clear that this is what is happening in practice: a 2018 *New York Times* report found that Khorgos was handling relatively low volumes of goods compared to the standard maritime route to Europe, and that most goods passing through Khorgos remained in Central Asia or ended up in nearby countries such as Iran.[149] In 2016, the rail route accounted for just 1 per cent of China-Europe trade by volume.[150]

Nevertheless, the Chinese presence at Khorgos provides evidence of heightened Chinese influence in the region. It also contributes to the steady drip of Chinese norms of interaction into regional affairs, which are also promoted by the significant presence of Chinese state oil and gas companies in the Central Asian energy sector. Indeed, the regional spread of Chinese practices, influence and economic diplomacy is likely to be a far more significant outcome of the implementation of the BRI in Central Asia than the development of the rail freight route to Europe.

At the same time, while Chinese influence expands, Russia still lurks in the background. A significant proportion of the population of Central Asian countries is Russian. As the January 2022 protests in Kazakhstan showed, the Russian military is ready to intervene and continues to maintain close contact with local regimes. None of the five Central Asian states voted to condemn Russia's invasion of Ukraine in a United Nations vote on 2 March 2022.[151] When combined with the local tendency to Sinophobia, there is always the likelihood that local leaders will back Russia over China when push comes to shove.

There is also the question of the mutual lack of trust between China and Russia. Although ostensibly close allies, in reality the partners are not as closely aligned as might be expected. The seeds of mistrust were sown during the Sino-Soviet split during the Cold War, when Khrushchev and Mao fell out over ideological and practical issues (such as Khrushchev's reluctance to give Mao nuclear weapons).[152] Although relations have improved since, the depth of relations should not be overestimated. Although supportive of cooperation at public events, both Chinese and Russian officials and experts tend to express disdain for their counterparts in private. In interviews, Pantucci and Petersen found that 'Russians were always quick to complain about the Chinese, and after a little prodding the Chinese would reciprocate'.[153]

It is therefore not wise to assume that the apparent axis between the two powers is as strong as it sometimes appears. For instance, although China has refrained from criticizing Russia over its invasion of Ukraine, Beijing has been quietly withdrawing some financial support.[154] A Russian official also claimed that China was refusing to supply aircraft parts; the official was later sacked for making the issue public.[155] In late May, *The Moscow Times* reported that China had closed its airports to Boeings operated by Russian companies, in the process complying with Western sanctions on Russia.[156] Russia is also a long-term supplier of military technology to India, China's arch-rival across the Himalayas: around 70 per cent of India's defence equipment has Russian origins.[157] Thus, even when the partners appear to be cooperating, on close inspection there are cracks in the façade of Sino-Russian 'friendship'.

As in Europe, questions related to the supply of fossil fuels and other natural resources tend to dominate China's relations with both Russia and Central Asia. Russia's economy is heavily focused on the export of natural resources. Since the invasion of Ukraine, it is natural to assume that China is an even more important market for Russian energy and other resources. However, it is not clear that China would desire to become over-dependent on Russia. The Chinese government has long been pursuing a policy of energy supply diversification to try to ensure China's energy security. Putting more eggs into the Russia basket by importing even more Russian oil and gas is therefore not part of China's long-term strategy. Nevertheless, Russian energy imported through pipelines does form a significant part of China's energy mix.[158]

Of the Central Asian states, Kazakhstan, Turkmenistan and Uzbekistan are the richest in natural resources. China is an important customer for each of them to varying degrees, with Turkmenistan being the most dependent on exports to China. A large proportion of Turkmenistan's natural gas production is managed by Chinese National Petroleum Corporation (CNPC). The key Galkynysh gas field has been developed by CNPC.[159] Three pipelines transport natural gas from Turkmenistan across Uzbekistan and Kazakhstan to Xinjiang province in northwest China. When Russia and Iran decided to stop buying Turkmen gas in 2016 and 2017, respectively, Turkmenistan became almost completely dependent on exports of gas to China.[160] In 2018, official figures stated that thirty-seven billion cubic metres (bcm) of gas were exported. Of this total, 34.5 bcm went to China: over 93 per cent of the total.[161] Given that hydrocarbons – primarily natural gas – constitute over 90 per cent of Turkmenistan's exports, the conclusion can only be that the nation's economy is overwhelmingly reliant on China. When the Chinese decided to reduce imports of fossil fuels from Central Asia during the

Covid-19 pandemic, the impact on Turkmenistan was dramatic: Turkmenistan's export revenues shrank by 30 per cent in 2020.[162]

Kazakhstan and Uzbekistan also contribute significantly to Central Asia's exports of hydrocarbons to China. However, they are by no means as dependent on China as Turkmenistan. Nevertheless, before the Covid-19 pandemic both countries were exporting ever-increasing amounts of energy to China. Energy exports consist of natural gas in the case of Uzbekistan, and both oil and gas in the case of Kazakhstan.[163]

Between 2003 and 2009, the Chinese National Petroleum Corporation (CNPC) constructed the Kazakhstan-China oil pipeline from western Kazakhstan to Xinjiang in cooperation with KazMunaiGaz, Kazakhstan's national energy company. The pipeline has a capacity of 12.5 million tonnes per year.[164] In 2005, CNPC assumed ownership of PetroKazakhstan, the country's largest independent oil producer.[165] CNPC also has an 8 per cent stake in the Kashagan offshore energy project in the Caspian Sea. Although details are difficult to obtain, Chinese oil companies reportedly own between 25 and 40 per cent of Kazakhstan's oil sector. At least ten companies in Kazakhstan's energy sector are entirely Chinese owned, and another eight have more than 50 per cent Chinese ownership.[166] Meanwhile, Kazakhstan's exports of gas to China rose markedly from 1.1 bcm in 2017 to 5.8 bcm in 2018.[167] This was out of a total of 33.3 bcm produced.[168]

In Uzbekistan's case, natural gas is the main fossil fuel export, some of which is transported via the pipelines which originate in Turkmenistan. Out of almost 60 billion bcm of gas produced in Uzbekistan in 2018, 6.5 bcm were exported to China. Around 4 bcm are purchased by Russia's Gazprom each year, while 1.5–4 bcm goes to Kazakhstan.[169] Most of the remainder is used for domestic consumption. Thus, although China has become the number one export market for Uzbek gas – providing a way for China to diversify away from Turkmenistan – the Uzbek economy does not rely solely on Chinese purchases. In short, at least in the pre-pandemic period, China was rapidly growing in importance as a customer for Uzbek and Kazakh gas and oil. Given the present uncertainties inherent in securing and selling energy supplies, it is unlikely that China will wean itself off Central Asian fossil fuels. It is also unlikely that Kazakhstan, Uzbekistan and, especially, Turkmenistan will diversify rapidly away from exports to China.

Kyrgyzstan and Tajikistan are not as blessed with natural resources as the other three Central Asian states, especially in terms of fossil fuels. Both are energy-poor and dependent on imports of gas and oil from Kazakhstan and Uzbekistan.[170] To alleviate this problem, Tajikistan has been developing hydroelectric power with some success.[171] The Nurik dam supplies 70 per cent of Tajikistan's electricity.[172] Nonetheless, Kyrgyzstan and Tajikistan's generally mountainous terrain and lack of fossil fuels mean that both nations are economically less developed than neighbouring Kazakhstan and Uzbekistan. In terms of resources, there is therefore little on offer which would obviously interest Beijing. As a result, most Chinese investment, as elsewhere in Asia, goes into the construction of transport and energy infrastructure.[173]

Both Kyrgyzstan and Tajikistan appear, along with Turkmenistan, on a list compiled by AidData of the twenty-five nations which are most economically dependent on Chinese development finance.[174] In the case of Tajikistan, out of $3.3 billion owed to international creditors by early 2022, almost $2 billion had been lent by China's Exim Bank.[175] The money was being used to fund the building of roads and power plants by Chinese companies. Thus, Chinese loans were producing visible results; but with the proviso that Chinese money circulated from Chinese state banks back into Chinese hands. In the meantime, Tajikistan was left with a sizeable debt that needed to be serviced, including the payment of interest. Indeed, out of Tajikistan's $131.9 million in debt repayments during 2021, $65.2 million went to China, including $22 million in interest.[176]

There are gold mining operations in both Kyrgyzstan and Tajikistan. Chinese companies have been operating mines in both countries with mixed results. While gold exports have been profitable, public perceptions of Chinese operations tend to be negative. Many locals see the Chinese as exploitative and having a lack of respect for Tajik employees and citizens. In both countries, there have been violent protests and attacks on Chinese operations and workers.[177] There have also been reports of Chinese companies investing in agricultural production in Kyrgyzstan and Tajikistan, but the reality is that given the two countries' unfavourable terrain such projects constitute a very minor proportion of total Chinese investment.[178] At the same time, the settling of a border dispute in 2011 resulted in Tajikistan apparently handing a large piece of territory to China.[179]

Given the fact that both countries have a land border with Xinjiang province, cooperation on security issues related to Uighur separatism is probably the main strategic priority for Beijing in cooperating with Tajikistan. As already discussed, China has established at least one border post within Tajikistan's territory. Under the auspices of the SCO, and with Russian knowledge, China's military regularly conducts training exercises and counter-terrorism operations with its Tajik and Kyrgyz counterparts focused on border security.[180] China's military aid to Central Asian countries has been at a lower level than that coming from Russia, but still at significant levels in the millions of dollars. China has supplied military equipment such as technological aid, communications equipment, night goggles, uniforms and vehicles to Tajikistan, Kyrgyzstan, Kazakhstan and Uzbekistan, with the most significant amounts of aid going to the first two countries. China has also sold surface to air missiles systems, drones, rifles and military aircraft to Central Asian countries.[181]

In short, China's influence in Central Asia is primarily connected to the areas of security cooperation and resource extraction. Cooperation occurs under the broad umbrella of the SCO, in the process ensuring that Russia is onside. Interactions take place 'through bilateral and multilateral structures at the same time'.[182] As elsewhere in Asia, 'corruption, weak checks on the executive branch, and lack of transparency … help China to secure its deals'.[183] While there is clearly a long way to go, Chinese norms and practices are gradually becoming established in Central Asia even as Sinophobia – a term describing negative perceptions of being exploited or 'flooded' by the Chinese – remains prevalent in the region.

In contrast to the focused Chinese approach to Central Asia, other major powers are losing out due to the absence of clarity and interest in their approach to the region. Richard Pomfret notes the 'inconsistencies and lack of focus in US policy towards Central Asia'.[184] Pantucci and Petersen describe the lack of 'a strong vision or strategy' in their conversations with US officials.[185] Similarly, despite some talk about cooperation, the EU's 'broader strategic vision has never been articulated' and there is 'little evidence of material progress'.[186] Despite the fact that the EU is Central Asia's largest trade partner, Boonstra concludes that 'the overall picture of the EU's engagement in Central Asia is one of limited to no impact'.[187] India also lacks a clear strategy and is therefore 'losing out' to China.[188] In this context, the Chinese engagement with Central Asia is on a different level of norm diffusion and material impacts. As elsewhere in Asia, China appears to be winning what used, in a previous era, to be called 'the Great Game' of geopolitical and geo-economic influence.

Conclusion: the BRI's impacts in China's neighbourhood

The analysis in this chapter reveals that Chinese influence – both material and ideational – is increasing through all three neighbouring regions. The Chinese approach is multidimensional: it attempts to address and encompass the complex needs of investor and recipient in a single investment package. To meet partner countries' needs, the Chinese supply the capital and infrastructure they lack. China's aims include establishing a degree of political influence, exporting excess industrial capacity and putting China's vast cash reserves to productive use. By utilizing its deep pockets and excess construction capacity in the service of comprehensive national security goals, China plugs an investment plus infrastructure gap to which other major powers have not been paying attention.

Obviously, the impacts of BRI investments vary between countries. The effects of Chinese influence-building and economic diplomacy tend to be greater in poorer countries which share land borders with China, most notably Laos, Cambodia, Myanmar, Tajikistan, Kyrgyzstan and Pakistan. Yet the fortunes of all China's neighbours are affected to one degree or another. The governments of each nation are forced to consider their policy towards China as a matter of priority. Only India, a state with a population of similar size to China's, has the luxury of maintaining an independent approach which actively resists Chinese influence. All other states are forced to cooperate with China to at least a certain degree, even if some of them – such as Vietnam – are highly suspicious of their outsized neighbour's intentions.

China is setting new norms of bilateral interaction throughout its economically developing Asian neighbourhood. With the support of the CCP, Chinese companies are active in many countries. Beijing is lending money for construction projects and building infrastructure under the banner of the BRI. This is generally done without necessarily revealing the financial terms established with national governments. In surprisingly many cases, the PLA is also pursuing security goals via cooperation with a neighbouring country's military. In short, China is an influential actor across all three Asian regions. Despite official protestations to the contrary, behind closed doors it has considerable influence in the internal affairs of many countries.

In contrast to China's growing influence, the position of the United States has become relatively weaker in recent years. The United States has withdrawn from Afghanistan and ceased financing Pakistan. It has neglected relations with countries such as Laos, Cambodia and Myanmar, leaving them open to China. Even the American approach to a potential partner like India is ambivalent and non-committal. Across the three regions, despite the supposed 'pivot to Asia' under Obama and the focus on the 'Indo-Pacific' under Trump, American influence has been weakening for years, if not decades. As for the EU, it was never a strong actor in Asia in the first place. Since decolonization after the Second World War, the European powers – chiefly Britain and France – have had a massively reduced role in the Asia-Pacific.

In short, China is establishing new norms of interaction and increasing influence in the developing regions of Asia. Many countries are still hedging between China and the United States, India or Russia. But the evidence reveals that this strategy, in many cases, is one of deferred bandwagoning: a delaying tactic designed to put off the inevitable as long as possible. And, in each region, the nation with which bandwagoning is being deferred is China. Since the West and China do not appear to be willing to work together, questions of influence in the Global South have assumed the characteristics of a zero-sum game. Such games are theoretically only supposed to have one winner, but this remains to be seen. Whether the course of history will keep running in China's direction depends on whether the United States and Europe can develop a coherent and attractive alternative to Chinese influence and investment.

Chapter 6

CHINA'S RELATIONS WITH THE REST OF THE GLOBAL SOUTH

To have friends come from afar is happiness, is it not?

— Confucius, the Analects

China's investment in the global South has a longer history than just the course of Xi Jinping's presidency. In fact, the BRI builds and expands on previous Chinese initiatives. As Aaron Friedberg points out,

> Contrary to the way he is sometimes portrayed in the West … Xi does not represent a break from the past. To the contrary, he is following in the footsteps of his forebears and attempting to attain the same objectives.[1]

More specifically, it is important to remember that the BRI is not China's first venture into investment and cooperation with the developing countries of the global South. The BRI built on the foundation of the 'Going Global' (*zou chuqu,* 走出去) initiative launched in 1999 under President Jiang Zemin. It was a strategy which

> … sought to build 'national champion' firms, reduce the cost of transporting goods to and from other countries, increase external demand for Chinese goods and services, wean the country off high levels of domestic infrastructure investment, acquire advanced technologies, and secure energy and raw materials.[2]

The 'Going Global' strategy was intended to anticipate the slowing of Chinese domestic economic growth and mitigate it by expanding the activity of Chinese commercial actors – most notably, construction firms – beyond China. It was conceived by the central government and implemented from the top down in a remarkably coordinated manner over an extended period, all the way up to the advent of the BRI.[3] Of course, problems with implementation should not be underestimated. In areas of detail, Chinese actors certainly interpreted their instructions in a range of different ways. Companies often took decisions which benefitted their own interests rather than those of the state. Yet the big picture of the Chinese approach to overseas economic activity at the macro-level retained an overall coherence during the decades over which 'Going Global' evolved into the

BRI. It contained a set of consistent, connected strategic goals including securing energy supplies, expanding the activity of Chinese commercial actors, as well as acquiring political and economic influence.

The extent of China's long-term top-down coordination undercuts perceptions among some Western experts and observers that China's authoritarian regime has become 'fractured' or 'fragmented' due to market pressures and competing actors.[4] To be clear: there is no doubt that the implementation of Chinese foreign policy is not as clear-cut as Beijing simply issuing orders and all commercial actors following suit. The principal-agent problem – in which the actions of an 'agent' do not match the expectations of the 'principal' – is a real concern for Beijing, as the case of CEFC going rogue in the Czech Republic demonstrates.[5] As Chapter 5 demonstrated, corruption is a problem in the implementation of the BRI in countries such as Sri Lanka. However, the overall thrust of Chinese economic diplomacy in the developing world has by no means been as scattered or inconsistent as some Western observers appear to believe. Indeed, as the meticulous analysis of a huge body of empirical data by an AidData team has demonstrated, there is a great deal of continuity from the 'Going Global' era to the BRI.[6]

The 'Going Global' era saw a huge expansion of Chinese investment and influence in the global South from a previously very low base. Between 2000 and 2014, development finance projects worth $350 billion were implemented in six regions: Africa, Asia, Central and Eastern Europe (CEE), Latin America, the Middle East and the Pacific. Two regions received the lion's share of the capital: Africa and Asia. Between them, these two regions absorbed two-thirds of China's development finance project funds. From 2000 to 2014, China's total investment of development finance in CEE, Latin America, the Middle East and the Pacific combined amounted to less than that in Africa. Subsequently, during the BRI era, while Chinese capital has continued to flow into Africa, more Chinese investments have focused on Latin America and the Middle East (see Table 6.1).[7] From 2015 to 2021, new investments across the six regions totalled $766 billion, with only CEE receiving less than in the preceding period. Thus, the BRI represents not only a

Table 6.1 China's investments in developing regions

Region	Value of development finance projects ($ billion), 2000–14	Value of large BRI investments ($ billion), 2015–21
Africa	118.1	160.9
Asia	116.5	303.3
Central and Eastern Europe	56.7	32.5
Latin America	53.4	105.7
Middle East	3.1	112.2
Pacific	2.8	3.4
Total	**350.6**	**766.0**

Source: author, based on data from Dreher et al (2022), p. 116, and the AEI China Global Investment Tracker

continuation of 'Going Global', but also an intensification and diversification of Chinese investments across most developing regions.

On the other hand, there are signs that the Chinese government has been shifting the focus of the BRI away from large-scale infrastructure investments since about 2017. China has reduced lending since an internal review in 2016–17 due to perceptions of wasteful spending and destabilization of the Chinese economy. Instead, Beijing has retooled the BRI in a more sustainable and less capital-intensive direction by focusing on areas such as media, academia and green energy – in line with the needs of partner countries. As a result, as Matt Schrader and J. Michael Cole point out, 'The United States and its industrialized partners will have to contend with a shifting paradigm of Chinese influence – one that is moving away from infrastructure megaprojects toward more diffuse, more sustainable engagement.'[8]

Developing this point, Lina Benabdallah suggests that a highly significant – but often ignored – aspect of Chinese power diffusion in Africa consists of 'investments in human resource development programs'.[9] These consist of what the Chinese government calls 'people-to-people relations' or 'people-to-people exchanges'. In practice, such exchanges are training programmes for elite groups such as military officers or journalists, often taking place in China. The aim of these training sessions is to diffuse Chinese norms, build relationships with elite groups and establish influence in partner countries. Benabdallah demonstrates that through this approach, the Chinese government has successfully constructed networks of contacts with elite groups across many African countries that are likely to be more sympathetic to China than before.[10]

Dawn Murphy confirms that 'China is building a new order that reflects its values' across regions such as the Middle East and Africa.[11] She further points out that the normative foundation of the BRI is based on policies such as state-backed economic activity, aid without strings attached, 'a strict interpretation of sovereignty' and South-South cooperation.[12] She shows that these norms diverge from those generally used by the United States and other developed nations in their approaches to development in the global South. Murphy demonstrates that China has a consistent strategy for building influence in the developing regions of the world containing 'specific features', many of which adhere to Chinese rather than Western norms.[13]

The Chinese government's portrayal of its BRI investments and other Chinese economic activities as 'South-South cooperation' has a clear purpose.[14] By doing this, Beijing is positioning itself ideationally as the leader of the global South rather than a member of the privileged elites in the global North. It is trying to distance itself, in the minds of its target audience in the developing world, from the European countries which previously colonized most countries that are now labelled the global South, and from the United States whose dominant population consists of the descendants of European colonists. In effect, as Murphy points out, China is presenting itself as a benefactor of poorer countries.[15] It is portraying itself and them as united in the process of emerging from poverty resulting from historically unequal economic processes of globalization and capitalism. China's appeal to the global South amounts to the following: 'Look – I am one of you. I was also colonised. But now I am free and getting richer, and I will help you to get rich too.'

The remainder of this chapter outlines the implementation and progress of Chinese economic- and influence-building activity via the BRI in five economically developing regions: Africa, Latin America, the Middle East, CEE and the Pacific. Outside Asia, these are the world's major developing regions. Given the high number of countries in these regions, it is not possible to be exhaustive about every single one of China's interactions. Instead, I will examine some representative examples of Chinese activity and interactions in each region with the aim of bringing out the key characteristics. The primary aim is to convey the depth and breadth of China's multidimensional engagement with less developed regions across an interconnected network of economic and political vectors. A wide range of data show that China's approach is strategic and long-term – and far more consistent and coherent than some analysts appear to believe.[16]

Africa

China's economic engagement with Africa preceded even the 'Going Global' strategy. Remarkably, China invested large sums in Africa during the Cultural Revolution, when the nation was in economic turmoil and had relatively little cash to spare. Among the Chinese projects carried out in Africa was the TAZARA railway linking Tanzania and Zambia.[17] Constructed at break-neck speed between 1970 and 1973, this was one of Africa's first railways. Tens of thousands of Chinese workers laboured alongside their Tanzanian counterparts.[18] Although this railway later experienced numerous problems related to its operation and maintenance, it is astonishing that even during a period of domestic turmoil and economic weakness China managed to build infrastructure in Africa that European colonial powers including Britain and France had not attempted to construct during their occupation of the continent.

After the end of the Cold War, China resumed its assistance to Africa, but this time on an ever-increasing scale, and with a shift, as Cheng and Taylor demonstrate in a book-length study, from aid (with no expectation of repayment) to loan-backed investments.[19] Although infrastructure construction was again on offer, resource extraction had become a priority. By the 1990s, China's oil consumption had overtaken its domestic production.[20] The government realized that more energy and raw materials would need to be imported, and that it was essential to ensure a diversity of suppliers to minimize risks to China's energy security. Chinese economic diplomacy therefore included offering collateralized loans and infrastructure in exchange for priority access to African natural resources at reduced prices. Other raw materials needed for industrial production in China included copper, zinc and cobalt. African countries with large reserves of natural resources – such as the Democratic Republic of the Congo (cobalt), Angola (oil), Nigeria (oil) and Zambia (copper) – therefore became attractive targets for Chinese energy and mining companies. After construction, mining is the second largest sector for Chinese FDI: the DRC, Zambia, Angola and Nigeria are among the top six recipients of Chinese investments.[21]

China's energy and resource diversification strategy in Africa produced dividends in the first two decades of the twenty-first century. Between them, Angola, Congo and Gabon supplied over 10 per cent of China's crude oil imports in 2020.[22] In Angola, China provided collateralized loans to the government and its state-owned oil company Sonangol which were to be repaid through oil exports.[23] As a result, 61 per cent of Angola's exports – mainly oil – end up in China.[24] Chinese companies also have a near-monopoly on oil exports from South Sudan.[25]

Research from the Massachusetts Institute of Technology (MIT) reveals that many African countries have become heavily reliant on exports of natural resources to China (see Figure 6.1). The MIT data reveal that Chinese companies have a dominant share in exports from Eritrea and Gambia. In the Democratic Republic of Congo (DRC), Chinese companies have gained a majority share in cobalt mining. DRC produces over 70 per cent of global cobalt output, most of which goes to China. China is the world's leading consumer of the metal due to its use in rechargeable batteries for electric vehicles.[26] Africa also possesses about half of the world's reserves of manganese, vital for steel production.[27] China is clearly the most significant nation-state partner for a number of African countries, giving Beijing a huge amount of political as well as economic influence.

Despite the large scale of resource imports, China is exporting sufficient goods to Africa to turn a profit amid growing two-way trade. An important point generally missed in analyses of China's global expansion is that Chinese companies are creating new export markets in the developing world as well as acquiring resources. This is certainly true of China's engagement with Africa. In

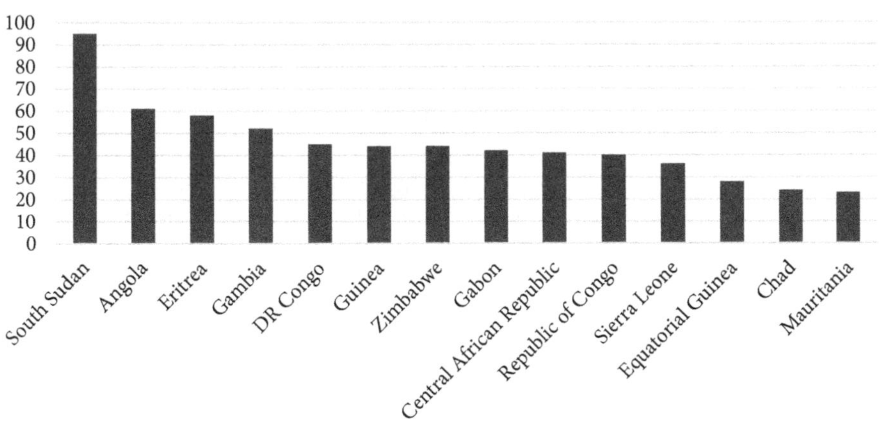

Figure 6.1 Percentage of 2017 exports going to China

Source: author, based on data from MIT's Observatory of Economic Complexity

2000, when economic relations began to take off, China-Africa trade was valued at $10.5 billion. By 2006, the figure had reached $55 billion.[28] Even at the height of the Covid-19 pandemic in 2021, China-Africa trade rose by 35 per cent to its highest-ever level of $254 billion, mainly because of an increase in Chinese exports. Nigeria, South Africa, Egypt, Ghana and Kenya were China's top African export markets during the year.[29] In the first three months of 2022, Chinese exports to Africa totalled $35.16 billion, compared to imports of $29.7 billion.[30] As a point of contrast, EU-Africa trade totalled 256 billion euro in 2011, but had increased only slightly to 288 billion euro ten years later.[31] Clearly, the volume of China's trade with Africa is rapidly catching up with the EU's.

Despite Western views of Africa as an impoverished continent rather than a business opportunity, some Chinese firms take the opposite view. For example, the Chinese mobile phone company Transsion – unknown in the West – dominates the African mobile phone market with its Tecno, Infinix and Itel brands. In 2021, Transsion had a 48.2 per cent share of the African smart phone market. Its nearest competitor – the South Korean electronics giant Samsung – was a distant second with 16 per cent.[32] Transsion also provides a music streaming service called Boomplay pre-installed in its mobile phones: it generates income through advertising and subscriptions. By mid-2020, Boomplay had 75 million African users.[33] Revenue from music streaming in sub-Saharan Africa reached $70.1 million in 2021 and is forecast to exceed $300 million by 2026.[34] African demand for affordable phones has created a business opportunity which a Chinese company has been swift to exploit.

Still, the size of the African market should not yet be overstated. Africa constitutes only 3.83 per cent of all China's global trade.[35] Nevertheless, the impressive growth rate in mutual trade indicates that Beijing's long-term Going Global/BRI strategy of the last two decades is beginning to bear fruit. China's ability to balance the books using its exports while obtaining access to vital energy supplies and raw materials makes investing in Africa a no-brainer as far as Beijing is concerned. With Western companies basically sitting on their hands as far as Africa is concerned, China has gained an advantage in market development and exploitation that bears witness to its venture capitalism credentials. Meanwhile, Europeans and Americans still tend to see Africa as a continent in need of aid and charity rather than a potential consumer market.

At the diplomatic level, Beijing's engagement with African leaders has also brought results in terms of nations switching allegiance from Taiwan to the PRC. African countries have steadily switched to China as the economic advantages of doing so became apparent. As of mid-2022, only one African nation – Eswatini (formerly Swaziland) still had full diplomatic relations with Taiwan.[36] As recently as 2006, six African nations still recognized Taiwan.[37] Burkina Faso became the second-to-last to switch allegiance in 2018.[38] In persuading African countries to formally acknowledge the 'One China' policy, Beijing has gained a valuable bloc of supporters in the United Nations. This support enables China to dampen Western pressure on Taiwan and on other issues such as the South China Sea. The Forum on

China-Africa Cooperation (FOCAC), a multilateral platform founded at China's instigation, is intended to cement ties at the regional level.

Beijing's diplomatic efforts have been complemented by a soft power campaign in Africa promoting the idea of China as a benefactor providing economic, educational and other opportunities. The campaign includes giving scholarships to African students to study in China. In 2018, over 80,000 African students were studying in China, many on Chinese-funded scholarships.[39] Many Africans also have employment opportunities in Chinese factories and mines, even if there are sometimes controversies about work conditions. At the same time, as with any major power's provision of public goods to citizens of other countries, China's apparent benevolence towards African students 'is not neutral, amoral and altruistic but laden with geopolitical meaning and objectives'.[40] In other words, Beijing's coordination of assistance to Africa is clearly given with long-term strategic goals in mind.

Nevertheless, while opinion polls in Europe and North America indicate overwhelming suspicion of China among the public, in Africa the picture is rather different. A 2015 Pew Global Attitudes survey found majority positive views of China (52–80 per cent favourable) in eight African countries (Ghana, Ethiopia, Burkina Faso, Tanzania, Senegal, Nigeria, Kenya, Uganda and South Africa).[41] A Pew survey conducted in spring 2019 found more positive than negative attitudes towards China in three African countries: Nigeria (70 per cent favourable), Kenya (58 per cent favourable) and South Africa (46 per cent favourable versus 35 per cent unfavourable). Professor Rhys Jenkins confirms that 'public opinion polls show that the majority of those surveyed in the region view China favourably' due to positive perceptions about infrastructure and business investments as well as affordable consumer goods.[42]

Such survey data contrast strongly with broadly unfavourable opinions of China in Western Europe and the United States.[43] It is possible that future surveys will reveal that African attitudes are becoming more negative towards China, but the evidence from 2015 to 2019 points to surprisingly high levels of positivity. Indeed, a 2022 survey of 4,507 young Africans in fifteen countries revealed that 76 per cent of the 18- to 24-year-old respondents saw China as having a positive influence on their lives. The comparable figure for the United States was 4 per cent lower.[44]

The Covid-19 pandemic undoubtedly damaged China's image. At the same time, it gave Beijing the opportunity to demonstrate largesse in the developing world through the provision of vaccines, healthcare and medical equipment. China had already been using health diplomacy as a soft power tool in Africa since dispatching a medical team to Algeria in 1963.[45] In March 2020, at the beginning of the global pandemic, China was quick to send medical teams, facemasks and protective suits to many African countries.[46] However, the apparent inferiority of Chinese vaccines and the controversy surrounding China's ongoing lockdowns likely reduced the effectiveness of China's 'health Silk Road' diplomacy.

Beyond such soft power efforts, China's infrastructure building in Africa has been significant. In 1990, American and European companies obtained contracts for more than 85 per cent of African construction projects. Thirty years later, their share had fallen to 12 per cent. According to a United Nations report, China had overtaken the United States as a holder of FDI stock in Africa by 2019.[47] Meanwhile, Chinese firms were responsible for 31 per cent of all infrastructure projects in 2020.[48] From 2007 to 2020, China's development banks lent $23 billion for infrastructure projects in sub-Saharan Africa. This was, according to a Center for Global Development report, more than twice the amount provided by American, German, Japanese and French banks combined.[49] As a specific example of Europe's inattention to sub-Saharan Africa, Deutsche Bundesbank reports that Germany's total FDI stock in Africa in 2019 was just over 12 billion euros. More than half of this was in South Africa, with most of the remainder concentrated in north Africa: only 619 million euros of stock were held in sub-Saharan African countries, and even then in only six of them.[50] As in the mobile phone market, Chinese construction companies were in the process of rapidly outcompeting Western firms in the sub-Saharan African market, using state-backed finance to do so. As an on-the-ground example, the independent journalist Katja Scherer reports a proliferation of high-rise blocks and roads being built in Ethiopia by Chinese construction companies when she toured the country in January 2020.[51]

While there have been problems with quality, transparency, debt loads and environmental impacts, the results of Chinese infrastructure projects remain striking. A railway now connects the Ethiopian capital Addis Ababa with Djibouti on the horn of Africa, where China established a naval base in 2017.[52] Another Chinese-financed railway connects Mombasa to Nairobi. Roads, dams, ports and power plants have also been constructed across the continent. Servicing the debt on Chinese loans is a problem for many partner countries. But, as the Chinese have long recognized, economic growth is difficult without adequate transport and energy infrastructure. Chinese banks and firms are providing it across Africa, and Chinese influence is increasing as a result. Meanwhile, the West's share in Africa's markets and investment projects is declining steadily – and with it the influence of the United States and Europe on the continent.[53]

Latin America and the Caribbean (LAC)

Since decolonization, Latin America and the Caribbean (LAC) have been thought of as the United States' backyard. However, the US influence in the region is perceived negatively in many countries.[54] For instance, in Venezuela, Ecuador and Bolivia, historical relations with the United States are generally regarded as having been unequal and exploitative.[55] In fact, the reality is more complex: experts point out that the United States has long neglected the region in its foreign policy apart from occasional military interventions.[56] This long-term American neglect has allowed China, which has the advantage of not having any negative historical associations locally, to enter the scene at the turn of the twenty-first century as a relatively new actor in the region. As Professor Carol Wise points out, Latin America is, compared to Africa and Asia, 'a latecomer to China's internationalized development strategy'.[57]

In those countries which perceive the United States negatively, China has a receptive audience for the introduction of new norms of interaction. Despite geographical distance and the lack of previously strong historical or cultural connections, Beijing has begun to build working relationships with some countries in the region. Most notable among China's partners are the oil-producing nations Brazil and Venezuela, with which strategic partnerships were signed in 1993 and 2001, respectively. Further strategic partnerships were signed with Mexico, Argentina, Peru and Chile between 2003 and 2012.[58] Consequently, Chinese influence in LAC is growing, especially in nations which have natural resources, which China needs to fuel its ongoing economic growth.

Eight countries in the region still retain formal relations with Taiwan, out of thirteen Taipei-supporting states worldwide. This group of eight consists of Belize, Guatemala, Haiti, Honduras, Paraguay, Saint Kitts and Nevis, Saint Lucia, plus Saint Vincent and the Grenadines. However, one should be careful not to overstate the Taiwanese influence in the region since the eight states listed in the previous sentence are not among the major regional players. The primary targets of Chinese economic statecraft are the larger states such as Brazil, Argentina and Venezuela. In these larger states, economic and political ties with China increased in the first two decades of the twenty-first century. Just four countries – Venezuela, Brazil, Argentina and Ecuador – accounted for 95 per cent of Chinese loans to Latin America between 2005 and 2015.[59] Thus, although it cannot be said that Chinese influence is increasing uniformly across the whole region, the overall picture is one in which Chinese banks and commercial actors are having a growing impact in the larger regional economies.

During the first two decades of the twenty-first century, Chinese economic statecraft in LAC had broadly the same package of goals as in other developing regions: to obtain supplies of natural resources (principally oil, but also metals and agricultural products such as soy beans), to open up markets for Chinese commercial interests, to export China's domestic industrial overcapacity by building loan-funded infrastructure and to increase China's influence in the region in support of the 'One China' policy and other political aims.[60] The record of Chinese economic diplomacy in the region bears witness to the implementation of these aims. For instance, in 2010, regional exports to the United States and Europe decreased by more than 25 per cent, while exports to China rose by 11 per cent.[61]

At the same time, there is a degree of uneven application due to the different characteristics and responses of individual countries, as well as the fact that Beijing has focused its economic diplomacy primarily on specific countries rich in natural resources such as Brazil, Venezuela and Argentina. Unevenness also arises from the domestic politics of individual nations, especially when they prioritize relations with Taiwan. However, it would be a mistake to see this unevenness as the result of supposed 'fragmented authoritarianism' within Chinese decision-making structures. In anonymous interviews conducted by the Chinese scholars Zhang and Chen, Chinese government officials responsible for the administration of economic cooperation with Brazil lamented their lack of input to decision-making processes.[62] Their experiences of powerlessness bear witness to the degree of top-down control exerted by Beijing in its economic statecraft in the region. This point was stressed by one official from the Ministry of Foreign Affairs, who stated that 'since political and strategic cooperation is the overriding priority in the Chinese-Brazilian partnership, any proposition for or directive on economic cooperation is always from the top down – and hence decision-making is fairly centralised'.[63]

LAC was not originally included in the BRI. It was added to the list of BRI regions only in 2018. This relabelling occurred just as BRI investment flows were slowing in a rationalization drive implemented by Beijing in response to what it – justifiably – saw as over-exuberance on the part of Chinese commercial actors. Irrational spending occurred during the peak 2015–17 period when investment funds flowed in a relatively unregulated fashion and on a large scale into regions which had already been included in the BRI. For instance, apart from infrastructure projects such as dams and ports, cash also poured into foreign football clubs and other non-essential assets.[64] Two years later, the Covid-19 pandemic hit, and China's overseas engagement was impacted. For these and other reasons, as Rhys Jenkins shows, being formally included in Xi Jinping's flagship foreign policy initiative has had a limited impact in terms of Chinese investment in LAC so far.[65]

On the other hand, Chinese economic relations with the region did not begin with the BRI. They have been growing rapidly since the early years of the 'Going Global' era. Total trade between China and LAC reached $306 billion in 2018, up from just a few billion dollars in 2000.[66] Over the same eighteen-year timespan, China's total foreign direct investment (FDI) in Argentina, Brazil, Chile, Mexico and Peru is estimated at around $130 billion. This constitutes about 15 per cent of total FDI inflows to these countries over the period.[67] Nevertheless, significant Chinese FDI flows only began to occur after the financial crisis of 2007–8.[68]

Despite the increase in investment, in 2019 China still held a far smaller amount of total FDI stock in the region than the United States or Europe. On the other hand, the proportion of Chinese investments in natural resources was far higher than that of its rivals – as high as 90 per cent of the total. Most notably, oil and gas account for about 40 per cent of Chinese investments between 2005 and 2015.[69] In addition, China imports around half of its copper, a quarter of its iron ore and more than half of its soybeans from the region (soybeans are obtained mainly from Brazil and Argentina).[70] Thus, the Chinese focus on LAC's natural resources is on a completely different level of than that of the United States or Europe.

Brazil represents an example of Chinese interest in Latin America's natural resources and the economic diplomacy used to access them. China's engagement with Brazil has been quite single-mindedly focused on gaining access to oil since Petrobras, the Brazilian state oil company, signed an initial export contract with its Chinese counterpart Sinopec in 2006.[71] The Brazilian side appears to have welcomed Chinese investment in the petroleum industry to boost economic growth. In 2000, Brazilian crude oil exports to China were just 1.7 million barrels per year. However, by 2019, China was importing 295 million barrels of Brazilian oil annually. In just under two decades, Brazil had become China's fifth largest supplier of crude, accounting for 8 per cent of China's total oil imports and 63 per cent of Brazil's oil exports.[72] This remarkable growth was achieved, as in other regions, through $36.8 billion in loans from Chinese state banks for investment in Brazilian oil and other infrastructure. Most of the funds were channelled to state-owned Petrobras.[73] China's involvement in the development of the Brazilian oil industry is clearly the result of strategic investment coordinated with the consent of the two states through state banks and state-owned commercial actors. China has achieved a dominant stake in the Brazilian oil industry while American and European commercial actors have thus far largely ignored it. Brazil is also, as already noted, one of China's largest suppliers of soybeans.

The tale of Chinese energy diplomacy through loans and deals is even more pronounced in Venezuela. Between 2004 and 2015, China's imports of Venezuelan oil increased from 14,000 to over 700,000 barrels per day.[74] Overall trade increased exponentially from a low base of $200 million in 1999 to a reported $169.8 billion in 2014.[75] Lending to Venezuela constituted more than half of all Chinese loans to the region after 2005.[76] Loans provided from 2008 onwards by the China Development Bank and other Chinese state lenders had reached more than $65 billion by 2016.[77] By that point, in less than a decade, Venezuela had become heavily indebted to China, with its fortunes tied to the Chinese oil industry. By 2014, oil made up a staggering 96 per cent of Venezuelan exports, leaving it about as dependent on energy exports as Turkmenistan.[78] Meanwhile, China's economic diplomacy in Venezuela had contributed to the overall strategic goal in Latin America of expanding and diversifying the nation's energy imports. As in Brazil, the United States and Europe had left Venezuela open to Chinese loans and oil companies, viewing the erstwhile president, Hugo Chávez, as someone with whom they could not do business.

Oil is not the only Latin American resource commodity exported to China. Like Brazil, Argentina is one of China's three main suppliers of soybeans (the other is the United States). Over 80 per cent of Argentina's unprocessed soybean exports go to China. Soybeans made up over two-thirds of Argentina's exports to China in 2012 and 2013.[79] Chile, whose leading export by far is copper, became increasingly reliant on exports to China in the first decade of the twenty-first century. By 2010, China had overtaken the United States as the leading importer of Chilean copper.[80] Copper is a vital material in the production of electronics and renewable energy systems and thus obtaining supplies is key for China's industry. Since 2007, more than 20 per cent of Chile's copper has ended up in China.[81]

As far as infrastructure building is concerned, the most extensive activity is reportedly in Ecuador, where eight dams were under construction or in the planning stage in 2014.[82] Chinese-constructed hydroelectric projects have also been implemented in Argentina, Belize, Bolivia, Brazil, Costa Rica, Honduras, Surinam and Venezuela.[83] Roads and railways have been built or refurbished in Brazil and Argentina to transport soybeans and other exports to ports.[84] Of course, there are environmental impacts of such projects – most notably on the Amazonian rainforest – but these tend to be difficult to measure.[85] What is not difficult to ascertain is the scale of Chinese infrastructure construction in LAC.

In short, China's economic statecraft has made major inroads in establishing relations with the larger Latin American countries since about 2005. While some countries in the region retain ties with Taiwan, this fact is less significant than it seems because they are not the major regional players. In countries such as Brazil, Argentina, Chile and Venezuela, resources have been secured, loans for infrastructure have been supplied and Chinese norms of political and economic interaction have been introduced. Following the pattern in other regions, a new regional cooperation forum – the China-CELAC Forum – was established by Beijing in 2015.[86] The long history of US neglect and perceived exploitation of LAC provided China with the opportunity to establish itself as arguably the most significant international actor in the region by the end of the twenty-first century's second decade.

The Middle East

The Middle East is a zone of increasing importance for Chinese foreign policy for three main reasons. Most obviously, countries in the Persian Gulf – Saudi Arabia, Iran, Iraq, Kuwait, Qatar, Oman, Bahrain and the UAE – have huge fossil fuel reserves which China covets. In addition, the region is geostrategically significant as far as the BRI is concerned in that it lies along the maritime route from Asia to Europe. All the same, it is advisable not to read too much into the geography: Europe-bound container ships pass through the Indian Ocean, the Red Sea and the Suez Canal, but of course not the Persian Gulf. On the other hand, there is little doubt that the Chinese government would like to establish good relations with as many states as possible in the region in support of its One China policy regarding the status of Taiwan, as well as other issues it regards as internal to the PRC, such as the Xinjiang/Uighur question. Thus, it is to be expected that the priorities of Beijing's economic statecraft in the Middle East will follow the same pattern as in other regions: obtaining natural resources, offering loans for infrastructure building as well as other assistance (for instance, medical aid during the Covid-19 pandemic) and increasing political influence by establishing ties with local leaders.

Like most other developing regions, the Middle East has had difficult historical relations with the West. Among the issues undermining cooperation – at least for Arab states – are the West's support for the formation of the state of Israel after the Second World War, the US invasion of Iraq and the history of European colonialism. In contrast, China has no such historical baggage. Instead, Beijing has a relatively clean slate in attempting to build influence and obtain resources in the region. Thus, while the West prevaricates over what to do about Iran, Syria and other countries sometimes classified as 'rogue' states, Beijing is not restricted in its economic diplomacy by any scruples of this type. It has a freer hand and can try to establish multilateral and bilateral cooperation frameworks and agreements based on Chinese norms rather than the Western rules-based 'liberal international order'.[87]

As in other developing regions, one of China's main priorities is to obtain supplies of fossil fuels and other resources to maintain domestic economic growth. To achieve this goal, Beijing aims to ensure that oil imports come from as diversified a set of exporters as possible.[88] In the Persian Gulf, this strategy means that China needs to cultivate good relations with oil-rich states even if there are bitter regional rivalries. Most notably this has not deterred the Chinese from hedging their bets with regard to Saudi Arabia and Iran.[89] Since the Islamic revolution of 1979, Washington has sided with Saudi Arabia against Iran. The Americans have supplied Saudi Arabia with arms over the long term, and even deployed troops on Saudi territory during the wars in Iraq. The United States even continued supporting the Saudi government after the much criticized 2018 killing of the Saudi journalist Jamal Khashoggi by Saudi agents.[90] Beijing takes a notably different tack to cooperation, seeking to minimize discussion of human rights issues or possible military alliances and instead emphasizing economic cooperation. In addition, and unlike the United States and Russia, China conspicuously avoids taking sides in the region's entrenched conflicts and proxy wars, most notably those in Yemen and Syria.

For two decades, cooperation between China and the Arab states has been supported by the China-Arab States Cooperation Forum (CASCF). This was founded in 2004 at the suggestion of President Hu Jintao during a tour of the region. Biannual meetings of the CASCF have helped to smooth the path for Chinese trade and investment in the region. As in the case of the SCO in Central Asia, the regional cooperation platform has allowed the Chinese government to cultivate relations with regional actors who do not necessarily see eye-to-eye, such as Qatar and Saudi Arabia.[91] The goal of obtaining a diverse set of fossil fuels suppliers in the region clearly underlies China's interest in building relations with the Gulf states through the medium of the CASCF.

In Chinese, the name for the Middle East is 'West Asia' (*xiya*, 西亚). By using this nomenclature, the Chinese give the region a status directly equivalent to 'East Asia', 'South Asia', 'Central Asia' and so on. This is important, because it includes the region firmly in Asia rather than leaving it – as the English name does – in a kind of conceptual no-man's-land in-between Europe and Asia. Using the 'West Asia' identifier allows space for a similar approach to the region as in other regions, introducing the same norms of interaction as in the other regions: regional cooperation platforms, loans and infrastructure, and negotiations at the leadership level. The Chinese leadership avoids stigmatizing any regional actors as problematic 'rogue states' which need to be punished or inculcated in how to behave. It tends to take the same underlying approach to bilateral relations with each individual country, insisting on standard points such as the non-recognition of Taiwan and acknowledging the Chinese government's right to deal with the Xinjiang issue as it sees fit, without outside 'interference'. The Chinese approach is thus in marked contrast to the US-led Western approach, which tends to categorize states dichotomously as allies or threats.

The characteristics of the Chinese approach – and the marked contrast to the US approach – emerge clearly with reference to Saudi Arabia's regional rivalry with Iran. Washington has sided with Saudi Arabia against Iran since the 1979 Iranian revolution, no matter who has been president. Even President Biden backtracked on his pre-election promise to make Saudi Arabia a 'pariah state' when he visited the Kingdom in July 2022 and bumped fists with Crown Prince Mohammed bin Salman.[92] Iran was still being classified by the United States as a security threat, even though both Saudi Arabia and the United Arab Emirates (UAE) indicated that they wanted to establish rapprochement with Tehran.[93] Beijing, in marked contrast, avoids picking sides. Roughly comparable packages of investments and trade deals are offered to both Saudi Arabia and Iran.[94] Within the limits set by Western sanctions and preferences, Beijing attempts to source oil from both countries. Somewhat surprisingly, China imports larger volumes of oil from Saudi Arabia than from its supposed ally, Iran.[95] Indeed, Saudi Arabia was China's number one oil supplier in 2019.[96] As the United States has increased its domestic oil production and reduced its Saudi imports, China has opportunistically taken up the slack in pursuit of the goal of achieving 'comprehensive national security'. Given the recurring Western-imposed sanctions on Iran, it is logical for China to cultivate oil-rich Saudi Arabia, even in the face of its erstwhile ties to the United States.

On the other hand, perceptions of China across the Middle East vary considerably depending on the country and depending on the issue. A 2019 Pew Global Attitudes survey revealed that roughly two-thirds of people in Israel and Lebanon had negative views of China. However, more people in Turkey had favourable than unfavourable views of China (44–37 per cent).[97] In an Arab Barometer survey conducted in 2018-2019, 73 per cent of Jordanians wanted aid from China to increase; but strangely only 34 per cent of them held a favourable or somewhat favourable view of the Middle Kingdom. In the same survey, 51 per cent of Iraqis wanted to build better economic ties with China; but only 30 per cent of Egyptians expressed such a preference.[98] Opinion polls thus project an image of uncertainty and unevenness across the region regarding the desirability of cooperation with China.

Nevertheless, deals regarding infrastructure projects and investments have continued to be struck under the umbrella of the BRI, regardless of the long-term allegiances of individual nations. As usual, Beijing has chiefly invested in nations rich in resources or with key geostrategic positions. According to the Arab Investment and Export Credit Guarantee Corp, driven by BRI projects, in 2016 China became the top investor in the Arab region with $29.5 billion of investments. Chinese investments can be contrasted with a figure of $6.9 billion for the United States. The PRC's holdings constitute 31.9 per cent of total FDI in Arab countries.[99]

Studying the details of China's relations with specific countries reveals the impact of Chinese investments. Throughout the region, Chinese investment projects have certainly not been implemented without difficulties. Nevertheless, albeit more slowly than expected, they are going ahead. In Egypt, Chinese companies are working on ports, railways, power plants and the ambitious Suez Canal Economic Zone. However, progress has been slower than anticipated due to structural weaknesses in Egypt's political and economic capacities.[100] In neighbouring Israel, Chinese companies have also been playing a major role in investments in start-ups and the installation of new infrastructure, even though local business, scientific and political communities tend to be suspicious of Chinese intentions. Transportation tunnels have been drilled, railways constructed and ports operated.[101] In 2015, Chinese companies invested about $500 million in Israeli startups.[102] Investments in Iran have progressed at a slower pace than anticipated: this is probably due to a combination of the sanctions imposed on the Islamic Republic during the Trump presidency and Chinese wariness about investing in a nation possessing a somewhat uncertain future. Still, as elsewhere, money has been committed to the energy and transport sectors, as well as resource extraction.[103] In late 2022, China established a direct shipping line to Iran's Chabahar port with the docking of the first Chinese container ship.[104] Meanwhile, at the strategic Omani port of Duqm, Chinese firms are building an industrial park designed to accommodate up to thirty-five special economic zone projects.[105]

As elsewhere, bilateral trade between China and individual countries has been growing exponentially. Saudi Arabia, despite supposedly being a US ally, is China's biggest trade partner in the Gulf, due principally to the fact that it supplies around 25 per cent of China's oil imports. In 2020, total imports and exports were valued at more than $67 billion. Trade with the United Arab Emirates (UAE) amounted to over $49 billion, while with Iraq the total was over $30 billion.[106] China's total trade with the Arab states reportedly amounted to around $330 billion in 2021.[107]

As far as military affairs and geopolitics are concerned, the Chinese government has been careful to ensure that China does not become entangled in the region's intractable problems. Beijing has observed the difficulties encountered by the United States and its allies during the occupation of Iraq and quietly sworn off committing Chinese forces to similar operations. The Chinese have also maintained a distance from the civil wars in Syria and Yemen. At the same time, Beijing needs to be engaged somehow in what has become a key region for its comprehensive national security due to its resources. To this end, the military base and port investments in Djibouti represent a step towards establishing a Chinese security presence in the region. Djibouti's strategic position at the entrance to the Red Sea is one that the Chinese cannot ignore. The Chinese military has been active in anti-piracy operations off Somalia, where privateers have targeted Chinese shipping. Security cooperation between China and states in the region is also increasing from a very low base: Chinese arms sales to Saudi Arabia increased by 386 per cent and to the UAE by 169 per cent in the period 2016–20.[108]

With the outbreak of the Covid-19 pandemic, China-Middle East relations transformed further with the advent of the so-called 'Health Silk Road'. By June 2020, China had rapidly supplied medical equipment and expertise to twenty-two countries in the Middle East and North Africa (MENA) region. Assistance sent included teams of doctors, testing kits, face masks, thermometers, protective suits, ventilators and prefabricated rooms.[109] Even though some of the equipment supplied turned out to be faulty, China's swift decision to send aid was acclaimed by the MENA states which received it. However, the increased Chinese involvement in the region did not please the West, which (correctly) saw the initiative as an attempt by Beijing to increase its political influence by deepening interstate ties.[110]

The diametrically opposed reactions of MENA and Western countries to China's Health Silk Road diplomacy constitute another indication of the split in perceptions of China between the West and the global South. While Western countries tend to criticize Beijing no matter how it acts, economically developing countries often take a very different position. China-Middle East relations are still evolving; but there is substantial evidence to indicate that China's influence and authority in the region are indeed rising.

Central and Eastern Europe

Central and Eastern Europe (CEE) represents a special case of China's relations with developing nations for four reasons. First, CEE cannot be classified as belonging to the Global South despite the Chinese including the region in the BRI alongside developing regions such as Southeast Asia and Africa. Second, since almost all CEE countries were under Soviet influence during the Cold War, the spectre of four decades of communism hangs over public perceptions of the People's Republic of China.[111] Third, some of them are EU members, while others are not.[112] Fourth, despite their shared Cold War history, they did not generally think of themselves as belonging together until China entered the scene: the idea of belonging to a larger regional grouping excluding Western Europe did not develop from among its supposed members.[113] These four factors combine to give China-CEE relations distinctly different characteristics from China's relations with other developing regions.

China's relations with CEE were limited during the Cold War because of the Sino-Soviet split. As signatories to the Warsaw Pact, the fortunes of CEE nations were tied to the Soviet mast. For this reason, they had limited contact with China. After the end of the Cold War, the newly independent nations tried to distance themselves from their communist past and orient towards the European Union as they sought membership. During the 1990s and 2000s countries such as the Czech Republic and Slovakia therefore tended to seek investment from other Asian investors such as Japan, South Korea and Taiwan rather than the PRC.[114]

The situation changed in 2012 when the '16+1' framework for cooperation between China and CEE countries was instituted in Warsaw. This format mimicked China's multilateral platforms in other regions such as the Forum on China-Africa Cooperation (FOCAC) and the Shanghai Cooperation Organization (SCO).[115] From its outset, the 16+1 platform was controversial because it contained a mix of nations which were EU members and ones which were not. Among the former were Poland, the Czech Republic, Hungary and the Baltic states. The latter included nations which had emerged from the break-up of the former Yugoslavia, such as Serbia, Albania and Macedonia. From the perspective of the EU, the Chinese-led cooperation mechanism aroused suspicions of an attempt to 'divide and conquer' Europe.[116]

For their part, the CEE countries initially welcomed the Chinese initiative. It appeared as if China was offering large-scale investment and infrastructure to assist with regional integration and development. The Chinese prime minister Wen Jiabao offered incentives to cooperation such as a $10 billion 'credit line' for the region.[117]

Proposed projects included a high-speed railway from Belgrade to Budapest and a 'Serbia-China friendship bridge' across the Danube.[118] Expectations of Chinese investments were high. In 2019, Greece joined the platform, making it '17+1'.[119]

However, from about 2017 onwards enthusiasm for the 16+1 began to cool in some countries when they realized that Chinese investments were not reaching the pledged levels. In the Czech Republic, media discourse about political influence and broken promises began to turn opinion against China.[120] In 2018, CEFC Energy, the company which had spearheaded China's investment drive in the country, failed to pay instalments on its acquisitions. Its Chief Financial Officer, Patrick Ho, was arrested on corruption charges in the United States. The company's CEO, Ye Jianming, was detained in China. The state-owned investment firm CITIC was sent in to take over CEFC's investments in a football club, a brewery and a media company.[121] That signalled both a halt to China's investment drive in the Czech Republic and an end to hope of any lingering Czech goodwill towards China. The mayor of Prague made overtures towards Taiwan and the leader of the Czech Senate visited Taipei.[122] Human rights agendas related to Xinjiang, Tibet and Hong Kong came to the fore.[123] Even President Miloš Zeman, who had initiated contact with China, began to express scepticism about the depth of Chinese commitment.[124] With the advent of the Covid-19 pandemic and apparent Chinese support for the Russian invasion of Ukraine, China's image deteriorated virtually beyond repair – a fact to which I can attest through my daily interactions with both Czech scholars and the Czech general public.

In 2021, there were signs that the Baltic states were also growing wary of China's influence. Amid an almost non-existent investment program and limited trade ties, the Lithuanian foreign minister signalled that the country was inclined to shift in the direction of Taiwan. Later in the year, Lithuania formally withdrew from the erstwhile 17+1, returning it to its original 16+1 format. Making things even worse, six heads of state refused to attend the annual meeting of state representatives, which was led for the first time by President Xi Jinping instead of Premier Li Keqiang. In mid-2022, Estonia and Latvia also withdrew from the platform. Within the space of a few years, the 16/17+1, initially so promising, had become a 'zombie mechanism'.[125]

In fact, Chinese influence attempts in CEE have overall been far less effective than in other developing global regions. In a data-driven study, Richard Turcsányi and his colleagues found that CEE countries – with the partial exception of Serbia – did not vote in line with China in the UN.[126] On the other hand, most developing countries in Asia and Africa did. The CEE countries were also closer to Germany than to China in terms of their political rhetoric. The authors of this study found that Serbia represents an exceptional case of relatively close cooperation with China which should not be taken as representative of the whole region. Thus, suggestions that China has successfully managed to 'divide and conquer' Europe through the 16/17+1 are exaggerated and wide of the mark.

In fact, warning signs regarding the problematic nature of China-CEE cooperation were present from the start and continued to appear at intervals. In 2011, a project in which a Chinese firm was hired to build a section of Polish highway collapsed acrimoniously amid misunderstandings and drastic under-estimates of costs.[127] In Montenegro, the construction of a Chinese-built highway has been controversial due to the high debt load for the micro-state and the project's tortuous progress.[128] In previously cooperative Hungary, protests erupted in 2021 against the foundation of a Budapest campus of China's Fudan University.[129]

The CEE region thus represents an example of a failed Chinese attempt to shape a region normatively. The 16+1 mechanism, which was intended to generate goodwill towards China, backfired: it came to be seen as a tool for divide and conquer tactics. By 2022, 16+1 lay in ruins as far as being a 'regional cooperation platform' was concerned. Chinese investments had been underwhelming; understandably, since the region is not endowed with either natural resources or obvious economic synergies. From the perspective of many CEE countries, China had broken its investment promises and was not to be trusted. The apparent Chinese backing of Russia in its invasion of Ukraine compounded the crime as far as countries such as the Czech Republic were concerned.

Yet just as Serbia is not representative of the whole region, observers should be careful to note that the failure of the 16+1 does not indicate the collapse of the whole BRI. As the previous chapter and the rest of this chapter indicate, China's economic diplomacy and norm diffusion across the rest of the developing world continue apace. China-CEE cooperation is the exception which proves the rule because it has characteristics which are distinct from China's cooperation with other developing regions. Most importantly, CEE countries do not perceive themselves as belonging to the global South or even to the developing world. They view themselves first and foremost as Europeans. Hence, their general priority is to gain and retain EU and NATO membership rather than to side with China and Russia. Their shared history of communism and occupation by foreign powers inclines many of them to be suspicious of Chinese influence attempts. It is for these reasons that China has gained far less traction for its commercial actors and political influence than in other developing regions. At the same time, the region is less strategically and commercially important for the Chinese than other regions examined in this chapter due to its distance from China, the absence of obvious business opportunities for Chinese companies and its relative lack of natural resources.

The Pacific Islands

China's engagement with the Pacific Islands attracted a great deal of attention in May and June 2022 due to Chinese foreign minister Wang Yi's tour of eight nations in the region.[130] Just a month prior to Wang's tour, details of a secret deal between the PRC and the Solomon Islands had leaked to the media, arousing fears that Beijing was planning to install a military base.[131] There seemed to be no doubt that the Chinese government was attempting to expand its influence in the region; but the purpose and precise characteristics of such expansion remained opaque even amidst the intense media coverage. The issue became even more contentious at the end of May when the Pacific Islands rejected a 'security pact' entitled the China-Pacific Island Countries Common Development Vision proposed by Beijing. At the same time, Island leaders agreed to cooperation with China in specific areas such as health and agriculture, muddying the Pacific waters further.[132]

While the geopolitical aspects of the region in terms of US-China rivalry are obvious, the reality is that these are very small, scattered islands with low populations, undeveloped economies and relatively limited natural resources. Just 2.3 million people live in the Pacific Islands, spread over an area equivalent to 15 per cent of the Earth's surface.[133] The primary industries are fishing and tourism. Thus, the rationale for Beijing to cultivate ties with regional leaders differs considerably from the motivation for economic statecraft in other regions more obviously endowed with large reserves of natural resources needed by China. In essence, as intuited by Western observers, politics and military security play an even more prominent role for China than in other regions. However, from the perspective of the relatively impoverished Pacific Islanders, cooperating with China is an attempt to boost economic development and environmental sustainability amidst local perceptions of lack of commitment from the West. Rising sea levels are an existential problem for many low-altitude island nations and per capita GDP in most nations remains at a fraction of that in neighbouring Australia and New Zealand.[134] Some in the Pacific Islands evidently see China as a potential benefactor bringing investments that have not necessarily been forthcoming from the Western powers – including their neighbours Australia and New Zealand.

As far as Beijing is concerned, the primary motivation for cooperation with the Pacific Islands is undoubtedly – despite official protestations to the contrary – focused on geopolitics. Since the Second World War, establishing and retaining military control of the Pacific Ocean has been a key part of US foreign policy. As far back as 1951, the US state department under the leadership of John Foster Dulles drew up a strategy for the collective defence of an 'island chain' in the Pacific. The document called for cooperation against possible aggression by the Soviet Union and the PRC against Japan and other allies, as well as the containment of the communist powers in northeast Asia.[135] Although this arrangement served mainly as a backdrop to the more dramatic events of the remainder of the Cold War, it has remained a cornerstone of US power projection in the Pacific up to the present. Chinese strategists are of course keenly aware of the United States' 'island chain' strategy and have been seeking to push back against it in recent decades, most notably in the South and East China Seas.[136]

The Pacific Islands are part of what is sometimes called the 'third island chain' (the first runs from Japan through Taiwan to the South China Sea, while the second island chain runs roughly from Guam to the western part of New Guinea). As such, in the minds of Chinese strategists, building influence in the Pacific Islands is part of a larger attempt to counter US containment of China. Thus, although Beijing denies that it is planning to build a military base in the region – according to reports, in the Solomon Islands – this denial should not preclude the possibility that such a base might be on the cards. China is already by far the Solomon Islands' leading trade partner, absorbing 58 per cent of all exports from the islands.[137] Given China's economic importance for the Solomons, it makes logical sense that China might push for a strategic foothold there. However, since in July 2022 the

Solomons' Prime Minister guaranteed that there would be no Chinese military base, it seems that the deal with China may have been part of an effort to attract more commitments from the West, especially from neighbouring Australia.[138]

In the meantime, as the West contemplates its reaction, China is offering its standard package of loans and infrastructure to the Pacific Islands. Although China is officially only the third-largest donor of aid to the region, the figure may not include all its loans and infrastructure packages. According to official government statistics, Chinese construction in the Pacific Islands amounted to $958 million in 2017.[139] As is the case in other regions, the Chinese offer to build infrastructure in consultation with local leaders. For instance, a Chinese company is building a stadium for the 2023 Pacific Games in Honiara, the capital of the Solomon Islands.[140] Proposed future projects include the upgrading of an airstrip in Kiribati, which is situated about 3,000 kilometres from Hawaii.[141]

In short, China's presence in the region, established over the last two decades, is growing as Chinese commercial actors and state lenders fill an infrastructure gap that the West has left open. The scramble by the United States to open new embassies in the region in July 2022, in the wake of Wang Yi's Pacific tour, reveals the West's belated understanding of the opportunity left to the Chinese and the need to counter it with an alternative offer.[142] What exactly that offer might be is not yet clear. However, it *is* clear that the Pacific Islands have now become a zone of contestation between China and the West in the Asia-Pacific. By courting local leaders and investing in infrastructure projects which the West did not offer, China has altered global perceptions of the role of the Pacific Islands in international affairs. Amid the complexities of rising sea levels, local concerns and geopolitics, the Chinese involvement has impacted Western perceptions of the islands – and perhaps also how the islands perceive themselves.

As of mid-2022, there was no certainty about how the struggle for influence was going to turn out. At the Pacific Islands Forum (PIF) in July 2022, leaders were all smiles as the incoming Australian Prime Minister, Anthony Albanese, took selfies. Yet the apparent bonhomie masked divisions between Polynesian and Micronesian islands.[143] Just days before the meeting, the Micronesian nation of Kiribati withdrew from the PIF, citing lack of power-sharing by the Polynesian islanders as the principal reason.[144] Amidst local divisions and uncertain levels of commitment from the West, China clearly still had an opportunity – despite the negative coverage of Wang Yi's tour – to exert influence and establish a presence in at least some of the Pacific islands. Without a shadow of doubt, by intervening in the region, China has become an agent of change amid the complexities of Asia-Pacific environmental issues and regional geopolitics.

Conclusion

Across the global South, China has made significant progress in establishing itself as a leader and partner of developing nations. Beijing has developed close ties with at least some national leaders in every region – not with every country, but with many significant regional actors. China is not universally admired; but its ability to stump up cash, provide companies which can build much-needed infrastructure and willingness to work with local regimes to generate solutions which suit both sides resonate with national elites across much of the developing world. These features of Chinese cooperation-building have given Beijing a degree of influence in many countries which the West can only envy.

Meanwhile, in exchange for investments and construction projects, China obtains resources which it needs to keep fuelling its economic rise. It also creates new opportunities and markets for its commercial actors. In so doing, China's BRI has become an agent of change. Beijing has altered the environment in which investment in the developing world takes place by introducing new norms of interaction. By playing the game of development by different standards – its own rather than the West's – China presents a challenge to the West's rules-based liberal international order. In the book's final chapter, we will examine some possible ways in which the United States and Europe can address China's growing influence in the global South with some cooperation-building of their own.

Chapter 7

CHINA AND THE WEST, REVISITED

On 24 February 2022, Russia invaded Ukraine. While Europe and the United States scrambled to protest Vladimir Putin's actions and support Ukraine, China's government did not immediately react. Voices inside China tended to blame the crisis on the US desire to include Ukraine in the North Atlantic Treaty Organization (NATO) – which would essentially expand the reach of US forces right up to the Russian border. While the West began to take measures – supplying arms to Ukraine and placing sanctions on Russia – China quietly continued to maintain relations with its long-time ally. The Ukraine crisis gave the West even more reason to be suspicious of China's intentions and influence-building.

Amidst the crisis, the biggest headache for the EU was its dependence on imports of Russian oil and natural gas. With alternative supplies available, it was relatively easy for Europe to cut back on Russian oil; but gas was more of a problem. Nevertheless, the EU began reducing its imports of gas as well, a painful process which looked set to continue throughout 2022 and into 2023. Apparently, the expectation in the West was that sanctions and cutting back on imports would undermine the Russian economy. This was supposed to bring Moscow to its knees and force President Vladimir Putin to end his invasion of Ukraine.

It was therefore something of a shock when economic data emerged in June 2022 revealing that the Russian rouble had risen sharply and was one of the world's best-performing currencies.[1] What had happened in the intervening months was that Asian countries, most notably China and India, had absorbed Russia's oil and gas supplies that had previously been earmarked for Europe.[2] Russia's imports from the West had also declined sharply, enabling the nation's trade balance to soar, boosting cash reserves and the economy. In essence, Western sanctions had backfired by forcing Russia to export more energy to China at discounted prices. Both countries benefited: China from more cheap energy imports and Russia from finding alternative customers to Europe. At least temporarily, Western sanctions had served to push them closer together and had fuelled Russia's economy rather than undermining it.

The unexpectedness of this development is indicative of the complexities in international affairs. It shows how an action can achieve the opposite of what was intended when not carefully planned and when the calculations of policymakers neglect to account for all circumstances and eventualities. It also demonstrates how difficult it is in today's intricately interconnected global economic system for the West to counter China and Russia using standard approaches such as economic sanctions. As complexity theory predicts, outcomes are difficult to forecast in the presence of the networks of interdependence inherent in today's globalized political economy. Complexity makes fools of those who seek simplistic black-and-white solutions to difficult problems.

Thus, although the Ukraine crisis cannot be classed in any sense as a victory for Beijing, it does reveal some of the issues involved in finding ways to counter China. Put simply, due to the complexity of policy implementation amidst globalization, the West does not have the hold over China and Russia that it expected to have. The two countries cannot be forced to behave as the West would like them to do. Relying on the rules-based liberal international order to right what the West sees as wrongs is no longer a given – if it ever was. The Ukraine crisis reveals that it is no longer the case that the West automatically has the upper hand over China and its allies – including those in the global South.

The twin aims of this final chapter are, first, to summarize the findings of the book concerning China's global expansion and influence-building in economically developing countries under the label of the BRI; and second, to identify the hard lessons the West needs to absorb concerning the ways and means through which China is altering the global economic and political landscape. I first present a summary of the book's main arguments, before moving on to a comparison of the strengths and weaknesses of China and the West. Finally, I conclude with an account of the substantial problems facing both China and the West in today's era of global disruption, explaining that the West has a great deal of work to do to compete with China.

China, catalyst of change

The previous three chapters have demonstrated that China is changing the landscape of development economics in the global South. The evidence of China's interactions with the developing world reveals a relatively consistent pattern of economic and political influence-building and norm diffusion which differs from standard Western approaches. By engaging with states on a bilateral basis under the umbrella of regional cooperation mechanisms and offering state-backed finance for BRI infrastructure projects built by Chinese companies, Beijing has introduced a new route to development for impoverished nations. Countries which previously lacked access to funds and expertise, or for whom Western offers have too many strings attached, have been able to plan and construct new roads, ports, dams and energy plants in an effort to transform their perennially troubled economies. What China offers under the label of 'BRI' is attractive to many states for the simple reason that many of them often lack any viable alternatives. For example, this is the case of Pakistan, Cambodia, Tajikistan and Montenegro: Western investors and the World Bank have been reluctant to invest in troubled countries such as these. Put quite simply, Western actors – in particular the United States and the

EU – have not offered countries in the global South anything similar to China's BRI-framed investments. Such countries have had no real choice but to turn to China for funds and expertise.

In the West, it is often suggested that the Chinese government's foreign policy is inconsistent, and that the BRI is vague and uncoordinated. However, the evidence presented in this book reveals that the Chinese approach to the global South is remarkably consistent and coherent at the level of overall policy and aims. This is true even when things do not run smoothly due to a complex range of factors. Such factors include the Covid-19 pandemic, wars such as the one in Ukraine, global heating and economic issues such as inflation and recessions. Despite the advent of 'black swans' or 'grey rhinos' – unlikely events which nevertheless could be anticipated – the Chinese government under Xi Jinping continues with a relatively consistent overall course of strategic implementation of the BRI across the global South. It knows that such known unknowns are beyond its direct control, and that it therefore needs an elastic overall framework which can be adjusted as needs demand.

Such considerations explain why the BRI appears loose and vague. It is intended to be a flexible envelope for the expansion of Chinese economic activity and political influence, especially across the global South. If its goals were specific and detailed, it could not be easily adapted to the changing circumstances of a complex world which is undergoing evolving processes of rapid change. If specific goals were not met, it would also appear that the BRI had failed. By being vague and loose, the government can stretch the BRI envelope easily, as it did by adding a 'Health Silk Road' to the BRI during the early days of the Covid-19 pandemic.[3]

To be clear: I am not saying that the Chinese government has every point of strategy perfectly mapped out. It does not. However, I *am* saying that the upper echelons of the Chinese Communist Party (CCP) appear to be more aware than Western strategists of the potential vagaries and grey areas in the globalized economy which threaten present and future prosperity. For instance, in December 2022 Xi Jinping reacted to global uncertainties by intensifying Chinese efforts to cement ties with oil-rich Saudi Arabia.[4] To put it bluntly: Chinese government strategizing is better attuned to the complex, intertwined problems of today's world, in which changes are occurring at an unprecedented rate and on an unprecedented scale.

The changes which are now in progress include emerging disruptions to the global economic and political systems through which the West has dominated global affairs for the last two centuries: the so-called liberal international order. Ineluctably, in the wake of the pandemic and in the presence of an unfolding global environmental catastrophe, things cannot just continue to be 'life as normal' (i.e., according to Western expectations and norms). The global order – the standard way of doing business and politics to which we have become accustomed since the end of the Second World War – is shifting as China and other countries in Asia and the remainder of the global South become more prominent global actors.

I contend that China's approach to the global South is putting it gradually but steadily into a better position to withstand the further unknown or semi-known shockwaves that are to come: the impacts of global environmental catastrophe; the probability of raging inflation and recession; further pandemics; competition between nations for resources; famines and water shortages; and, tragically, the inevitability of more wars. There will also certainly be other 'black swans' and 'grey rhinos' that you and I are not even able to imagine. Amidst the complexities of our era of global disruption, the Chinese government's overriding aim is to achieve what it calls 'comprehensive national security': a term encompassing an intertwined set of issues including energy security, food security, health security, environmental security and military security. It is not an easy task to meet all these security needs at once in a nation of China's massive size and population. To do so requires a broad, holistic strategic approach which attempts to address a range of needs simultaneously.

The BRI and China's other engagements with the world are intended to contribute as much as possible to achieving the long-term goals of national rejuvenation and the China dream. According to Xi's vision, China is supposed to come out on top. The Chinese government is working as it sees fit to ensure that this happens. Of course, the Party also seeks to preserve its own position at the head of the state. The CCP knows it cannot maintain its grip on power without convincing the majority of the population that they are better off than before, and that their lives will continue to improve. Public relations campaigns and propaganda, as well as control of the internet, have the aim of persuading the Chinese people that its government is promoting such goals and giving them the opportunity to lead more fulfilling lives.

The BRI is supposed to be the international face of Xi Jinping's PR campaign. For existential reasons it is more important for the government to persuade the Chinese people of its value than it is to convince foreign audiences. This also explains why the BRI is presented in a way which is more intuitively understandable for Chinese rather than global publics. And as Bruce Dickson's survey data demonstrate, the Chinese public has so far been mostly receptive to what it has been told, with around 70 per cent of the population on board with the China dream.[5]

Despite frequent claims that the BRI is not working, is an empty shell or is prone to fragmentation due to the conflicting interests of a raft of actors, there is evidence that Chinese investments and other commercial activity – whether labelled 'BRI' or otherwise – have been relatively coordinated and have made a significant impact in the global South. Infrastructure has been built in many countries. Chinese commercial actors are present and developing new markets. As the main emphasis of the BRI shifts from large-scale infrastructure projects to smaller, more sustainable projects, relationships are being built with regimes that the West shuns, such as those in Zimbabwe, Myanmar and Iran.

The fact that the United States and the EU are now scrambling to present their own infrastructure investment initiatives – the EU's 'Global Gateway' and the US Partnership for Global Infrastructure and Investment (PGII) – is indicative of a belated recognition on the part of the West that there is a need to offer an alternative to the BRI. However, as of mid-2022, amidst the many other problems and priorities facing Western countries, it is unclear how much progress has been made on advancing these initiatives towards realization. If the West wishes to establish a genuine platform for cooperation with the developing world, it is going to have to put its money where its mouth is and coordinate its investments and corporations in a way that it has not done previously.

At the same time, I do not intend to claim that the Chinese government is in full control of the developments it has unleashed under the BRI and 'Going Global' labels. Chinese investments have turned sour in Sri Lanka, for example. China's involvement in Montenegro is controversial due to the debt incurred in the construction of a highway. It is not clear whether poor countries such as Laos, Pakistan and Tajikistan will be able to service the debts they have accrued, and it is not clear what this means for their long-term relations with China. In short, there are many problems with the BRI. However, these problems do not negate the initiative nor the substantial progress that has been made in constructing infrastructure and building ties and influence with many developing countries.

Of course, China's image varies across the global South. There is enthusiasm in some quarters: for instance, a majority of people in Pakistan and some African countries welcome the Chinese presence as a force for positive change. However, others have acquired a poor impression of China's involvement in their countries. In Central Asia, despite understanding the need for economic cooperation, people worry about being 'flooded' by Chinese immigrants and goods, or about Chinese companies or the Chinese state acquiring too much control over their countries' internal affairs.[6] There are fears about Chinese expansionism in the East and South China Seas and the Indian Ocean. Nevertheless, merely by introducing a framework for trade, investment and cooperation that is distinctly non-Western and which does not adhere to the standard rules of what is sometimes called the 'liberal international order', China has altered the global development landscape. By emerging onto the world stage and engaging with countries according to its own norms, China has acted as a catalyst for change. Arguably, it has also shown that its approach to development is better suited to coping with the vagaries and complexities of managing relations with emerging economies than the West's approach over the last half century since European decolonization.

Such is the complexity of global affairs that nobody can predict the long-term consequences of specific actions and events. International affairs evolve and shift for many reasons. Industrialization, capitalism and the consequences of European colonization have been among the main driving forces of global change over the last two centuries. Wars, economic crises and pandemics are black swans thrown like spanners into the engine of history. Today, humanity is dealing with climate change resulting from exponential population growth and industrialization. There is also another novel force of change: China's rise as an economic powerhouse and its global expansion under the BRI label. The fact of China becoming a catalyst for change reveals that the West no longer has the dominant influence in global affairs which it once enjoyed. This is difficult for the West to accept; but accept it must. The West cannot simply continue as before, assuming that it can dictate to the rest of the world how to do business. There is a need to develop partnerships with developing countries, to treat them as equals rather than subordinates. Within this process of adaptation to changed circumstances, the West must also develop clearer ideas for how to react to Chinese initiatives, most notably Xi Jinping's BRI.

Strengths and weaknesses: China versus the West

It is obvious that both China and the West – the United States and Europe – have their strengths and weaknesses. Regardless of whether the West is going to counter, compete or cooperate with China, it needs to understand the relative positions and characteristics of each side clearly. Only on a basis of clear understanding can coherent strategies be formulated, meaningful decisions taken. Accordingly, this section outlines the main strengths and weaknesses of the two sides and evaluates their respective positions in relation to each other.

As Chapters 4, 5 and 6 demonstrated, China's strengths emerge from the state's ability to coordinate, with relative efficiency, the activities of Chinese commercial actors in the service of national security goals. Since it is an authoritarian regime, the Chinese state does not have to lose time passing legislation to endorse its decisions. It does not have to campaign in democratic elections, so can be relatively patient and consistent over the long term. It can simply decide on a strategy, behind closed doors, and then direct its agents to follow its general policy direction. At the same time, the general vagueness of Chinese official texts gives actors flexibility to decide on details within the overall strategic envelope (in foreign policy this is represented by the BRI). If Beijing can maintain the support of the majority of the Chinese people, it can ensure a substantial amount of legitimacy for its policies without having to contest direct elections.

In terms of its engagement with the global South, Beijing utilizes China's large, relatively 'tight' and homogeneous population, substantial cash reserves and infrastructure construction capabilities in the service of national goals. It uses these to build relations with individual regimes on a bilateral basis and steadily increase its influence in the developing world. The Beijing government can engage effectively with authoritarian regimes, coordinating their interests and its own. Summit diplomacy via regional cooperation forums smooths relations even amidst local rivalries. From a pivotal position in Asia, Chinese companies can fan out across the region and beyond. Beijing can enlist the support of Russia, which has been blacklisted by the West and hence pushed towards China. It does this most notably as a supplier of much-needed energy and resources. Such are China's advantages when compared with the West.

Undoubtedly, China also has substantial weaknesses. Some would say these outweigh its strengths. Not least among China's vulnerabilities is the nation's poor international image and consequent lack of soft power. Its image tends to be poor overseas due to global perceptions of issues such as its human rights record and the Covid-19 pandemic. Taiwan, Xinjiang and Tibet also weigh down China's ability to generate soft power abroad, especially in liberal democracies. The lack of transparency surrounding commercial transactions also impacts China's image (although secrecy is an advantage in pushing through deals without obstruction). Worldwide, China's image varies from country to country, and seems to lack a firm foundation even in nations which are ostensibly allies. As an extension of this point, China has few firm friends, and tends to have partners rather than close allies (although in fact this can be said of almost any nation).

Materially, China lacks sufficient domestic supplies of energy and other natural resources to fuel its continuing economic rise (this is also true of Europe). It is therefore forced import supplies from as wide a range of suppliers as possible to ensure that it can obtain enough imports even if some supply routes are cut. Beijing thus seeks to mitigate this key weakness through supply diversification and cultivation of relations with the leaders of resource-rich nations. Nevertheless, the insufficiency of domestic resources – apart from polluting coal and rare earths – is certainly a weakness in comparison to the resource-rich United States, which is more or less self-sufficient in oil and gas due to recently developed fracking technologies.

China's army lacks experience due to the fact that the nation has not fought a full-scale war since its brief invasion of Vietnam in 1979. The state of Chinese military technology is certainly inferior to that possessed by the United States: China is trying to close the gap but is probably still far behind. China still spends far less on its military than the United States. Still, China's ability to project military power internationally has increased in the last two decades as it has expanded its reach through the South China Sea and into the Indian Ocean. China's military still has a long way to go; but Beijing is prepared to play a long game. Chinese political and military leaders carefully refrain from becoming entangled in large-scale conflicts while making the point that the nation's military is not to be taken lightly: for instance, by displays of force in the waters off Taiwan.

In terms of China's approach to economics, there are several weaknesses. Chief among these is the built-in inefficiency of the state capitalism model, which tends to prioritize monolithic state-owned enterprises (SOEs) and other large national champions over smaller, more dynamic firms. Because of this issue, China's domestic economy is encumbered with debt emanating from the activities of SOEs, banks, real estate firms and local governments.[7] In the international sphere, the looseness of the BRI and limited state oversight of commercial actors' overseas activities can result in the principal-agent problem: this is when individual commercial actors seek immediate profit by pursuing their own interests rather than behaving in tune with the long-term expectations of the state.[8] Another point is that China's investment model of state-backed loans funding infrastructure projects built by Chinese firms generates debt loads for already impoverished partner countries. In some cases, these may be unsustainable, leading to accusations of 'debt-trap diplomacy'. Whether these accusations are correct or not is something of a moot point, with some scholars explaining that 'debt-trap diplomacy' is a 'meme' or a 'myth' which is unrepresentative of Chinese lending practices.[9] Be this as it may, damage is done to China's image as partner nations such as Sri Lanka and Pakistan run into cashflow problems.

Finally, there is China's relationship with Russia. Whether this is truly a weakness is hard to evaluate; but it is certainly a vulnerability of sorts. Closeness to Russia certainly does not enhance China's image in the West or other countries striving to become full-fledged democracies. Yet for those outside the Western orbit who may be at least somewhat sympathetic to Russia it does not necessarily present a problem. In an October 2022 UN vote about the Ukraine invasion, many Asian and African countries abstained from condemning Russia, showing that they are not necessarily supportive of the Western approach to Russia and China.[10] At any rate, association with Russia may present Beijing with assorted future problems, tarnishing its claim that China is a model for the global South. Over-reliance on Russian resources is also not desirable because it acts against the effort to diversify resource suppliers in the name of comprehensive national security.

China's weaknesses may seem more numerous than its strengths. The question is whether they are more numerous than the West's. As we shall see, the West is facing its fair share of problems. First, however, let us summarize the West's strengths, compared to China. Of course, 'the West' is no more a monolithic entity than China. One therefore has to be careful not to 'flatten' differences between the EU and the United States, as well as internal differences and divisions within and between states. Nevertheless, it is possible to draw out some general points about where the West has advantages or vulnerabilities relative to China.

Foremost among the West's strengths is its generally positive image. Democratic institutions, individual freedoms and rule of law make the United States and Europe attractive, as do their economic strength and quality of life. Powerful private companies with global presence enhance the West's soft power. The United States has the world's largest economy and the highest military spending. Western business practices are far more transparent than China's. The EU is viewed as a 'normative power', transmitting ideas about human rights and freedoms to the world. In short, the West has an impressive set of positive attributes to project, none of which are possessed by China.

On the other hand, the West also has a range of noticeable vulnerabilities relative to China. For instance, while democracy at first sight appears to be a strength, frequent changes of government after elections undermine the possibility of implementing policy over the long term. In the United States, huge swings in foreign policy occur when a new president is elected, making Washington look inconsistent and unreliable. For instance, Donald Trump withdrew the United States from the Iran nuclear deal, the Trans-Pacific Partnership and the Paris climate agreement, all of which had been ratified by the Obama administration. Within the United States, differences of opinion between the two main political parties have created an ever-widening schism between right and left.

In the EU, it can be difficult to establish consensus on policy across such a large number of nations. The EU is not a single unified actor, but twenty-seven separate polities. Some of these – for instance, Hungary – appear to have national goals which are drastically at odds with the stated goals of the EU. Some EU states – such as Lithuania or the Czech Republic – take an actively critical stance towards China, while others – such as Germany – appear willing to engage, at least economically.[11] The disunity and frequent inconsistency of the EU – and the West as a whole – undermine efforts at coordinated action. This lack of unity places the EU and the United States at a disadvantage relative to China.

An additional issue is that the most powerful Western actor, the United States, also often tends to act against the interests of the collective (if such a thing can even be said to exist in the West). The United States undermines collective interests when it refuses to conform to the decisions of international institutions such as the UN (for example in its invasion of Iraq in 2003) or the International Criminal Court (Washington denies that the ICC has jurisdiction over serving members of the US military). The United States also looks like a hypocrite in the eyes of the developing world when it insists on a 'rules-based international order', then fails to sign up to agreements such as the UN Convention on the Laws of the Sea (UNCLOS). This looks like a case of 'do as I say, not as I do': not a great image for a nation which thinks of itself as 'a shining city on a hill'.

Beyond the West's inherent disunity, there are other problems. The interests of private and state actors are not well aligned due to the focus on market forces and profit-seeking. It often seems that Western countries have difficulties obtaining and coordinating funds from private investors for large-scale projects. The United States is not strong in infrastructure, as the poor condition of many of the nation's roads and bridges reveals. It is difficult to coordinate efforts to improve this situation, as the inefficiencies inherent in funding and implementing President Biden's 2021 infrastructure bill demonstrate.[12] Above all, it seems to be difficult for Western nations to generate the political will to follow through with projects that do not have a direct impact on their internal affairs, such as investment in developing countries. Promises are made, but these are not translated into actions. Documents are published expressing the intention to do something, but there is limited or no follow-up. When a course of action is decided, the implementation can be slow or non-existent. All these issues undermine the image of the West as a potential partner and investor in the global South.

Comparing the strengths and weaknesses of China and the West is revealing. While China recognizes many of its strategic vulnerabilities and has developed policies to mitigate them (as in the case of energy supply diversification), the West has been very slow to address its shortcomings. While China recognizes that it has a range of complex and interconnected problems which require an integrated strategic approach, the West seems reluctant even to acknowledge that it has weaknesses. The assumption, prevalent in the West, that the United States and Europe somehow have moral superiority is undermined by their inability to acknowledge relative disadvantages, let alone to draw any lessons from China's success in gaining more influence in the global South. The notion that China is an irresponsible actor which does not follow the rules-based order becomes meaningless in the face of China's relative success at building relations using Chinese norms which do not fit the Western conception of correctness. De facto, the West's 'liberal international order' is no longer necessarily the dominant system through which international affairs are conducted – if it ever, in its hypothetical form, was.

Difficulties for China, difficulties for the world

In July 2022 it was reported that China's housing market was in dire straits. Prices had collapsed and the finances of major real estate contractors such as Evergrande were on the rocks.[13] Purchasers of unconstructed apartments were protesting, refusing to pay their mortgages until they received assurances about their investments. The government subsequently promised to guarantee that homes would be delivered to buyers.[14] It seemed that the Chinese property bubble had finally burst. Nevertheless, in view of the fact that the government had for years been looking to cool down the overheated property market, the situation was neither unexpected nor completely disastrous as far as Chinese policymakers were concerned. It seemed they believed they could, at least to an extent, control the problems.

China's overall economy was also being impacted by the continued enforcement of the government's zero-Covid approach. Although there were signs of a recovery in June 2022 as industrial output and retail sales grew over 3 per cent, analysts remained pessimistic. They were forecasting that China might be on the verge of economic contraction as a result of the slumping property market and declining global growth.[15] Indeed, the figures for July showed a slight but significant decrease in industrial production and consumption.[16] More worryingly, by mid-2022, youth unemployment reached almost 20 per cent.[17] At the same time, the emerging global recession was not likely to do the West many favours relative to China. The situation regarding China and the world's economic future remained murky and complex. Any downturn for China would not necessarily mean a victory for the West, but rather a further downwards pressure on the overall global economy.

As far as geopolitics were concerned, in the wake of Russia's invasion of Ukraine, and apparent Chinese support for the Russians, tensions with the United States were building. In August, Nancy Pelosi, the Speaker of the US House of Representatives visited Taiwan, intensifying the standoff. China conducted military exercises and missile firings in the Taiwan Straits to demonstrate that the United States could not dictate what it should do. Beijing decided to withdraw cooperation with Washington on the climate crisis and other matters. On the other hand, Western sanctions on Russia meant more energy supplies for China as Europe turned its back on Moscow. Adding fuel to the fire, in February 2023 the US military shot down a suspected Chinese 'spy balloon' which had traversed the country.[18] The situation was volatile, but the advent of numerous 'grey rhinos' charging through the global political economy was something that Beijing appeared to have anticipated better than Washington or Brussels.

In November 2022, Xi Jinping was reappointed Party General Secretary at the annual Communist Party Congress after securing firm support within the Party over the summer.[19] Shortly after this, there were protests against the government's continuing zero-Covid policy. Xi took the decision to relax the lockdown and allow the virus to spread.[20] This caused short-term confusion, but it soon became clear that China was beginning to emerge from the pandemic. In February 2023, the International Monetary Fund (IMF) projected a rebound in China's economy, with higher growth for the year than in 2022.[21] Among the Chinese public, even if Xi's image had been somewhat tarnished by the sudden U-turn, there was no evidence of increased resistance to his regime. He appeared to have weathered the crisis, retaining a solid grip on power. While some have suggested China's pandemic response was chaotic, the sudden policy shift can also be interpreted as another sign of the Chinese government's willingness to be pragmatic and flexible, changing course when necessary while seeking to retain the coherence of overall strategy. China's future is uncertain, but Xi and his Party are still in charge amidst apparent economic recovery.

At the same time, amidst the emerging global economic downturn and geopolitical uncertainties, the opportunity was there for the West to strike out on a new course: one which might better account for the inherent complexities of our globalized world. A strategy was needed which approached the global South with an altered mindset, treating developing countries with respect rather than as basket cases which should simply listen obediently to supposedly sage Western advice. Western finance and investment can transform the South if they are coordinated properly and implemented in consultation with the governments of impoverished countries. China's success at building relations shows that developing countries will respond enthusiastically if they can get the sense that they are being treated as equals rather than subordinates and that long-term commitment from the West is on offer. This is how the West can best learn from and react to China and its BRI: by presenting a better offer and sticking to it. Only time will tell if the American PGII and the EU's Global Gateway can be coordinated to present a viable alternative to China's BRI. At the time of writing, in the face of mounting crises and domestic pressures, it appears that there is a long way to go before the political will, coherence and consistency can be found to develop a unified Western approach to the much-needed investment in infrastructure and technology which the global South so urgently needs – and which China has so far done a better job of offering.

As an important side note, as far as science and technology research is concerned, China is rapidly overtaking the West. A study by the Australian Strategic Policy Institute (ASPI) published in March 2023 revealed that China leads the world in thirty-seven out of forty-four critical technologies, including hypersonic missiles, electric batteries and 5G internet. The United States is still ahead in areas such as vaccines and quantum computing; but overall 'China has built the foundations to position itself as the world's leading science and technology superpower, by establishing a sometimes stunning lead in high-impact research across the majority of critical and emerging technology domains.'[22] China's advantage in science and technology is based on the Chinese government's focus on scale and efficiency in manufacturing – an area long neglected by the United States.[23] If the West wishes to reduce China's influence in the global South and increase its own, it will have to move rapidly to improve domestic manufacturing capacities rather than continuing down the route of focusing chiefly on research and development while outsourcing manufacturing to developing countries such as China.

Thus, it is a moot point whether the West can get its act together and compete with China. The structure of the EU – essentially, a loose confederation of states with individual polities, tax regimes and foreign policies – weighs against a coherent and viable European approach. It also seems unlikely that the United States and the EU will sit down together and hammer out a coordinated global investment, infrastructure and technology initiative. It seems even more unlikely that subsequent leaders – inevitably different ones – will thereafter persist unabated with such an initiative. The West's reliance on market forces, democratic elections and independent actors undercut the idea of developing a long-term coordinated response enforced from the top down. Indeed, the very idea of a coordinated, top-down strategic initiative seems alien to Western notions of how things are supposed to be done. For many, the very idea of top-down coordination smacks of autocracy and authoritarianism. It seems unlikely that it will be an easy sell, whether labelled PGII, Global Gateway or something else.

At the same time, there is another point which is surely more important for the future of the world. In the face of today's entrenched and often contradictory problems – global warming, geopolitical conflicts, energy crises and complex issues emerging from economic interdependence – it seems essential for the United States, Europe and China (and other significant actors such as India, Japan and Russia) to work together to find solutions. Yet the prospect of such cooperation seems further away than ever, especially when even blocks of supposed allies find it so difficult to pull together. Put simply: groups of humans continue to fight each other when they should be working together to save the planet. As John Mearsheimer perceptively points out, it seems impossible for humanity to overcome what he calls the 'tragedy of great power politics': the inevitability of competition – and war – between rival states such as the United States and China.[24] The problem is now that in the face of impending environmental catastrophe, the tragedy is likely to expand beyond mere politics and war to encompass a raft of environmental, economic and other existential issues as well. The coming disaster will be greater than we can even imagine if the West and China do not find ways to overcome their differences and cooperate on strategies for global development which can generate positive outcomes for all.

The 2022 Ukraine and Taiwan Straits crises appear to reveal a deep schism between the West on the one hand and China/Russia on the other. Cooperation seems impossible. Yet to overcome the climate crisis and the fragilities inherent in the globalized, interdependent economy, cooperation is needed more than ever. Geopolitics may seem like a zero-sum game; but economics and the climate are not. Ideally, even it seems unlikely, ways should be found for the United States and Europe to work with China rather than against it. Failing this, if competition is deemed the best course of action, the West should develop a clear and consistent approach to the global South which aims to develop it in the interests of all parties. Yet, at the present time, neither cooperation with China nor a clear-sighted approach to global development seems to be on the cards. While the West fails to take action on these two vital issues, China is left with a continued advantage in the global marketplace of ideas and investments in the developing world. To the extent that the future must unfortunately be considered a zero-sum game of geopolitics and influence rather than a positive-sum game of saving the world for everybody, it appears that China may be better equipped to come out on top of whatever is left of the world at the end of the contest.

Ultimately, whatever China's intentions may be, there can be little doubt that its emergence onto the international stage as a major player has altered the course of history – and continues to do so. Amidst uncertainty, complexity and disruption, China has become a catalyst for change, especially in the global South. As China transforms the global landscape of investment and ideas, the previously dominant West is forced to react. China holds some aces; but the game is not yet over. If the West can find ways to coordinate its response, it may be possible to wrest back the advantage. At the same time, this is a big ask, and it is not clear that the West is up to it. What is sure is that, as the twenty-first century unfolds, whatever Beijing's plans and intentions, China will continue to be an agent of change in an era of global disruption.

NOTES

Introduction

1   Stephen L. Morgan (2021) *The Chinese Economy*, Newcastle upon Tyne: Agenda Publishing, p. 74.
2   Morgan (2021), p. 77.
3   Morgan (2021), p. 79.
4   Stockholm International Peace Research Institute (2022) 'World military expenditure passes \$2 trillion for first time', 25 April. Available at: https://www.sipri.org/media/press-release/2022/world-military-expenditure-passes-2-trillion-first-time (accessed 17 August 2022).
5   Felix Richter (2021) 'China is the world's manufacturing superpower', *Statista*, 4 May. Available at: https://www.statista.com/chart/20858/top-10-countries-by-share-of-global-manufacturing-output/ (accessed 17 August 2022).
6   Morgan (2021), p. 167.
7   Axel Dreher, Andreas Fuchs, Bradley Parks, Austin Strange, and Michael J. Tierney (2022) *Banking on Beijing: The Aims and Impacts of China's Overseas Development Program*, Cambridge: Cambridge University Press, pp. 9–22.
8   Dreher et al (2022), p. 23.
9   Dreher et al (2022), p. 32.
10 Lee Jones and Shahar Hameiri (2022) *Fractured China: How State Transformation is Shaping China's Rise*, Cambridge: Cambridge University Press.
11 Kjeld Erik Brødsgaard (ed.) (2017) *Chinese Politics as Fragmented Authoritarianism: Earthquakes, Energy and Environment*, Abingdon: Routledge.
12 Jones and Hameiri (2022).
13 Shu G. Zhang and Ni Chen (2021) 'Beijing's institutionalised economic statecraft towards Brazil: a case study', *Journal of Current Chinese Affairs*, Vol. 50, Issue 3, p. 356.
14 Dreher et al (2022), p. 24.
15 Dreher et al (2022), p. 129.
16 Jeremy Garlick (2019) 'China's principal-agent problem in the Czech Republic: the curious case of CEFC', *Asia Europe Journal*, Vol. 17, Issue 4, pp. 437–51.
17 David Shambaugh (2021) *China's Leaders: From Mao to Now*, Cambridge: Polity, p. 141.
18 Susan L. Shirk (2007) *China: Fragile Superpower*, New York: Oxford University Press.
19 Gordon G. Chang (2002) *The Coming Collapse of China*, London: Arrow.
20 Erin Mendell (2021) 'What is China Evergrande, and why is its crisis worrying markets?', *The Wall Street Journal*, 6 December. Available at: https://www.wsj.com/articles/evergrande-china-crisis-11632330764 (accessed 17 August 2022).
21 Zeng Ming, Liu Ximei, Li Yulong, and Peng Lilin (2014) 'Review of renewable energy investment and financing in China: status, mode, issues and countermeasures', *Renewable and Sustainable Energy Reviews*, Vol. 31, pp. 23–37.

22 Bruce J. Dickson (2016) *The Dictator's Dilemma: The Chinese Communist Party's Strategy for Survival*, New York: Oxford University Press, Chapter 2.

23 Tristan Kenderdine and Han Ling (2018) 'International capacity cooperation: Financing China's export of industrial overcapacity', *Global Policy*, Vol. 9, Issue 1, pp. 41–52.

24 Ching Kwan Lee (2017) *The Specter of Global China: Politics, Labor, and Foreign Investment in Africa*, Chicago: University of Chicago Press, p. 13.

25 Ching Kwan Lee (2017), p. 6.

26 Dreher et al (2022).

27 Robert Haddick (2012) 'Salami slicing in the South China Sea', *Foreign Policy*, 3 August. Available at: https://foreignpolicy.com/2012/08/03/salami-slicing-in-the-south-china-sea/ (accessed 18 August 2022).

28 Xiaoming Zhang (2005) 'China's 1979 war with Vietnam: a reassessment', *The China Quarterly*, Vol. 184, pp. 851–74.

29 Rush Doshi (2021) *The Long Game: China's Grand Strategy to Displace American Order*, New York: Oxford University Press.

30 See for instance Bruce Gilley (2004) *China's Democratic Future: How It Will Happen and Where It Will Lead*, New York: Columbia University Press.

31 Chang (2002).

32 Francis Fukuyama (1992) *The End of History and the Last Man*, New York: Free Press.

33 Martin Jacques (2009) *When China Rules the World: The Rise of the Middle Kingdom and the End of the Western World*, London: Allen Lane, p. 265.

34 Dreher et al (2022), p. 6.

35 Dreher et al (2022), p. 302.

Chapter 1

1 Examples of books advancing the argument that China is strategically undermining the United States – and European-led international order include the following: Rush Doshi (2021) *The Long Game: China's Grand Strategy to Displace American Order*, New York: Oxford University Press; Philippe Le Corre and Alain Sepulchre (2016) *China's Offensive in Europe*, Washington, D.C.: Brookings Institution Press; Michael Pillsbury (2015) *The Hundred-Year Marathon: China's Secret Strategy to Replace America as the Global Superpower*, New York: Henry Holt; and Martin Jacques (2009) *When China Rules the World: The Rise of the Middle Kingdom and the End of the Western World*, London: Allen Lane. These are just a sample of the many publications advancing arguments of this type.

2 The 'yellow peril' was a racist discourse of exclusion prevalent in the Americas in the late nineteenth and early twentieth centuries. See Erika Lee (2007) 'The "yellow peril" and Asian exclusion in the Americas', *Pacific Historical Review*, Vol. 76, Issue 4, pp. 537–62.

3 Edward W. Said (1978) *Orientalism*, New York: Pantheon.

4 John Hobson (2012) *The Eurocentric Conception of World Politics: Western International Theory, 1760–2010*, Cambridge: Cambridge University Press.

5 The concept of Europe as a normative power was introduced by Ian Manners in his seminal (2002) 'Normative power Europe: a contradiction in terms?', *Journal of Common Market Studies*, Vol. 40, Issue 2, pp. 235–58.

6   Amitav Acharya has argued this in many of his publications, including his (2014) *Rethinking Power, Institutions and Ideas in World Politics: Whose IR?* Abingdon, UK: Routledge.

7   For more on this, see: Amitav Acharya (2011) 'Norm subsidiarity and regional orders: sovereignty, regionalism, and rule-making in the Third World', *International Studies Quarterly*, Vol. 55, Issue 1, pp. 95–123; and Emilian Kavalski (2010) 'Shanghaied into cooperation: framing China's socialization of Central Asia', *Journal of Asian and African Studies*, Vol. 45, Issue 2, pp. 131–45.

8   Jonathan Spence (1980) *To Change China: Western Advisers in China*, New York: Penguin.

9   'Mike Pompeo says free world must change China or "China will change us"', *The Guardian*, 24 July 2020. Available at: https://www.theguardian.com/world/2020/jul/24/mike-pompeo-says-free-world-must-change-china-or-china-will-change-us (accessed 3 March 2023).

10 Spence (1980).

11 Jacques (2009).

12 Kerry Brown (2018) *China's Dream: The Culture of Chinese Communism and the Secret Sources of Its Power*, Cambridge: Polity Press.

13 Jeremy Garlick (2013) 'A critical analysis of EU-China relations: towards improved mutual understanding', *Contemporary European Studies*, Vol. 1, pp. 51–70.

14 The first wave included books such as Bill Gertz (2000) *The China Threat: How the People's Republic Targets America*, Washington, D.C.: Regnery. The current wave includes media articles such as Gordon Corera (2022) 'China: MI5 and FBI heads warn of "immense" threat', *BBC News*, 7 July. Available at: https://www.bbc.com/news/world-asia-china-62064506 (accessed 19 August 2022) and Sylvia Hui (2022) '"China threat" emerges in elections from UK to Australia', *AP News*, 14 August. available at: https://apnews.com/article/inflation-boris-johnson-taiwan-china-australia-f977bdcaa2aa3287d34231efcc682b03 (accessed 19 August 2022).

15 For instance, the primary aim of the China Observers in Central and Eastern Europe (CHOICE) organization and its affiliate MapInfluenCE is to critique Chinese influence attempts in Europe, especially individual countries in Central and Eastern Europe. See articles such as Liisi Karindi (2020) 'How China is buying influence in Europe', CHOICE, 7 July, Available at: https://chinaobservers.eu/how-china-is-buying-influence-in-europe/ (accessed 19 August 2022) and Edit Zgut-Przybylska (2022) 'A lucrative relationship: clientelist corruption underpins Orbán's China policy', MapInfluenCE, 30 June, Available at: https://mapinfluence.eu/en/a-lucrative-relationship-clientelist-corruption-underpins-orbans-china-policy/ (accessed 19 August 2022). There are many others.

16 See Igor Rogelja and Konstantinos Tsimonis (2020) 'Narrating the China threat: securitising Chinese economic presence in Europe', *The Chinese Journal of International Politics*, Vol. 13, Issue 1, pp. 103–33.

17 Most notably in Francois Godement and Abigael Vasselier (2017) *China at the Gates: A New Power Audit of EU-China Relations*, London: European Council on Foreign Relations.

18 Hans von der Burchard (2019) 'EU slams China as "systemic rival" as trade tension rises', *Politico*, 12 March. Available at: https://www.politico.eu/article/eu-slams-china-as-systemic-rival-as-trade-tension-rises/ (accessed 15 February 2023).

19 The text of this document is available at: https://eeas.europa.eu/archives/docs/china/docs/eu-china_2020_strategic_agenda_en.pdf.

20   Available at: https://ec.europa.eu/energy/sites/ener/files/documents/FINAL_EU_CHINA_ENERGY_ROADMAP_EN.pdf.

21   Movies containing pandemics as a central part of the story include 1995's Outbreak (starring Dustin Hoffmann) and 2010's remake of Planet of the Apes. There is even a popular series of board games entitled Pandemic.

22   Arthur R. Kroeber (2016) *China's Economy: What Everyone Needs to Know*, New York: Oxford University Press, p. 5.

23   Jonathan Spence (1990) *The Search for Modern China*, New York: W.W. Norton, pp. 262–8.

24   John Keay (2008) *China: A History*, London: HarperPress, pp. 513–14.

25   Spence (1990), p. 510.

26   Spence (1990), p. 631.

27   Henry Kissinger (2012) *On China*, London: Penguin, p. 276.

28   Spence (1990), p. 598.

29   Stephen L. Morgan (2021) *The Chinese Economy*, Newcastle upon Tyne: Agenda Publishing, p. 58.

30   Morgan (2021), p. 64.

31   The World Bank, GDP growth (annual per cent) – China. Available at: https://data.worldbank.org/indicator/NY.GDP.MKTP.KD.ZG?locations=CN.

32   Morgan (2021), p. 66.

33   Spence (1990), pp. 122–3.

34   William A. Callahan (2010) *China: The Pessoptimist Nation*, Oxford: Oxford University Press, pp. 34–5.

35   Kissinger (2012), pp. 330–1.

36   Lucian W. Pye (1997) 'Chinese democracy and constitutional development', in Fumio Itoh (ed.) *China in the Twenty-First Century: Politics, Economy, and Society*, Tokyo: United Nations University Press, p. 209.

37   Callahan (2010).

38   Bruce J. Dickson (2016) *The Dictator's Dilemma: The Chinese Communist Party's Strategy for Survival*. New York: Oxford University Press.

39   Zheng Wang (2008) 'National humiliation, history education, and the politics of historical memory: patriotic education campaign in China', *International Studies Quarterly*, Vol. 52, Issue 4, pp. 783–806.

40   Dickson (2016).

41   Callahan (2010).

42   Kai-Fu Lee (2018) *AI Superpowers: China, Silicon Valley, and the New World Order*, New York: Mariner Books.

43   Statista (2022) 'Global smartphone market share from 4th quarter 2009 to 1st quarter 2022', 11 August. Available at: https://www.statista.com/statistics/271496/global-market-share-held-by-smartphone-vendors-since-4th-quarter-2009/ (accessed 21 August 2022).

44   Michael Malakata (2022) 'China's Transsion Holdings dominates Africa smartphone market', ITWeb, 28 March. Available at: https://itweb.africa/content/Kjlyr7w1WE4qk6am (accessed 27 January 2023).

45   Will Knight (2021) 'TikTok a year after Trump's ban: no change, but new threats', Wired.com, 26 July. Available at: https://www.wired.com/story/tiktok-year-trump-ban-no-change-new-threats/ (accessed 21 August 2022).

46   Sarah Frier (2022) 'Facebook bets its users really want a TikTok clone', *Bloomberg*, 27 July. Available at: https://www.bloomberg.com/news/articles/2022-07-27/why-facebook-instagram-look-like-tiktok (accessed 21 August 2022).

47　Albee Zhang and Farah Master (2023) 'China's first population drop in six decades sounds alarm on demographic crisis', *Reuters*, 18 January. Available at: https://www.reuters.com/world/china/chinas-population-shrinks-first-time-since-1961-2023-01-17/ (accessed 27 January 2023).

48　David Shambaugh (2008) *China's Communist Party: Atrophy and Adaptation*, Washington, D.C.: Woodrow Wilson Center Press.

49　Rongbin Han (2015) 'Manufacturing consent in cyberspace: China's "fifty-cent army"', *Journal of Current Chinese Affairs*, Vol. 44, Issue 2, pp. 105–34.

50　Yuen Yuen Ang (2018) 'Autocracy with Chinese characteristics: Beijing's behind-the-scenes reforms', *Foreign Affairs* 97 (May/June), pp. 39–46.

51　Dragan Pavlićević argues this in his (2018) article '"China threat" and "China opportunity": politics of dreams and fears in China-Central and Eastern European relations', *Journal of Contemporary China*, Vol. 27, Issue 113, pp. 688–702.

52　Helen Davidson (2023) 'Chinese spy balloon may have been blown off intended course – report', *The Guardian*, 15 February. Available at: https://www.theguardian.com/world/2023/feb/15/japan-says-aerial-objects-spotted-in-recent-years-were-likely-chinese-spy-balloons (accessed 15 February 2023).

53　Sergei Klebnikov (2020) 'Here's what China says about TikTok being sold to Microsoft, potential ban', *Forbes*, 4 August. Available at: https://www.forbes.com/sites/sergeiklebnikov/2020/08/04/heres-what-china-says-about-tiktok-being-sold-to-microsoft-potential-ban/#18bf432c746e (accessed 3 March 2023).

54　Andrew Tillett (2020) 'China's "wolf warriors" abandon diplomatic niceties', *Australian Financial Review*, 23 May. Available at: https://www.afr.com/politics/federal/china-s-wolf-warriors-abandon-diplomatic-niceties-20200521-p54v5v (accessed 3 March 2023).

55　John J. Mearsheimer (2001) *The Tragedy of Great Power Politics*, New York: W.W. Norton; Graham T. Allison (2017) *Destined for War: Can America and China Escape Thucydides's Trap?* Boston: Houghton Mifflin Harcourt.

56　Graham Allison (2015) 'The Thucydides Trap: are the U.S. and China headed for war?' *The Atlantic*, 24 September. Available at: https://www.theatlantic.com/international/archive/2015/09/united-states-china-war-thucydides-trap/406756/ (accessed 3 March 2023). Allison claims to show that war has resulted in twelve out of sixteen past cases analysed in which a rising power challenged a ruling power.

57　The notion of a 'pivot to Asia' was first formulated in a 2011 article written by Obama's Secretary of State, Hilary Clinton 'America's Pacific Century', *Foreign Policy*, 11 October 2011. Available at: https://foreignpolicy.com/2011/10/11/americas-pacific-century/ (accessed 3 March 2023).

58　See Kat Devlin, Laura Silver, and Christine Huang (2020) 'U.S. views of China increasingly negative amid coronavirus outbreak', Pew Research Center, 21 April. Available at: https://www.pewresearch.org/global/2020/04/21/u-s-views-of-china-increasingly-negative-amid-coronavirus-outbreak/ (accessed 3 March 2023).

59　For analysis of some of the effects of this, see Pavlićević (2018), pp. 688–702.

60　Angela Stanzel (2019) 'Merkel's visit to China: freedom, trade, but no Europe', *Institut Montaigne*, 11 September. Available at: https://www.institutmontaigne.org/en/blog/merkels-visit-china-freedom-trade-no-europe (accessed 3 March 2023).

61　Maximiliane Koschyk (2019) 'Angela Merkel in China: a trip fraught with difficulties', *Deutsche Welle (DW)*, 6 September. Available at: https://www.dw.com/en/angela-merkel-in-china-a-trip-fraught-with-difficulties/a-50296876 (accessed 3 March 2023).

62 Most notably: Gordon G. Chang (2002) *The Coming Collapse of China*, London: Arrow; and Minxin Pei (2006) *China's Trapped Transition: The Limits of Developmental Autocracy*, Cambridge, MA: Harvard University Press.

63 See Kerry Brown (2016) *CEO China: The Rise of Xi Jinping*, London: I.B. Tauris, pp. 24–5.

64 Emilian Kavalski (2012) 'Waking IR up from its "deep Newtonian slumber"', *Millennium: Journal of International Studies*, Vol. 41, Issue 1, 137–50.

65 I developed a framework for this called 'complex eclecticism' in my previous book about the BRI, *The Impact of China's Belt and Road Initiative: From Asia to Europe*, Abingdon: Routledge, 2020).

66 Tang Shiping (2013) *The Social Evolution of International Politics*, Oxford: Oxford University Press.

67 Rudra Sil and Peter J. Katzenstein (2010) *Beyond Paradigms: Analytic Eclecticism in the Study of World Politics*, Houndmills, UK: Palgrave Macmillan.

68 For more on black swans, see Nicholas Nassim Taleb (2008) *The Black Swan: The Impact of the Highly Improbable*, London: Penguin. For more on grey rhinos, see Michele Wucker (2016) *The Gray Rhino: How to Recognize and Act on the Obvious Dangers we Ignore*, New York: St Martin's Press.

69 For an accessible account of theories of the social construction of identity in international relations, see: Felix Berenskoetter (2010) 'Identity in International Relations', *Oxford Research Encyclopedia of International Studies*. Available at: https://oxfordre.com/internationalstudies/view/10.1093/acrefore/9780190846626.001.0001/acrefore-9780190846626-e-218 (accessed 21 August 2022). For a more scholarly approach, see: Timothy Dunne (1995) 'The social construction of international society', *European Journal of International Relations*, Vol. 1, Issue 3, pp. 367–89.

70 Yuen Yuen Ang (2016) *How China Escaped the Poverty Trap*, Ithaca and London: Cornell University Press.

71 Jonathan Fenby (2017) *Will China Dominate the 21st Century?*, Cambridge: Polity Press, p. 31.

72 Ang (2016), pp. 239–40.

73 Shambaugh (2008).

Chapter 2

1 James Kynge (2006) *China Shakes the World: The Rise of a Hungry Nation*, London: Weidenfeld & Nicolson, p. 7.

2 Spence (1990), pp. 484–512.

3 Spence (1990), pp. 574–617.

4 Helen Davidson (2023) 'Xi's authority dented by sudden Covid U-turn, but grip on power is as strong as ever', *The Guardian*, 20 January. Available at: https://www.theguardian.com/world/2023/jan/20/xis-authority-dented-by-sudden-covid-u-turn-but-iron-grip-on-power-is-undimmed (accessed 30 January 2023).

5 Jeremy Garlick (2020) *The Impact of China's Belt and Road Initiative: From Asia to Europe*, Abingdon: Routledge.

6 Kenderdine and Ling (2018).

7 Timothy R. Heath (2016) 'China's evolving approach to economic diplomacy', *Asia Policy*, Vol. 11, Issue 22, pp. 157–92.

8 Siegfried Jäger (2001) 'Discourse and knowledge: theoretical and methodological aspects of a critical discourse and dispositive analysis'; Ruth Wodak (2001) 'The discourse-historical approach', both in Ruth Wodak and Michael Meyer (eds.) *Methods of Critical Discourse Analysis*, London: Sage.

9 Spence (1990), pp. 569–73.

10 Spence (1990), p. 606.

11 Doshi (2021), pp. 59–60.

12 Doshi (2021), p. 12.

13 There are many books expounding the 'China threat' hypothesis. See for instance: Bill Gertz (2000) *The China Threat: How the People's Republic Targets America*, Washington, D.C.: Regnery; Peter Navarro (2008) *The Coming China Wars: Where They Will Be Fought and How They Can Be Won*, Upper Saddle River, NJ: FT Press; and Jonathan Holslag (2015) *China's Coming War with Asia*, Cambridge: Polity.

14 Zhao Tingyang (2006) 'Rethinking empire from a Chinese concept "All-under-Heaven" (Tian-xia, 天下)', *Social Identities*, Vol. 12, Issue 1, pp. 29–41.

15 William A. Callahan (2008) 'Chinese visions of world order: post-hegemonic or a new hegemony?' *International Studies Review*, Vol. 10, Issue 4, pp. 749–61.

16 For instance, Xi used the phrase 'community of shared interests' in the speech during which he introduced the BRI to the world. See Xi Jinping (2014) *The Governance of China*, Beijing: Foreign Languages Press, p. 317.

17 In a 2014 speech promoting the CASCF, Xi talked of the 'shared interests and destiny' of China and Arab states. See Xi (2014), p. 348.

18 Xi (2014), p. 351.

19 Doshi (2021), p. 2.

20 Doshi (2021), p. 265.

21 Li Jie (2018) 'Deeply understand and grasp the world's "great changes not seen in a century"', *Study Times* (学习时报), 3 September. Available at: https://web.archive.org/web/20200624172344/http://www.qstheory.cn/llwx/2018-09/03/c_1123369881.htm (accessed 3 March 2023); Zhu Feng (2019) 'A summary of recent academic research on "great changes unseen in a century"', *People's Forum – Academic Frontier* (人民论坛-学术前沿), Vol. 167, Issue 7, pp. 6–12; Zhang Yuyan (2019) 'Understanding the great changes unseen in a century', *International Economic Review* (国际经济评论), 18 September. Available at: http://www.qstheory.cn/llwx/2019-09/18/c_1125010363.htm (accessed 3 March 2023).

22 Li Jie (2018).

23 For more on classical Aristotelian logic, see William T. Parry and Edward A. Hacker (1991) *Aristotelian Logic*, Albany, NY: State University of New York Press.

24 A good introduction to quantum physics is Alastair I.M. Rae (2005) *Quantum Physics: A Beginner's Guide*, Oxford: Oneworld.

25 An attempt by a Chinese author to reconcile Marxist dialectics, Chinese thought, and the natural sciences is Zhang Yibing (2011) *The Subjective Dimension of Marxist Historical Dialectics* (2nd) ed., London: Canut Publishers.

26 Qin Yaqing (2016) 'A relational theory of world politics', *International Studies Review*, Vol. 18, Issue 1, pp. 33–47.

27 For more on the differences between Western and Chinese relationalism, see: Siyang Liu, Jeremy Garlick, and Fangxing Qin (2021) 'Towards guanxi? Reconciling the "relational turn" in Western and Chinese international relations scholarship', *All Azimuth*, Vol. 11, Issue 1, pp. 67–85.

28 See Antonio R. Damasio's classic (1994) *Descartes' Error: Emotion, Reason, and the Human Brain*, London: Penguin.

29 Andrew P. Allen, Timothy G. Dinan, Gerard Clarke, and John F. Cryan (2017) 'A psychology of the human brain-gut-microbiome axis', *Social and Personality Psychology Compass*, Vol. 11, Issue 4, e12309.

30 Emilian Kavalski calls the reluctance of the Western social sciences – and the field of international relations in particular – to abandon classical Cartesian logic and Newtonian assumptions a 'deep Newtonian slumber': see his (2012) 'Waking IR up from its "deep Newtonian slumber"', *Millennium: Journal of International Studies*, Vol. 41, Issue 1, pp. 137–50.

31 Robert Lawrence Kuhn (2011) *How China's Leaders Think* (revised) ed., Singapore: John Wiley & Sons, pp. xix–xx.

32 See: Henry Kissinger (2011) *On China*, London: Allen Lane, pp. 94–95; and Jonathan D. Spence (2000) *Mao*, London: Phoenix.

33 Kissinger (2011), p. 274.

34 Garlick (2020), p. 36.

35 Shambaugh (2008); Pei (2006).

36 Carl E. Walter and Fraser J.T. Howie (2011) *Red Capitalism: The Fragile Financial Foundation of China's Extraordinary Rise*, Singapore: John Wiley & Sons.

37 Garlick (2020), p. 36.

38 Vincent Ni (2022) 'Growing pains: China's faltering economy tests leadership's nerve', *The Observer*, 20 August. Available at: https://www.theguardian.com/business/2022/aug/20/growing-pains-chinas-faltering-economy-tests-leaderships-nerve (accessed 25 August 2022).

39 See Shambaugh (2008) for more on what he calls China's 'atrophy and adaptation'.

40 Callahan (2010).

41 Lyle J. Morris et al. (2019) *Gaining Competitive Advantage in the Gray Zone: Response Options for Coercive Aggression below the Threshold of Major War*, RAND Corporation, p. 8. Available at: https://www.rand.org/pubs/research_reports/RR2942.html (accessed 25 August 2022).

42 State Council of the People's Republic of China (2015) *China's Military Strategy*, 27 May. Available at: http://english.www.gov.cn/archive/white_paper/2015/05/27/content_281475115610833.htm (accessed 25 August 2022).

43 David Santoro (2019) 'Beijing's South China Sea aggression is a warning to Taiwan', *Foreign Policy*, 16 September. Available at: http://www.viet-studies.net/kinhte/SCSeaWarningTaiwan_FP.pdf (accessed 25 August 2022).

44 Bill Hayton (2014) *The South China Sea: The Struggle for Power in Asia*, New Haven: Yale University Press, pp. 82–3.

45 Michael Grow (2008) *U.S. Presidents and Latin American Interventions: Pursuing Regime Change in the Cold War*, Lawrence, Kansas: University Press of Kansas.

46 See for instance: Noam Chomsky and Andre Vltchek (2013) *On Western Terrorism: From Hiroshima to Drone Warfare*, London: Pluto Press.

47 Keay (2008), p. 530.

48 Kissinger (2012), pp. 271–2.

49 Andrea Shalal, Michael Martina, David Brunnstrom, and Yew Lun Tian (2021) 'Biden raises human rights, Xi warns of Taiwan "red line" in three hour talk'. *Reuters*, 16 November. Available at: https://www.reuters.com/world/biden-raised-concerns-over-xinjiang-tibet-hong-kong-xi-warns-taiwan-red-line-2021-11-16/ (accessed 16 November 2021).

50   Chip Gregson, Russell Hsiao, and Stephen M. Young (2020) 'David and Goliath:
      strengthening Taiwan's deterrence and resiliency', *Global Taiwan Institute*, November,
      p. 15. Available at: https://globaltaiwan.org/wp-content/uploads/2020/11/GTI-David-
      and-Goliath-Strengthening-Taiwan-Deterrence-and-Resiliency-Nov-2020-final.pdf
      (accessed 16 November 2021).

51   Li Li (2022) 'China's US debt holdings fall below $1 trillion', *Asia Times*, 22 July.
      Available at: https://asiatimes.com/2022/07/chinas-us-debt-holdings-fall-below-1-
      trillion/ (accessed 26 August 2022).

52   For more on structural violence and centre-periphery relations, see: Johan Galtung
      (1980) 'A structural theory of imperialism', in Richard A. Falk and Samuel S. Kim
      (eds.) *The War System: An Interdisciplinary Approach*, New York: Routledge.

53   Gary King, Robert O. Keohane, and Sidney Verba (1994) *Designing Social Inquiry:
      Scientific Inference in Qualitative Research*. Princeton: Princeton University Press.

54   Emilian Kavalski (2015) 'Complexifying IR: disturbing the "deep Newtonian
      slumber" of the mainstream', in Emilian Kavalski (ed.) *World Politics at the Edge of
      Chaos: Reflections on Complexity and Global Life*, Albany: State University of New
      York Press, pp. 253–72.

55   M. Mitchell Waldrop (1993) *Complexity: The Emerging Science at the Edge of Order
      and Chaos*, London: Viking.

56   Steven Johnson (2002) *Emergence: The Connected Lines of Ants, Brains, Cities and
      Software*, London: Penguin.

57   John H. Miller and Scott E. Page (2007) *Complex Adaptive Systems: An Introduction
      to Computational Models of Social Life*, Princeton: Princeton University Press, p. 9.

58   Robert Jervis (1997) *System Effects: Complexity in Political and Social Life*, Princeton:
      Princeton University Press.

59   Ben Ramalingam (2013) *Aid on the Edge of Chaos: Rethinking International
      Cooperation in a Complex World*, Oxford: Oxford University Press.

60   Taleb (2007); Wucker (2016).

61   Sidney Leng (2017) 'Beijing watches out for "grey rhino" and "black swan" in the
      jungle of financial risks', *South China Morning Post*, 19 July. Available at: https://www.
      scmp.com/news/china/economy/article/2103186/beijing-watches-out-grey-rhino-
      and-black-swan-jungle-financial (accessed 3 March 2023); Kelsey Munro (2019)
      'China cabinet: black swans, grey rhinos, and elephant in the room', *The Interpreter*
      (Lowy Institute), 24 January. Available at: www.lowyinstitute.org/the-interpreter/
      china-cabinet-black-swans-grey-rhinos-elephant-room (accessed 3 March 2023).

62   Shuxiu Zhang (2016) *Chinese Economic Diplomacy: Decision-Making Actors and
      Processes*, London and New York: Routledge, p. 12.

63   Kissinger (2012), p. 274.

64   For a full discussion of complexity thinking, see Emilian Kavalski (2015)
      'Introduction: Inside/outside and around: observing the complexity of global life', in
      Emilian Kavalski (ed.) *World Politics at the Edge of Chaos: Reflections on Complexity
      and Global Life*, Albany: State University of New York Press, pp. 1–27.

65   J. Bradford De Long and Barry Eichengreen (1991) *The Marshall Plan: History's
      Most Successful Structural Adjustment Program*, Cambridge, MA: National Bureau of
      Economic Research. Available at: https://www.nber.org/papers/w3899 (accessed 26
      August 2022).

66   Concerning China's use of the SCO to 'socialize' Central Asia, see: Emilian Kavalski
      (2010) 'Shanghaied into cooperation: framing China's socialization of Central Asia',
      Journal of Asian and African Studies, Vol. 45, Issue 2, pp. 131–45. For analysis of

China's use of regional multilateral cooperation platforms, see: Jakub Jakóbowski (2018) 'Chinese-led regional multilateralism in Central and Eastern Europe, Africa and Latin America: 16+1, FOCAC, and CCF', *Journal of Contemporary China*, Vol. 27, Issue 113, pp. 659–73.

67   Sean Golden (2011) 'China's perception of risk and the concept of comprehensive national power', *The Copenhagen Journal of Asian Studies*, Vol. 29, Issue 2, pp. 79–109.

68   William J. Norris (2016) *Chinese Economic Statecraft: Commercial Actors, Grand Strategy, and State Control*, Ithaca, NY: Cornell University Press.

69   David Shambaugh (2013) *China Goes Global: The Partial Power*, New York: Oxford University Press, pp. 174–83.

70   Wade Shepard (2016) 'The story behind the world's emptiest international airport', *Forbes*, 28 May. Available at: https://www.forbes.com/sites/wadeshepard/2016/05/28/the-story-behind-the-worlds-emptiest-international-airport-sri-lankas-mattala-rajapaksa/?sh=46de0fa87cea (accessed 26 August 2022).

71   John Hurley, Scott Morris, and Gailyn Portelance (2018) *Examining the Debt Implications of the Belt and Road Initiative from a Policy Perspective*, Washington, D.C.: Center for Global Development, Policy Paper 121.

72   Deborah Brautigam (2020) 'A critical look at Chinese "debt-trap diplomacy": the rise of a meme', *Area Development and Policy*, Vol. 5, Issue 1, pp. 1–14.

73   Zhenjie Yang (2013) '"Fragmented authoritarianism" – the facilitator behind the Chinese reform miracle: a case study in central China', *China Journal of Social Work*, Vol. 6, Issue 1, pp. 4–13.

74   Jeremy Garlick (2019) 'China's principal-agent problem in the Czech Republic: the curious case of CEFC', *Asia Europe Journal*, Vol. 17, Issue 4, pp. 437–51.

75   Jeremy Garlick and Radka Havlová (2020) 'China's "Belt and Road" economic diplomacy in the Persian Gulf: strategic hedging amidst Saudi-Iranian regional rivalry', *Journal of Current Chinese Affairs*, Vol. 49, Issue 1, pp. 82–105.

76   Lee Jones and Jinghan Zeng (2019) 'Understanding China's "Belt and Road Initiative": beyond "grand strategy" to a state transformation analysis', *Third World Quarterly*, Vol. 40, Issue 8, pp. 1415–39.

77   World Bank, Historical GDP by country, 1960–2020. Available at: https://knoema.com/mhrzolg/historical-gdp-by-country-statistics-from-the-world-bank-1960-2019 (accessed 1 December 2021).

78   Dickson (2016), p. 259.

79   International Monetary Fund (2022) 'GDP, current prices'. Available at: https://www.imf.org/external/datamapper/PPPGDP@WEO/OEMDC/ADVEC/WEOWORLD/AFQ (accessed 26 August 2022).

80   Simon Constable (2021) 'When investors mention "decoupling", what do they mean?' *The Wall Street Journal*, 2 October. Available at: https://www.wsj.com/articles/what-does-decoupling-mean-to-investors-11633112138 (accessed 23 November 2021).

81   Niall Ferguson and Xiang Xu (2018) 'Making Chimerica great again', *International Finance*, Vol. 21, Issue 3, pp. 239–52.

82   Laura Silver, Kat Devlin, and Christine Huang (2021) 'Large majorities say China does not respect the personal freedoms of its people', Washington, D.C.: Pew Research Center, 30 June. Available at: https://www.pewresearch.org/global/2021/06/30/large-majorities-say-china-does-not-respect-the-personal-freedoms-of-its-people/ (accessed 26 August 2022).

83	Alexandria Williams (2019) 'China is making more of Africa's phones than you think', *Quartz*, 12 December. Available at: https://qz.com/africa/1764356/china-makes-majority-of-africas-smartphones/ (accessed 26 August 2022).

84	Pete Pattisson and Febriana Firdaus (2021) '"Battery arms race": how China has monopolised the electric vehicle industry', *The Guardian*, 25 November. Available at: https://www.theguardian.com/global-development/2021/nov/25/battery-arms-race-how-china-has-monopolised-the-electric-vehicle-industry (accessed 30 November 2021).

Chapter 3

1	Burton Watson (trans.) (2013) *The Complete Works of Zhuangzi*, New York: Columbia University Press, pp. 135–6.

2	Such is the assumption made by the influential neorealist scholar Kenneth Waltz, in his (1979) *Theory of International Politics*, New York: Addison-Wesley. Waltz exclusively attributes the behaviour of states to the anarchic nature of the international system. This explanation of state behaviour has tended to prevail in theoretically orientated academic IR ever since.

3	Martin Jacques makes this important point in his 2009 book *When China Rules the World: The Rise of the Middle Kingdom and the End of the Western World* (London: Allen Lane).

4	Samuel P. Huntington (2005) *Who Are We?: The Challenges to America's National Identity*, New York: Simon & Schuster.

5	Ipek S. Burnett (2020) *A Jungian Inquiry into the American Psyche: The Violence of Innocence*, Abingdon: Routledge.

6	Cornel West (2005) *Democracy Matters: Winning the Fight against Imperialism*, New York: Penguin Books, p. 41.

7	Karl Polanyi (1957) *The Great Transformation: The Political and Economic Origins of Our Time*, Boston: Beacon Press.

8	One of the first former slaves to raise awareness of these issues was Frederick Douglass. See his (2008) *My Bondage and My Freedom*, Urbana, IL: Project Gutenberg. Available at: http://www.gutenberg.org/files/202/202-h/202-h.htm (accessed 27 August 2022).

9	Paul H. Rubin (2010) 'More money into bad suits', *The New York Times*, 16 November. Available at: https://www.nytimes.com/roomfordebate/2010/11/15/investing-in-someone-elses-lawsuit/more-money-into-bad-suits (accessed 4 March 2023).

10	Alain Ehrenberg (2010) *The Weariness of the Self: Diagnosing the History of Depression in the Contemporary Age*, Montreal & Kingston: McGill-Queen's University Press, p. 10.

11	First so called by J. Halford Mackinder in his (1904) 'The geographical pivot of history', *The Geographical Journal*, Vol. 23, Issue 4, pp. 421–37.

12	Franklin L. Lavin (1996) 'Isolationism and U.S. foreign policy', *The Brown Journal of World Affairs*, Vol. 3, Issue 1, pp. 271–7.

13	Burnett (2020), p. 2.

14	Quoted by Francis Fukuyama (2004) 'Nation-building 101', *The Atlantic*, January/February issue. Available at: https://www.theatlantic.com/magazine/archive/2004/01/nation-building-101/302862/ (accessed 29 December 2021).

15   Craig Whitlock (2019) 'Built to fail', *Washington Post*, 9 December. Available at: https://www.washingtonpost.com/graphics/2019/investigations/afghanistan-papers/afghanistan-war-nation-building/ (accessed 28 December 2021).

16   *Al Jazeera* (2021) 'Afghan president Ghani flees country as Taliban enters Kabul', 16 August. Available at: https://www.aljazeera.com/news/2021/8/15/afghan-president-ghani-flees-country-as-taliban-surrounds-kabul (accessed 28 December 2021).

17   Natasha Turak (2021) 'Weeks after fleeing Afghanistan, former president Ashraf Ghani issues "explanation" statement to Afghan people – only in English', CNBC, 9 September. Available at: https://www.cnbc.com/2021/09/09/ashraf-ghani-afghanistan-ex-president-issues-explanation-after-fleeing.html (accessed 4 March 2024).

18   Joseph S. Nye (2004) *Soft Power: The Means to Success in World Politics*, New York: Public Affairs.

19   Stephen M. Walt (2021) 'What comes after the forever wars', *Foreign Policy*, 28 April. Available at: https://foreignpolicy.com/2021/04/28/what-comes-after-the-forever-wars/ (accessed 28 December 2021).

20   Richard Wike, Jannell Fetterolf, and Mara Mordecai (2020) 'U.S. Image Plummet Internationally as Most Say Country Has Handled Coronavirus Badly', Washington, D.C.: Pew Research Center, September 2020. Available at: https://www.pewresearch.org/global/2020/09/15/us-image-plummets-internationally-as-most-say-country-has-handled-coronavirus-badly/ (accessed 17 February 2022).

21   Bruce Stokes (2017) 'Taking the measure of America's powers of attraction', RealClearWorld.com, 20 December. Available at: https://www.realclearworld.com/articles/2017/12/20/taking_the_measure_of_americas_powers_of_attraction_112668.html?utm_source=rcp-today&utm_medium=email&utm_campaign=mailchimp-newsletter&utm_source=RC+World+Today&utm_campaign=42d64bb899-RSS_EMAIL_CAMPAIGN&utm_medium=email&utm_term=0_d519acabbf-42d64bb899-83781601 (accessed 17 February 2022).

22   Stephen M. Walt (2021) 'The myth of American exceptionalism', *Foreign Policy*, 11 October. Available at: https://foreignpolicy.com/2011/10/11/the-myth-of-american-exceptionalism/ (accessed 28 December 2021).

23   Burnett (2020), p. 2.

24   Whitlock (2019).

25   Whitlock (2019).

26   Whitlock (2019).

27   The White House (2022) *The Build Back Better Framework: President Biden's Plan to Rebuild the Middle Class*, Washington, D.C. Available at: https://www.whitehouse.gov/build-back-better/ (accessed 13 January 2022).

28   Samuel Stebbins, Michael B. Sauter and Evan Comen (2020) 'Infrastructure crisis across the US: assessing the conditions of roads, bridges and railways by state', *USA Today*, 16 July. Available at: https://eu.usatoday.com/story/money/2020/07/16/infrastructure-states-bridges-roads-falling-apart/112127156/ (accessed 13 January 2022).

29   Hannah Sarisohn and Jay Croft (2022) 'Pennsylvania officials agree to spend $25 million to replace a Pittsburgh bridge one week after it collapsed', *CNN*, 4 February. Available at: https://edition.cnn.com/2022/02/04/us/pennsylvania-bridge-repair/index.html (accessed 10 February 2022).

30   Adie Tomer, Caroline George, and Joseph W. Kane (2023) 'The start of America's infrastructure decade: how macroeconomic factors may shape local strategies'. Washington, D.C.: The Brookings Institution, 1 February. Available at: https://www.brookings.edu/research/the-start-of-americas-infrastructure-decade-how-macroeconomic-factors-may-shape-local-strategies/ (accessed 5 February 2023).

31   De Long and Eichengreen (1991).

32   Ruth Benedict (1989) *The Chrysanthemum and the Sword: Patterns of Japanese Culture*, Boston: Houghton Mifflin.

33   Robert E. Wood (1986) *From Marshall Plan to Debt Crisis: Foreign Aid and Development Choices in the World Economy*, Berkeley: University of California Press, p. 1.

34   Jervis (1997), p. 6.

35   Burnett (2020), p. 2.

36   Manners (2002), pp. 235–58.

37   The term 'structural violence' was introduced by Johan Galtung (1969) in his paper 'Violence, peace, and peace research', *Journal of Peace Research*, Vol. 6, Issue 3, pp. 167–91.

38   Shada Islam (2023) 'The taboos are falling fast as the EU embraces the far-right racist approach to migration', *The Guardian*, 15 February. Available at: https://www.theguardian.com/world/commentisfree/2023/feb/15/eu-far-right-migration-fortress-europe (accessed 16 February 2023).

39   Richard Perkins and Eric Neumayer (2010) 'The organized hypocrisy of ethical foreign policy: human rights, democracy and Western arms sales', *Geoforum*, Vol. 41, Issue 2, pp. 247–56.

40   Dan Stone (2017) *Concentration Camps: A Short History*, Oxford: Oxford University Press, pp. 11–12.

41   Andrew Moravcsik (2005) 'The European constitutional compromise and the neofunctionalist legacy', *Journal of European Public Policy*, Vol. 12, Issue 2, pp. 349–86.

42   Moravscik (2005), p. 350.

43   Moravscik (2005), p. 351.

44   Zosia Wanat and Lili Bayer (2021) 'Brussels takes step toward rule-of-law penalty process with Poland, Hungary', *Politico*, 19 November. Available at: https://www.politico.eu/article/eu-rule-of-law-penalty-process-poland-hungary/ (accessed 13 January 2022).

45   Anh Thu Nguyen (2020) 'Macron's call for a European army: still echoing or forgotten?', European Law Blog, 22 June. Available at: https://europeanlawblog.eu/2020/06/22/macrons-call-for-a-european-army-still-echoing-or-forgotten/ (accessed 13 January 2022).

46   Sébastian Seibt (2021) 'With its "Global Gateway", EU tries to compete with China's Belt and Road Initiative', *France24*, 3 December. Available at: https://www.france24.com/en/europe/20211203-with-its-global-gateway-eu-tries-to-compete-with-the-china-s-belt-and-road (accessed 13 January 2022).

47   Mikaela Gavas and Samuel Pleeck (2021) 'The EU's global gateway is not a groundbreaking plan for domination in global infrastructure', *Center for Global Development*, 6 December. Available at: https://www.cgdev.org/blog/eus-global-gateway-not-groundbreaking-plan-domination-global-infrastructure (accessed 13 January 2022).

48 Andrea Moreschi (2021) 'The EU Global Gateway: the narrow path between relevance and invisibility', *Observer Research Foundation*, 23 December. Available at: https://www.orfonline.org/expert-speak/the-eu-global-gateway/ (accessed 13 January 2022).

49 Islam (2023).

50 Annette Jünemann, Nikolas Scherer, Nicolas Fromm (eds.) (2017) *Fortress Europe? Challenges and Failures of Migration and Asylum Policies*, Wiesbaden: Springer VS.

51 Islam (2023).

52 Deutsche Press-Agentur (2019) 'New EU commission: what challenges await von der Leyen?', 2 December. Available at: https://ednh.news/new-eu-commission-what-challenges-await-von-der-leyen/ (accessed 27 August 2022).

53 M. Rodrigues, I. Hindriks, A. Burgess, et al. (2021) *Support study for the TEN-T policy review, concerning relevant national plans and programs in Member States: Final report*, Publications Office, European Commission, Directorate-General for Mobility and Transport, pp. 90–3. Available at: https://data.europa.eu/doi/10.2832/27595 (accessed 18 January 2022).

54 Frédéric Simon (2022) 'Electricity market "not to blame for current crisis", EU agency concludes', EURACTIV, 29 April. Available at: https://www.euractiv.com/section/electricity/news/electricity-market-not-to-blame-for-current-crisis-eu-agency-concludes/ (accessed 27 August 2022).

55 Jacques (2009), pp. 240–4.

56 Michele Gelfand (2018) *Rule Makers, Rule Breakers: Tight and Loose Cultures and the Secret Signals That Direct Our Lives*, New York: Scribner.

57 Geert Hofstede and Gert Jan Hofstede (2005) *Cultures and Organizations: Software of the Mind*, New York: McGraw-Hill.

58 The peer-reviewed paper upon which Gelfand's book is based is Michele J. Gelfand et al (2011) 'Differences between tight and loose cultures: A 33-nation study', *Science*, Vol. 332, Issue 6033, pp. 1100–4.

59 Dickson (2016).

60 Byung-Chul Han (2017) *In the Swarm: Digital Prospects*, Cambridge, MA: The MIT Press, p. 17.

61 David Shambaugh (2021) *China's Leaders: From Mao to Now*, Cambridge, UK: Polity Press.

62 Nina Lakhani (2021) 'Why the collapse of Biden's Build Back Better would be a major blow to the climate fight', *The Guardian*, 22 December. Available at: https://www.theguardian.com/us-news/2021/dec/22/joe-biden-build-back-better-climate-crisis-consequences (accessed 28 December 2021).

63 Tanya Snyder (2022) 'Biden's incredible shrinking infrastructure plan', *Politico*, 17 June. Available at: https://www.politico.com/news/2022/06/17/democrats-shrinking-infrastructure-plan-00039588 (accessed 16 February 2023).

64 Simone Tagliapietra (2021), 'The Global Gateway: a real step towards a stronger Europe in the world?', Bruegel, 7 December. Available at: https://www.bruegel.org/blog-post/global-gateway-real-step-towards-stronger-europe-world (accessed 27 August 2022).

65 Shambaugh (2013), pp. 174–5.

66 Mercy A. Kuo (2021) 'Global Gateway: the EU's alternative to China's BRI'. *The Diplomat*, 28 September. Available at: https://thediplomat.com/2021/09/global-gateway-the-eu-alternative-to-chinas-bri/ (accessed 9 November 2021).

67 Pamela Blackmon (2014) 'Determinants of developing country debt: the revolving door of debt rescheduling through the Paris Club and export credits', *Third World Quarterly*, Vol. 35, Issue 8, pp. 1423–40.

68 Kenderdine and Ling (2018).

69 Tomer et al (2023).

70 Yang Wanli (2021) 'High-speed rail network expands past 40,000 km', *China Daily*, 31 December. Available at: https://www.chinadailyhk.com/article/254073 (accessed 19 January 2022).

71 Alexander Lew (2007) 'Today in history: Train Grand Vitesse (TGV) delivers first passengers to Lyon', *Wired*, 27 September. Available at: https://www.wired.com/2007/09/today-in-hist-3/ (accessed 19 January 2022).

72 Ben Jones (2021) 'Past, present and future: the evolution of China's incredible high-speed rail network', *CNN*, 27 December. Available at: https://edition.cnn.com/travel/article/china-high-speed-rail-cmd/index.html (accessed 19 January 2022).

73 Sharon LaFraniere (2011) 'Design flaws cited in deadly train crash in China', *New York Times*, 28 December. Available at: https://www.nytimes.com/2011/12/29/world/asia/design-flaws-cited-in-china-train-crash.html (accessed 19 January 2022).

74 Jones (2021).

75 Sukhan Jackson and Adrian Sleigh (2000) 'Resettlement for China's Three Gorges Dam: socio-economic impact and institutional tensions', *Communist and Post-Communist Studies*, Vol. 33, Issue 2, pp. 223–41.

76 Jonathan Hillman (2021) *The Digital Silk Road: China's Quest to Wire the World and Win the Future*, London: Profile Books, p. 56.

77 International Monetary Fund (2022) GDP, current prices (by region). Available at: https://www.imf.org/external/datamapper/NGDPD@WEO/OEMDC/ADVEC/WEOWORLD (accessed 18 January 2022).

78 Iyanatul Islam and Anis Chowdhury (1997) *Asia-Pacific Economies: A Survey*, London and New York: Routledge.

79 International Monetary Fund (2021) *Asia and Pacific: Navigating Waves of New Variants: Pandemic Resurgence Slows the Recovery*, World Economic and Financial Surveys, Washington, D.C., p. 1. Available at: https://www.imf.org/en/Publications/REO/APAC/Issues/2021/10/15/regional-economic-outlook-for-asia-and-pacific-october-2021 (accessed 18 January 2022).

80 Garlick and Havlová (2020).

81 M. Taylor Fravel (2019) *Active Defense: China's Military Strategy since 1949*, Princeton: Princeton University Press.

82 *China's Military Strategy* (2015), Defence White Paper, Beijing: the State Council, 27 May. Available at: http://english.www.gov.cn/archive/white_paper/2015/05/27/content_281475115610833.htm (accessed 21 January 2022).

83 Weiying Zhang (2018) *Game Theory and Society*, Abingdon: Routledge, p. 34.

Chapter 4

1 Xi Jinping (2014) 'Work together to build the Silk Road Economic Belt', in *The Governance of China*, Beijing: Foreign Languages Press, pp. 315–9.

2 Xi Jinping (2014) 'Work together to build a 21st-century Maritime Silk Road', in *The Governance of China*, Beijing: Foreign Languages Press, pp. 320–4.

3   Xi (2014), pp. 317–8.

4   The speech was filmed and can be viewed at https://www.youtube.com/
watch?v=1jEco0VWYig (accessed 10 February 2022).

5   *Vision and Actions on Jointly Building Silk Road Economic Belt and 21st-Century
Maritime Silk Road* (2015) Ministry of Foreign Affairs of the People's Republic of
China, 28 March. Available at: https://www.fmprc.gov.cn/eng/topics_665678/2015zt/
xjpcxbayzlt2015nnh/201503/t20150328_705553.html (accessed 4 March 2023).

6   Jeremy Garlick (2022) *Reconfiguring the China-Pakistan Economic Corridor: Geo-
Economic Pipe Dreams versus Geopolitical Realities*, Abingdon: Routledge, p. 40.

7   Kerry Brown (2015) 'The security implications of China's Belt and Road', *The
Diplomat*, 27 November. Available at: https://thediplomat.com/2015/11/the-security-
implications-of-chinas-belt-and-road/ (accessed 2 March 2022); Natasha Kuhrt
(2015) 'Is sinocentrism putting Russia's interests at risk?' *East Asia Forum Quarterly*,
Vol. 7, Issue 3, pp. 21–3; Justyna Szczudlik-Tatar (2015) '"One Belt, One Road":
Mapping China's new diplomatic strategy', *PISM Bulletin*, Vol. 67, Issue 799, 2 July.
Available at: https://www.files.ethz.ch/isn/192200/Bulletin%20PISM%20no%20
67%20(799)%202%20July%202015.pdf (accessed 2 March 2022).

8   There are two music videos made by New China TV (a subsidiary of the state
news channel Xinhua) promoting the BRI on YouTube: 'The Belt and Road Is
How'. Available at: https://www.youtube.com/watch?v=M0lJc3PMNIg (accessed
17 February 2022); and 'The Belt and Road, Sing Along'. Available at: https://www.
youtube.com/watch?v=98RNh7rwyf8 (accessed 17 February 2022).

9   For an entertaining example of the 'sinister bid' perspective, see China Uncensored
(2017) 'China's global domination plan: One Belt, One Road'. Available at: https://
www.youtube.com/watch?v=zLKgGyBO5x8 (accessed 2 March 2022). For an
example of an optimistic interpretation at the other end of the spectrum, see
Michael Dunford and Weidong Liu (2019) 'Chinese perspectives on the Belt and
Road Initiative', *Cambridge Journal of Regions, Economy and Society*, Vol. 12, Issue 1,
pp. 145–67.

10 Chinese scholars who visited Prague in March 2016 at the time of Xi Jinping's visit to
the city insisted that the BRI had purely economic goals.

11 Stephen Hoadley and Jian Yang (2007) 'China's cross-regional FTA initiatives:
towards comprehensive national power', *Pacific Affairs*, Vol. 80, Issue 2, pp. 327–48.

12 For a transportation-centric account of the BRI, see Richard T. Griffiths (2017)
Revitalising the Silk Road: China's Belt and Road Initiative, Leiden: HIPE
Publications.

13 Sean Golden (2011) 'China's perception of risk and the concept of comprehensive
national power', *The Copenhagen Journal of Asian Studies*, Vol. 29, Issue 2, pp. 79–109.

14 Xi Jinping (2014) 'New Asian Security Concept for New Progress in Security
Cooperation', Ministry of Foreign Affairs (PRC), 21 May. Available at: https://www.
fmprc.gov.cn/mfa_eng/wjdt_665385/zyjh_665391/201405/t20140527_678163.html
(accessed 4 March 2023).

15 Jeremy Mark (2021) 'China's real "debt trap" threat', *New Atlanticist*, 13 December.
Available at: https://www.atlanticcouncil.org/blogs/new-atlanticist/chinas-real-debt-
trap-threat/ (accessed 28 August 2022).

16 Emilian Kavalski (2013) 'The struggle for recognition of normative powers:
normative power Europe and normative power China in context', *Cooperation and
Conflict*, Vol. 48, Issue 2, pp. 247–67.

17 Weifeng Zhou and Mario Esteban (2018) 'Beyond balancing: China's approach towards the Belt and Road Initiative', *Journal of Contemporary China*, Vol. 27, Issue 112, pp. 487–501.

18 Lina Benabdallah (2020) *Shaping the Future of Power: Knowledge Production and Network-Building in China-Africa Relations*, Ann Arbor: University of Michigan Press.

19 Important books on BRI include the following: Jonathan Hillman (2020) *The Emperor's New Road: China and the Project of the Century*, New Haven and London: Yale University Press; Bruno Maçães (2018) *Belt and Road: A Chinese World Order*, London: Hurst & Co.; Nadège Rolland (2017) *China's Eurasian Century? Political and Strategic Implications of the Belt and Road Initiative*, Seattle: The National Bureau of Asian Research; Li Xing (ed.) (2019) *Mapping China's 'One Belt One Road' Initiative*, Cham: Palgrave Macmillan; Alfred Gerstl and Ute Wallenböck (eds.) (2021) *China's Belt and Road Initiative: Strategic and Economic Impacts on Central Asia, Southeast Asia, and Central Eastern Europe*, Abingdon: Routledge; and Igor Rogelja and Konstantinos Tsimonis (2023) *Belt and Road: The First Decade*, Newcastle Upon Tyne: Agenda Publishing.

20 Feng Huiyun (2009) 'Is China a Revisionist Power?' *Chinese Journal of International Politics*, Vol. 2, Issue 3, pp. 313–34.

21 At the time of writing, it appeared that Xi Jinping was almost certain to be reappointed Chairman of the CCP and President of China for another five years at the Party's 20th National Congress in November 2022. Official discourse was anointing him the 'unquestionable "core" leader of the CCP'. See Bill Bishop (2022) 'China's political discourse July 2022: Setting the tone for the 20th National Congress', *Sinocism*, 27 August. Available at: https://sinocism.com/p/chinas-political-discourse-july-2022?utm_source=email&triedSigningIn=true (accessed 28 August 2022).

22 Garlick (2020, 2022).

23 Kong Soon Lim (2018) 'China's Arctic policy and the Polar Silk Road vision', in Lassi Heininen and Heather Exner-Pirot (eds.) *Arctic Yearbook 2018*, Akureyri: Northern Research Forum, pp. 420–32. Available at: SSRN: https://ssrn.com/abstract=3603710.

24 See for instance: Go Yamada and Stefania Palma (2018, 28 March) 'Is China's Belt and Road working?' Washington, D.C.: Center for Strategic and International Studies (CSIS). Available at: https://reconasia.csis.org/is-china-belt-and-road-working/ (accessed 24 February 2022).

25 David Shambaugh (2013) *China Goes Global: The Partial Power*, New York: Oxford University Press, pp. 174–5.

26 David Shambaugh (2021) *China's Leaders: From Mao to Now*, Cambridge: Polity Press, p. 335.

27 George T. Yu (1971) 'Working on the railroad: China and the Tanzania-Zambia railway', *Asian Survey*, Vol. 11, Issue 11, pp. 1101–17.

28 Garlick (2022), p. 59.

29 Garlick (2022), p. 16.

30 See Garlick (2022) and Chapter 5 of this book for more details.

31 Ayman Falak Medina (2021) 'The completed China-Laos railway: bringing opportunities for ASEAN and the Asia-Pacific', *ASEAN Briefing*, 21 December. Available at: https://www.aseanbriefing.com/news/the-completed-china-laos-railway/ (accessed 18 February 2022).

32 Garlick (2022).

33 Siegfried O. Wolf (2020) *The China-Pakistan Economic Corridor of the Belt and Road Initiative: Concept, Context and Assessment*, Cham: Springer, pp. 45–6.

34 Hans-Peter Brunner (2013) *What Is Economic Corridor Development and What Can It Achieve in Asia's Subregions?* Asian Development Bank Working Paper No. 117. Available at: https://www.econstor.eu/bitstream/10419/109610/1/wp-117.pdf (accessed 4 March 2023).

35 Garlick (2020), p. 106.

36 Joanna Lillis (2022) 'Kyrgyzstan, Kazakhstan: billions vanish into black hole on border with China', *Eurasianet*, 17 February. Available at: https://eurasianet.org/kyrgyzstan-kazakhstan-billions-vanish-into-black-hole-on-border-with-china (accessed 18 February 2022).

37 Joanna Lillis (2022) 'Kazakhstan promises to smash smuggling rings on Chinese border', *Eurasianet*, 2 February. Available at: https://eurasianet.org/kazakhstan-promises-to-smash-smuggling-rings-on-chinese-border.

38 Alessandro Rippa (2019) 'Cross-border trade and "The Market" between Xinjiang (China) and Pakistan', *Journal of Contemporary Asia*, Vol. 49, No. 2, p. 260.

39 Jamil Nagri (2021) 'Closure of China border brings economic woes for GB people', *Dawn*, 11 January. Available at: https://www.dawn.com/news/1600923 (accessed 23 March 2022).

40 This point is covered at more length in my 2022 book, *Reconfiguring the China-Pakistan Economic Corridor: Geo-Economic Pipe Dreams Versus Geopolitical Realities* (Abingdon: Routledge), p. 39.

41 Garlick (2020).

42 John W. Garver and Fei-Ling Wang (2010) 'China's anti-encirclement struggle', *Asian Security*, Vol. 6, Issue 3, pp. 238–261.

43 Rush Doshi (2021) *The Long Game: China's Grand Strategy to Displace American Order*, New York: Oxford University Press, pp. 106–107.

44 Kavalski (2010).

45 Garlick and Havlová (2020).

46 David Shambaugh (2021) *Where Great Powers Meet: America & China in Southeast Asia*, New York: Oxford University Press, p. 143.

47 Jakub Jakóbowski and Marcin Kaczmarski (2017) 'Beijing's mistaken offer: the "16+1" and China's policy towards the European Union', Centre for Eastern Studies, *OSW Commentary* No. 250, 15 September. Available at: https://www.osw.waw.pl/en/publikacje/osw-commentary/2017-09-15/beijings-mistaken-offer-161-and-chinas-policy-towards-european (accessed 4 March 2022).

48 Horia Ciurtin (2019) 'The "16+1" becomes the "17+1": Greece joins China's dwindling cooperation framework in Central and Eastern Europe', *China Brief*, Vol. 19, Issue 10. Available at: https://jamestown.org/program/the-161-becomes-the-171-greece-joins-chinas-dwindling-cooperation-framework-in-central-and-eastern-europe/ (accessed 4 March 2022).

49 Stuart Lau (2021) 'Lithuania pulls out of China's "17+1" bloc in Eastern Europe', *Politico*, 21 May. Available at: https://www.politico.eu/article/lithuania-pulls-out-china-17-1-bloc-eastern-central-europe-foreign-minister-gabrielius-landsbergis/ (accessed 4 March 2022).

50 Finbarr Bermingham and Robert Delaney (2022) 'Estonia and Latvia leave China's 16+1 trade group for central and eastern European nations', *South China Morning Post*, 12 August. Available at: https://www.scmp.com/news/china/diplomacy/

article/3188599/estonia-and-latvia-leave-chinas-161-trade-group-central-and (accessed 28 August 2022).

51 Sudha Ramachandran (2020) 'Bangladesh buries the Sonadia deep-sea port project', *The Diplomat*, 12 October. Available at: https://thediplomat.com/2020/10/bangladesh-buries-the-sonadia-deep-sea-port-project/ (accessed 4 March 2022).

52 Garlick (2019), p. 445.

53 Agatha Kratz, Max J. Zenglein, and Gregor Sebastian (2021) *Chinese FDI in Europe: 2020 Update*, Berlin: Mercator Institute for China Studies (MERICS), p. 11. Available at: https://rhg.com/wp-content/uploads/2021/06/MERICSRhodium-GroupCOFDIUpdate2021.pdf (accessed 24 February 2022).

54 See: Ariel Cohen (2019) 'China's giant $400 billion Iran investment complicates U.S. options', *Forbes*, 19 September. Available at: https://www.forbes.com/sites/arielcohen/2019/09/19/chinas-giant-400-billion-iran-investment-snubs-trump/?sh=14aa37c084d1; and Farnaz Fassihi and Steven Lee Myers (2021) 'China, with $400 billion Iran deal, could deepen influence in Mideast', *The New York Times*, 27 March, available at: https://www.nytimes.com/2021/03/27/world/middleeast/china-iran-deal.html (both accessed 2 March 2022).

55 Jeremy Garlick and Radka Havlová (2021) 'The dragon dithers: assessing the cautious implementation of China's Belt and Road Initiative in Iran', *Eurasian Geography and Economics*, Vol. 62, Issue 4, p. 470.

56 Derek Scissors (2022) *China Global Investment Tracker*, Washington, D.C.: American Enterprise Institute. Available at: https://www.aei.org/china-global-investment-tracker/ (accessed 24 February 2022).

57 Asian Infrastructure Investment Bank (2021) Condensed Financial Statements (Unaudited) for the Nine Months Ended 30 September 2021. Available at: https://www.aiib.org/en/about-aiib/financial-statements/.content/index/pdf/AIIB_Q3-2021-Financial-Statements.pdf (accessed 24 February 2022).

58 Scissors (2022).

59 Scissors (2022).

60 John Hurley, Scott Morris, and Gailyn Portelance (2018) *Examining the Debt Implications of the Belt and Road Initiative from a Policy Perspective*, Washington, D.C.: Center for Global Development, Policy Paper 121. Available at: https://www.cgdev.org/publication/examining-debt-implications-belt-and-road-initiative-a-policy-perspective (accessed 4 March 2022).

61 See: Deborah Brautigam (2020) 'A critical look at Chinese "debt-trap diplomacy": The rise of a meme', *Area Development and Policy*, Vol. 5, Issue 1, pp. 1–14; Pádraig Carmody (2020) 'Dependence not debt-trap diplomacy', *Area Development and Policy*, Vol. 5, Issue 1, pp. 23–31; Lee Jones and Shahar Hameiri (2020) *Debunking the Myth of 'Debt-Trap Diplomacy': How Recipient Countries Shape China's Belt and Road Initiative*, London: Chatham House. Available at: https://www.chathamhouse.org/sites/default/files/2020-08-19-debunking-myth-debt-trap-diplomacy-jones-hameiri.pdf (accessed 4 March 2022); Ajit Singh (2021 'The myth of "debt-trap diplomacy" and realities of Chinese development finance', *Third World Quarterly*, Vol. 42, Issue 2, pp. 239–53.

62 Garlick (2022), p. 43.

63 Sezgi Cemiloğlu (2015) *China's Economic Engagement in Africa: A Case Study of Angola*, Frankfurt: Peter Lang.

64 Dionne Searcey, Michael Forsythe, and Eric Lipton (2021) 'A power struggle over cobalt rattles the clean energy revolution', *The New York Times*, 20 November.

Available at: https://www.nytimes.com/2021/11/20/world/china-congo-cobalt.html (accessed 27 February 2022).

65 Scissors (2022).

66 The phrase 'community of shared destiny' and its close relative 'community of shared interests' have been frequently used by Chinese leaders – most notably Xi Jinping – when speaking about the BRI, as has the expression 'mutually beneficial cooperation'. For instance, see Xi Jinping (2014) *The Governance of China*, Beijing: Foreign Languages Press, p. 317.

67 Mark Langan (2018) *Neo-Colonialism and the Poverty of Development in Africa*, Cham: Palgrave Macmillan.

68 Bräutigam (2020).

69 Jian Junbo and Donata Frasheri (2014) 'Neo-colonialism or de-colonialism? China's economic engagement in Africa and the implications for world order', *African Journal of Political Science and International Relations*, Vol. 8, Issue 7, pp. 185–201.

70 Zhao Tingyang (2006) 'Rethinking Empire from a Chinese Concept "All-under-Heaven" (Tian-xia, 天下)', *Social Identities*, Vol. 12, Issue 1, pp. 29–41.

71 Immanuel Wallerstein expounds upon what he calls the 'capitalist world system' in his 1979 collection of essays, *The Capitalist World-Economy* (Cambridge: Cambridge University Press). Susan Strange introduces the concept of structural power in her 1988 book *States and Markets* (London: Bloomsbury).

72 Hurley et al (2018).

73 Hurley et al (2018), p. 19.

74 Hurley et al (2018), pp. 4-5.

75 Hurley et al (2018), p. 21.

76 Bräutigam (2020), p. 12.

77 Bräutigam (2020), p. 7.

78 Bräutigam (2020), p. 8.

79 Bräutigam (2020), pp. 8-11.

80 See: Imtiaz Gul (2018) 'Pakistan's elite capture and the state of insecurity', in Aparna Pande (ed.) *Routledge Handbook of Contemporary Pakistan*, Abingdon, UK: Routledge, p. 196; and Feisal Khan (2018) 'The banking and financial sector of Pakistan', in Pande (ed.), p. 259.

81 Jones and Hameiri (2020).

82 Jones and Hameiri (2020), p. 27.

83 Jones and Hameiri (2020), p. 19.

84 Garlick and Havlová (2021), p. 470; Garlick (2022), p. 40.

85 Frank Holmes (2016) 'How gold helped South Korea repay its debt', *Business Insider*, 29 September. Available at: https://www.businessinsider.com/how-gold-helped-south-korea-repay-its-debt-2016-9 (accessed 30 March 2022).

86 *People's Daily*, 24 August 2001, 'South Korea pays off debt to IMF'. Available at: http://en.people.cn/english/200108/24/eng20010824_78160.html (accessed 30 March 2022).

87 Jonathan Holslag (2017) 'How China's New Silk Road Threatens European Trade', *The International Spectator*, Vol. 52, Issue 1, pp. 48–52.

88 Timothy R. Heath (2016) 'China's Evolving Approach to Economic Diplomacy', *Asia Policy*, Vol. 22, pp. 157–192.

89 William J. Norris (2016) *Chinese Economic Statecraft: Commercial Actors, Grand Strategy, and State Control*, Ithaca: Cornell University Press.

90	Shahar Hameiri and Lee Jones (2016) 'Rising powers and state transformation: the case of China', *European Journal of International Relations*, Vol. 22, Issue 1, pp. 72–98.
91	Garlick (2019).
92	Thomas J. Shattuck (2022) 'Lithuania fever in Taiwan: can China break it?' Philadelphia: Foreign Policy Research Institute, 26 January. Available at: https://www.fpri.org/article/2022/01/lithuania-fever-in-taiwan-can-china-break-it/ (accessed 30 March 2022).
93	Andrius Sytas and John O'Donnell (2021) 'China targets Lithuania by urging car firm to cut out pro-Taiwan country', *The Independent*, 17 December. Available at: https://www.independent.co.uk/asia/china/china-lithuania-car-continental-taiwan-b1977983.html (accessed 30 March 2022).
94	For a recent analysis of the 'fragmented authoritarianism' hypothesis from a range of angles, see Kjeld Erik Brødsgaard (ed.) (2017) *Chinese Politics as Fragmented Authoritarianism: Earthquakes, Energy and Environment*, Abingdon: Routledge. See also Andrew Mertha (2009) '"Fragmented authoritarianism 2.0": Political pluralization in the Chinese policy process', *The China Quarterly*, Vol. 200, pp. 995–1012.
95	William J. Norris (2021) 'China's post-Cold War economic statecraft: a periodization', *Journal of Current Chinese Affairs*, Vol. 50, Issue 3, pp. 294–316.
96	Richard Turcsányi and Eva Kachlíková (2020) 'The BRI and China's soft power in Europe: why Chinese narratives (initially) won', *Journal of Current Chinese Affairs*, Vol. 49, Issue 1, p. 60.
97	Joseph S. Nye Jr. (2004) *Soft Power: The Means to Success in World Politics*, New York: Public Affairs, p. 5.
98	Joseph S. Nye, Jr. (1990) 'Soft power', *Foreign Policy*, Issue 80, pp. 153–71.
99	Joseph S. Nye, Jr. (2011) *The Future of Power*, New York: Public Affairs, p. 82.
100	Nye (2011), p. 81.
101	Richard Wike, Janell Fetterolf, and Mara Mordecai (2020) 'U.S. image plummets internationally as most say country has handled coronavirus badly', Washington, D.C.: Pew Research Center, 15 September. Available at: https://www.pewresearch.org/global/2020/09/15/us-image-plummets-internationally-as-most-say-country-has-handled-coronavirus-badly/ (accessed 6 April 2022).
102	Laura Silver, Kat Devlin, and Christine Huang (2020) 'Unfavorable views of China reach historic highs in many countries', Washington, D.C.: Pew Research Center, 6 October. Available at: https://www.pewresearch.org/global/2020/10/06/unfavorable-views-of-china-reach-historic-highs-in-many-countries/ (accessed 6 April 2022).
103	Peter Martin (2021) *China's Civilian Army: The Making of Wolf Warrior Diplomacy*, New York: Oxford University Press.
104	For an account of the purported advantages of the BRI in terms of removing trade barriers, see Lianbiao Cui and Malin Song (2019) 'Economic evaluation of the Belt and Road Initiative from an unimpeded trade perspective', *International Journal of Logistics Research and Applications*, Vol. 22, Issue 1, pp. 25–46.
105	Ian Manners (2002) 'Normative power Europe: a contradiction in terms?' *Journal of Common Market Studies*, Vol. 40, Issue 2, pp. 235–58.
106	Thomas Diez (2013) 'Normative power as hegemony', *Cooperation and Conflict*, Vol. 48, Issue 2, pp. 194–210; Emilian Kavalski (2013) 'The struggle for recognition of normative powers: normative power Europe and normative power China in context', *Cooperation and Conflict*, Vol. 48, Issue 2, pp. 247–67.
107	Manners (2002), p. 253.

108 Emilian Kavalski (2010) 'Shanghaied into cooperation: framing China's socialization of Central Asia', *Journal of Asian and African Studies*, Vol. 45, Issue 2, pp. 131–145.

109 Dawn C. Murphy (2022) *China's Rise in the Global South: The Middle East, Africa, and Beijing's Alternative World Order*, Stanford: Stanford University Press, p. 277.

110 Daniel Deudney and G. John Ikenberry (1999) 'The nature and sources of liberal international order', *Review of International Studies*, Vol. 25, Issue 2, pp. 179–96.

111 John J. Mearsheimer (2019) 'Bound to fail: the rise and fall of the liberal international order', *International Security*, Vol. 43, Issue 4, pp. 7–50.

112 Hilary Clinton (2011) 'America's Pacific century', *Foreign Policy*, 11 October. Available at: https://foreignpolicy.com/2011/10/11/americas-pacific-century/ (accessed 5 April 2022).

113 Murphy (2022, p. 269) points out that 'BRI can be seen as a direct result of Sino-American competition.'

114 Tobita Chow and Jake Werner (2022) 'Don't assume Russia and China are on the same page. The US can work with China', *The Guardian*, 4 April. Available at: https://www.theguardian.com/commentisfree/2022/apr/04/us-china-relationship-xi (accessed 5 April 2022).

115 Murphy (2022), p. 252.

116 For an account of China's norm diffusion via the BRI, see Anastas Vangeli (2019) 'A framework for the study of the One Belt One Road initiative as a medium of principle diffusion', in Li Xing (ed.) *Mapping China's 'One Belt One Road' Initiative*, Cham: Palgrave Macmillan, pp. 57–89.

Chapter 5

1 Valentina Romei and John Reed (2019) 'The Asian century is set to begin', *Financial Times*, 26 March. Available at: https://www.ft.com/content/520cb6f6-2958-11e9-a5ab-ff8ef2b976c7 (accessed 12 April 2022).

2 Kishore Mahbubani (2022) *The Asian 21st Century*, Singapore: Springer, p. 11.

3 As Pál Nyíri and Danielle Tan point out in their introduction to their multi-authored study of China's influence in Southeast Asia, it is surprising and disappointing that there has been far less focus in the English-language literature on China's interactions with its neighbouring regions such as Southeast Asia than on Africa. See Pál Nyíri and Danielle Tan (2017) 'Introduction: China's "rise" in Southeast Asia from a bottom-up perspective', in Pál Nyíri and Danielle Tan, *Chinese Encounters in Southeast Asia: How People, Money, and Ideas from China Are Changing a Region*, Seattle: University of Washington Press, p. 7.

4 Australian Government (2017) 'ASEAN's economic growth'. Available at: https://www.austrade.gov.au/asean-now/why-asean-matters-to-australia/asean-economic-growth/ (accessed 28 April 2022).

5 Axel Berkofsky (2018) 'US freedom of navigation operations (FONOPs) in the South China Sea: able to keep Chinese territorial expansionism in Check?', in Marco Clementi, Matteo Dian and Barbara Pisciotta, *US Foreign Policy in a Challenging World: Building Order on Shifting Foundations*, Cham: Springer, pp. 339–56.

6 For a thorough review of the literature and analysis of the hedging behaviour of Southeast Asian states in the face of US-China regional rivalry, see David Shambaugh (2021) *Where Great Powers Meet: America & China in Southeast Asia*, New York: Oxford University Press.

7   The concept of hedging was first applied to Southeast Asia by Evelyn Goh and Cheng-Chwee Kuik. See: Evelyn Goh (2005) *Meeting the China Challenge: The U.S. in Southeast Asian Regional Security Strategies*, Washington, D.C.: East-West Center; and Cheng-Chwee Kuik (2008) 'The essence of hedging: Malaysia and Singapore's response to a rising China', *Contemporary Southeast Asia*, Vol. 30, Issue 2, pp. 159–85. For a recent update of the concept and critique of the debate so far, see David Martin Jones and Nicole Jenne (2022) 'Hedging and grand strategy in Southeast Asian foreign policy', *International Relations of the Asia-Pacific*, Vol. 22, Issue 2, pp. 205–35.

8   Wang Yuzhu (2021) 'Hedging strategy: concept, behavior, and implications for China-ASEAN relations', *East Asian Affairs*, Vol. 1, Issue 2, p. 31.

9   Shambaugh (2021) *Where Great Powers Meet*.

10   Nyíri and Tan (2017), p. 5.

11   Goh (2005), Kuik (2008) and Shambaugh (2021).

12   Shambaugh (2021) *Where Great Powers Meet*, p. 243.

13   Nie Wenjuan (2015) 'Dengmeng duihua de shenfen dingwei yu zhanlue fenxi' ['An analysis of ASEAN views of and strategies towards China'], *Dangdai Yatai* (Journal of Contemporary Asia-Pacific Studies), vol. 1, pp. 21–37.

14   Jeffrey Becker (2017) 'What is the PLA's role in promoting China-Cambodia relations?', *The Diplomat*, 29 April. Available at: https://thediplomat.com/2017/04/what-is-the-plas-role-in-promoting-china-cambodia-relations/ (accessed 28 April 2022).

15   Megha Bahree (2014) 'In Cambodia, a close friendship with the PM leads to vast wealth for one power couple', *Forbes*, 24 September. Available at: https://www.forbes.com/sites/meghabahree/2014/09/24/who-you-know-inc-in-cambodia-a-close-friendship-with-the-pm-leads-to-vast-wealth-for-one-power-couple/ (accessed 23 April 2022).

16   Bill Hayton (2014) *The South China Sea: The Struggle for Power in Asia*, New Haven: Yale University Press, p. 83.

17   There are many people of Vietnamese origin who are citizens of the Czech Republic. Those I have taught at Prague University of Economics and Business have confirmed the general Vietnamese mistrust of China.

18   Jason McMann (2022) 'In the Indo-Pacific, Country Favorability Is Closely Tied to Business Opportunities for U.S. and Chinese Companies', Morning Consult, 14 June. Available at: https://morningconsult.com/2022/06/14/indo-pacific-relations-country-favorability/ (accessed 9 February 2023).

19   Stephen L. Morgan (2021) *The Chinese Economy*, Newcastle upon Tyne: Agenda Publishing, p. 102.

20   Ayman Falak Medina (2021) 'The completed China-Laos railway: bringing opportunities for ASEAN and the Asia-Pacific', *ASEAN Briefing*, 21 December. Available at: https://www.aseanbriefing.com/news/the-completed-china-laos-railway/ (accessed 24 April 2022).

21   Latsamy Phonevilay (2022) 'Over 1 million passengers ride Laos-China railway', *The Laotian Times*, 1 February. Available at: https://laotiantimes.com/2022/02/01/over-1-million-passengers-ride-laos-china-railway/#:~:text=Over%201%20million%20passengers%20have,cargo%20since%20its%20official%20opening (accessed 12 June 2022).

22   Shambaugh (2021) *Where Great Powers Meet*, p. 204.

23   John Hurley, Scott Morris and Gailyn Portelance (2018) *Examining the Debt Implications of the Belt and Road Initiative from a Policy Perspective*, Washington, D.C.: Center for Global Development, Policy Paper 121, p. 17.

24 Axel Dreher, Andreas Fuchs, Bradley Parks, Austin Strange and Michael J. Tierney (2022) *Banking on Beijing: The Aims and Impacts of China's Overseas Development Program*, Cambridge: Cambridge University Press, p. 119.

25 Marimi Kishimoto (2017) 'Laos merely a bystander as China pushes Belt and Road ambitions', *Nikkei Asian Review*, 6 October. Available at: https://asia.nikkei.com/ Economy/Laos-merely-a-bystander-as-China-pushes-Belt-and-Road-ambitions (accessed 25 April 2022).

26 Luke Hunt (2021) 'In the face of criticism, Laos pushes ahead with four Mekong dams', *The Diplomat*, 14 January. Available at: https://thediplomat.com/2021/01/in-the-face-of-criticism-laos-pushes-ahead-with-four-mekong-dams/ (accessed 25 April 2022).

27 Sebastian Strangio (2021) 'Chinese casino magnate's empire set to expand in Laos', *The Diplomat*, 8 April. Available at: https://thediplomat.com/2021/04/chinese-casino-magnates-empire-set-to-expand-in-laos/ (accessed 25 April 2022).

28 Dreher et al (2022), p. 117.

29 Davis Florick (2021) 'Cambodia is China's leverage point on ASEAN', *East Asia Forum*, 15 December. Available at: https://www.eastasiaforum.org/2021/12/15/ cambodia-is-chinas-leverage-point-on-asean/ (accessed 25 April 2022).

30 Hannah Ellis-Petersen (2018) '"No Cambodia left": how Chinese money is changing Sihanoukville', *The Guardian*, 31 July. Available at: https://www.theguardian.com/ cities/2018/jul/31/no-cambodia-left-chinese-money-changing-sihanoukville (accessed 25 April 2022).

31 *Bloomberg* (2022) 'China signs deal with Cambodia army, rebuffing U.S. warnings', 31 March. Available at: https://www.bloomberg.com/news/articles/2022-03-31/china-signs-cooperation-deal-with-cambodia-army-amid-u-s-strain (accessed 25 April 2022).

32 Florick (2021) 'Cambodia is China's leverage point on ASEAN'.

33 *Bloomberg* (2022) 'China signs deal with Cambodia army'.

34 Beth Walker (2014) 'Anti-Chinese sentiment on rise in Myanmar', *China Dialogue*, 13 May. Available at: https://chinadialogue.net/en/business/6969-anti-chinese-sentiment-on-rise-in-myanmar/ (accessed 28 August 2022).

35 Anne Barker (2021) 'China and the Philippines' tense stand-off over Scarborough Shoal leaves fishermen in fear', *ABC News*, 25 May. Available at: https://www.abc.net. au/news/2021-05-26/china-philippines-stand-off-over-scarborough-shoal/100145586 (accessed 2 May 2022).

36 Cliff Venzon (2020) 'Philippines set to fix airstrip on South China Sea island', *Nikkei Asia*, 9 June. Available at: https://asia.nikkei.com/Politics/International-relations/ South-China-Sea/Philippines-set-to-fix-airstrip-on-South-China-Sea-island (accessed 2 May 2022).

37 Shambaugh (2021) *Where Great Powers Meet*, p. 236.

38 McMann (2022).

39 Shambaugh (2021) *Where Great Powers Meet*, p. 218.

40 McMann (2022).

41 Philip Wen (2018) 'Mahathir says China will sympathize with Malaysia's problems', *Reuters*, 20 August. Available at: https://www.reuters.com/article/us-china-malaysia-trade-idUSKCN1L5070 (accessed 2 May 2022).

42 Stefania Palma (2018) 'Malaysia cancels China-backed pipeline projects', *Financial Times*, 9 September. Available at: https://archive.ph/AUCVK (accessed 2 May 2022).

43 State Council of the People's Republic of China (2018) 'State councilor meets with Malaysian PM', 2 August. Available at: http://english.www.gov.cn/state_council/state_councilors/2018/08/02/content_281476245621468.htm (accessed 2 May 2022).

44 Shambaugh (2021) *Where Great Powers Meet*, p. 169.

45 Shambaugh (2021) *Where Great Powers Meet*, p. 218.

46 Alfred Gerstl (2020) 'Malaysia's hedging strategy towards China under Mahathir Mohamad (2018-2020): direct engagement, limited balancing, and limited bandwagoning', *Journal of Current Chinese Affairs*, Vol. 49, Issue 1, pp. 106–131.

47 Shambaugh (2021) *Where Great Powers Meet*, p. 188.

48 Benjamin Zawacki (2021) *Thailand: Shifting Ground between the US and a Rising China* (2nd ed.), London: Zed Books.

49 Shambaugh (2021) *Where Great Powers Meet*, p. 192.

50 Shambaugh (2021) *Where Great Powers Meet*, p. 187.

51 Ian Storey (2015) *Thailand's Post-Coup Relations with China and America: More Beijing, Less Washington* (Trends in Southeast Asia, no. 20), Singapore: ISEAS-Yusof Ishak Institute, p. 17.

52 Shambaugh (2021) *Where Great Powers Meet*, p. 189.

53 Ian Storey (2019) 'Thailand's military relations with China: moving from strength to strength', *Perspective*, No. 43, 27 May, p. 2. Available at: https://www.iseas.edu.sg/images/pdf/ISEAS_Perspective_2019_43.pdf (accessed 4 May 2022).

54 Patrick Jory (2017) 'Enter the dragon: Thailand gets closer to China', *The Lowy Interpreter*, 7 July. Available at: https://www.lowyinstitute.org/the-interpreter/enter-dragon-thailand-gets-closer-china (accessed 4 May 2022).

55 Storey (2019), pp. 6-8.

56 Shambaugh (2021) *Where Great Powers Meet*, pp. 191-192.

57 Neill Fronde (2022) 'Rail to connect Thailand to China delayed 3 years to 2026', *Thaiger*, 19 January. Available at: https://thethaiger.com/hot-news/transport/rail-to-connect-thailand-to-china-delayed-3-years-to-2026 (accessed 5 May 2022).

58 Shambaugh (2021) *Where Great Powers Meet*, p. 228.

59 Shambaugh (2021) *Where Great Powers Meet*, p. 163.

60 Shambaugh (2021) *Where Great Powers Meet*, p. 131.

61 McMann (2022).

62 David Rogers (2022) 'Indonesia's high-speed railway to start commissioning in November', *Global Construction Review*, 13 April. Available at: https://www.globalconstructionreview.com/indonesias-high-speed-railway-to-start-commissioning-in-november/ (accessed 5 May 2022).

63 Ronna Nirmala (2021) 'Indonesia breaks ground on China-backed "green" industrial zone on Borneo', *Benar News*, 21 December. Available at: https://www.benarnews.org/english/news/indonesian/kalimantan-industrial-zone-12212021135837.html (accessed 5 May 2022).

64 Shambaugh (2021) *Where Great Powers Meet*, p. 230.

65 Shambaugh (2021) *Where Great Powers Meet*, p. 222.

66 U.S. Department of State (2021) 'U.S. relations with Singapore', 1 October. Available at: https://www.state.gov/u-s-relations-with-singapore/ (accessed 7 May 2022).

67 Wong Wee Kim (2010) *Census of Population 2010 Advance Census Release*, Singapore: Department of Statistics, Ministry of Trade & Industry, p. 5. Available at: https://web.archive.org/web/20120327064912/http://www.singstat.gov.sg/pubn/popn/c2010acr.pdf (accessed 7 May 2022).

68 Shambaugh (2021) *Where Great Powers Meet*, p. 222.

69   Observatory of Economic Complexity (OEC) (2021) *Singapore and China Trade*. Available at: https://oec.world/en/profile/bilateral-country/sgp/partner/chn?redirect=true (accessed 7 May 2022).

70   Graham Allison, Robert D. Blackwill and Ali Wyne (2013) *Lee Kuan Yew: The Grand Master's Insights on China, the United States, and the World*, Cambridge, MA: MIT Press, p. 7.

71   McMann (2022).

72   Derek Scissors (2022) *China Global Investment Tracker*, Washington, D.C.: American Enterprise Institute. Available at: https://www.aei.org/china-global-investment-tracker/ (accessed 7 May 2022).

73   Ministry of Foreign Affairs of the People's Republic of China (2019) 'Xi Jinping meets with Sultan Haji Hassanal Bolkiah of Brunei', 26 April. Available at: https://www.fmprc.gov.cn/mfa_eng/wjb_663304/zzjg_663340/yzs_663350/gjlb_663354/2691_663386/2693_663390/201904/t20190429_510445.html (accessed 7 May 2022).

74   Shambaugh (2021) *Where Great Powers Meet*, p. 221.

75   Ian Storey (2011) *Southeast Asia and the Rise of China: The Search for Security*, Abingdon: Routledge, p. 274.

76   David Hutt (2020) 'Timor-Leste's costly oil and gas ambitions grind to a halt', *The Diplomat*, 2 October. Available at: https://thediplomat.com/2020/10/timor-lestes-costly-oil-and-gas-ambitions-grind-to-a-halt/ (accessed 7 May 2022).

77   Storey (2011), pp. 282–3.

78   Kate Lyons and Dorothy Wickham (2022) 'The deal that shocked the world: inside the China-Solomons security pact', *The Guardian*, 20 April. Available at: https://www.theguardian.com/world/2022/apr/20/the-deal-that-shocked-the-world-inside-the-china-solomons-security-pact (accessed 7 May 2022).

79   Tess McClure (2022) 'New Zealand foreign minister blames "relationship failure" for China-Solomons security deal', *The Guardian*, 5 May. Available at: https://www.theguardian.com/world/2022/may/05/new-zealand-foreign-minister-blames-relationship-failure-for-china-solomons-security-deal (accessed 7 May 2022).

80   Nyíri and Tan (2017).

81   Jeremy Garlick (2022) *Reconfiguring the China-Pakistan Economic Corridor: Geo-Economic Pipe Dreams versus Geopolitical Realities*, London: Routledge.

82   McMann (2022).

83   Andrew Small (2015) *The China-Pakistan Axis: Asia's New Geopolitics*, Oxford: Oxford University Press.

84   See for instance: Gurpreet S. Khurana (2008) 'China's "string of pearls" in the Indian Ocean and its security implications', *Strategic Analysis*, Vol. 32, Issue 1, pp. 1–39; or Sumanta Bhattacharya, Jayanta Kumar Ray, Shakti Sinha and Bhavneet Kaur Sachdev (2021) 'Can India's necklace of diamonds strategy defeat the China's string of pearls', *International Journal of Recent Advances in Multidisciplinary Topics*, Vol. 2, Issue 11, pp. 105–8.

85   Tehran Times (2023) 'China launches direct shipping line to Iran's Chabahar port', 1 January. Available at: https://www.tehrantimes.com/news/480298/China-launches-direct-shipping-line-to-Iran-s-Chabahar-port (accessed 9 February 2023).

86   Soroush Aliasgary and Marin Ekstrom (2021) 'Chabahar port and Iran's strategic balancing with China and India', *The Diplomat*, 21 October. Available at: https://thediplomat.com/2021/10/chabahar-port-and-irans-strategic-balancing-with-china-and-india/ (accessed 9 February 2023).

87   Tehran Times (2023).

88   Hillary Clinton (2011) 'America's Pacific Century', *Foreign Policy*, 11 October. Available at: https://foreignpolicy.com/2011/10/11/americas-pacific-century/ (accessed 15 May 2022).

89   Savita Pande, Shefali Dhar and Sidhanta Mehra (2018) 'Introduction', in Aparna Pande (ed.) *Routledge Handobook of Contemporary Pakistan*, Abingdon, UK: Routledge, p. 2.

90   Garlick (2022).

91   Ayesha Siddiqa (2007) *Military Inc.: Inside Pakistan's Military Economy*, London: Pluto Press.

92   Sanskar Shrivastava (2009) 'US report: China gifted nuclear bomb and Pakistan acquired the technology', *The World Reporter*, 18 November. Available at: http://www.theworldreporter.com/2009/11/us-report-china-gifted-nuclear-bomb-and.html (accessed 13 May 2022).

93   Lu Shulin (2014/2015) 'China-Pakistan Economic Corridor: a flagship and exemplary project of "One Belt and One Road"', *Strategic Studies*, Vol. 34, Issue 4 / Vol. 35, No. 1, pp. 165–73.

94   CPEC official website (2022). Available at: http://cpec.gov.pk/ (accessed 15 May 2022).

95   Garlick (2022), p. 101.

96   Khalid Hasnain, Aamir Yasin, Manzoor Ali and Tahir Siddiqui (2022) 'Country swelters as power outages disrupt daily life', *Dawn*, 29 April. Available at: https://www.dawn.com/news/1687371 (accessed 13 May 2022).

97   Lu (2014/2015), p. 165.

98   Garlick (2022), p. 41.

99   Kazim Alam (2021) 'Short supply from Iran behind outages in Balochistan: minister', *Dawn*, 30 July. Available at: https://www.dawn.com/news/1637671 (accessed 13 May 2022).

100 Garlick (2022), p. 88.

101 Alessandro Rippa (2019) 'Cross-border trade and "the market" between Xinjiang (China) and Pakistan', *Journal of Contemporary Asia*, Vol. 49, Issue 2, p. 260.

102 Garlick (2022), p. 17.

103 Jeremy Garlick (2018) 'Deconstructing the China-Pakistan Economic Corridor: pipe dreams versus geopolitical realities', *Journal of Contemporary China*, Vol. 27, Issue 112, p. 526.

104 Kristina Kironska and Jeremy Garlick (2022) 'Pakistanis perceive China as their "best friend"', *The Diplomat*, 14 October. Available at: https://thediplomat.com/2022/10/pakistanis-perceive-china-as-their-best-friend/ (accessed 9 February 2023).

105 Safdar Khokhar (2022) 'Pak-China joint statement and future of Pakistani students', *Pakistan Observer*, 13 February. Available at: https://pakobserver.net/pak-china-joint-statement-and-future-of-pakistani-students-by-safdar-khokhar/ (accessed 12 June 2022).

106 Garlick (2022), p. 50.

107 Dreher et al (2022), p. 9.

108 Maria Abi-Habib (2018) 'How China got Sri Lanka to cough up a port', *The New York Times*, 25 June. Available at: https://www.nytimes.com/2018/06/25/world/asia/china-sri-lanka-port.html (accessed 15 May 2022).

109 Dreher et al (2022), p. 288 n16.

110 Saikiran Kannan (2021) 'Exclusive: revival of Hambantota port in Sri Lanka may strengthen China's position in Indian Ocean', *India Today*, 19 March.

Available at: https://www.indiatoday.in/world/story/revival-hambantota-port-sri-lanka-strengthen-china-position-indian-ocean-1781171-2021-03-19 (accessed 15 May 2022).

111 Larry Elliott (2022) 'Sri Lanka is the first domino to fall in the face of a global debt crisis', *The Guardian*, 9 May. Available at: https://www.theguardian.com/world/2022/may/09/sri-lanka-is-the-first-domino-to-fall-in-the-face-of-a-global-debt-crisis (accessed 15 May 2022).

112 Abi-Habib (2018).

113 Skandha Gunasekara and Mujib Mashal (2022) 'In blow to ruling family, Sri Lanka's prime minister quits in face of unrest', *The New York Times*, 9 May. Available at: https://www.nytimes.com/2022/05/09/world/asia/mahinda-rajapaksa-resigns-sri-lanka.html (accessed 15 May 2022).

114 Indrana Bagchi (2016) 'Dhaka cancels port to be built by China, India eyes another', *Times of India*, 8 February. Available at: https://timesofindia.indiatimes.com/india/dhaka-cancels-port-to-be-built-by-china-india-eyes-another/articleshow/50894554.cms (accessed 15 May 2022).

115 Dipanjan Roy Chaudhury (2020) 'Bangladesh drops plan to develop a deep-sea port at Sonadia island', *The Economic Times*, 15 October. Available at: https://economictimes.indiatimes.com/news/international/world-news/bangladesh-drops-plan-to-develop-a-deep-sea-port-at-sonadia-island/articleshow/78688376.cms (accessed 14 May 2022).

116 Shahidul Islam, Wuyi Wang and Laping Sheng (2022) 'The construction of Bangladesh-China-India-Myanmar Economic Corridor: current situation, problem, and countermeasures', *Asian Journal of Social Science Studies*, Vol. 7, Issue 4, pp. 10–24.

117 McMann (2022).

118 Hurley et al (2018), p. 17.

119 Anirban Bhaumik (2021) 'India pips China, inks deal to develop, support, maintain harbour at naval base in Maldives', *Deccan Herald*, 21 February. Available at: https://www.deccanherald.com/national/india-pips-china-inks-deal-to-develop-support-maintain-harbour-at-naval-base-in-maldives-953675.html (accessed 15 May 2022).

120 Lekhanath Pandey (2022) 'How infrastructure financing disagreements are hindering closer China-Nepal ties', *Deutsche Welle*, 28 March. Available at: https://www.dw.com/en/how-infrastructure-financing-disagreements-are-hindering-closer-china-nepal-ties/a-61282250 (accessed 16 May 2022).

121 Dipanjan Roy Chaudhury (2021) 'Nepalese businessmen launch protests against China's blockade of cross-border trade', *The Economic Times*, 30 January. Available at: https://economictimes.indiatimes.com/news/international/world-news/nepalese-businessmen-launch-protests-against-chinas-blockade-of-cross-border-trade/articleshow/80598132.cms?from=mdr (accessed 16 May 2022).

122 Hari Bansh Jha (2022) 'Nepal-China relations under the shadow of geopolitics', *Observer Research Foundation*, 5 April. Available at: https://www.orfonline.org/expert-speak/nepal-china-relations-under-the-shadow-of-geopolitics/ (accessed 16 May 2022).

123 Pandey (2022).

124 Manoj Joshi (2021) 'The China-Bhutan border deal should worry India', *Observer Research Foundation*, 22 October. Available at: https://www.orfonline.org/research/the-china-bhutan-border-deal-should-worry-india/ (accessed 16 May 2022).

125 Sudhi Ranjan Sen and Archana Chaudhary (2021) 'Bhutan struggles to defend territory in India-China border spat', *Bloomberg*, 8 December. Available at: https://www.bloomberg.com/news/articles/2021-12-08/bhutan-struggles-to-defend-territory-in-india-china-border-spat (accessed 16 May 2022).

126 Joshi (2021).

127 Ruby Osman (2021) 'Navigating the "graveyard of empires": what next for China-Afghan relations?' *Tony Blair Institute for Global Change*, 21 September. Available at: https://institute.global/institute/navigating-graveyard-empires-what-next-china-afghan-relations (accessed 17 May 2022).

128 Tao Mingyang and Chu Daye (2021) 'GT exclusive: Chinese firm's copper mine project in Afghanistan hasn't started, despite Taliban's push', *Global Times*, 16 December. Available at: https://www.globaltimes.cn/page/202112/1241686.shtml (accessed 17 May 2022).

129 Velina Tchakarova (2021) 'Will China get embroiled in the graveyard of empires?', *9dashline*, 29 July. Available at: https://www.9dashline.com/article/will-china-get-embroiled-in-the-graveyard-of-empires (accessed 17 May 2022).

130 Ermek Baisalov (2021) 'Territorial disputes in Central Asia on the threshold of the 30th anniversary of independence', *Central Asian Bureau for Analytical Reporting*, 31 May. Available at: https://cabar.asia/en/territorial-disputes-in-central-asia-on-the-threshold-of-the-30th-anniversary-of-independence (accessed 18 May 2022).

131 *The Economist* (2019) 'Convoluted borders are hampering Central Asian integration', 31 October. Available at: https://www.economist.com/asia/2019/10/31/convoluted-borders-are-hampering-central-asian-integration (accessed 19 May 2022).

132 Kemel Toktomushev (2018) 'Understanding cross-border conflict in post-Soviet Central Asia: The case of Kyrgyzstan and Tajikistan', *Connections*, Vol. 17, Issue 1, pp. 21–41.

133 Aude Mazoue (2022) 'Russian intervention in Kazakhstan risks "destabilising" ethnic divides', *France24*, 7 January. Available at: https://www.france24.com/en/asia-pacific/20220107-russian-intervention-in-kazakhstan-risks-destabilising-its-ethnic-divides (accessed 18 May 2022).

134 Isabelle Khurshudyan (2022) 'Kazakhstan officials say 164 are dead in protests, country now "stabilized"', *The Washington Post*, 9 January. Available at: https://www.washingtonpost.com/world/2022/01/09/kazakhstan-protests-stabilized-russia/ (accessed 18 May 2022).

135 *Eurasianet* (2022) 'Tajikistan: at least one killed in Pamirs unrest', 17 May. Available at: https://eurasianet.org/tajikistan-at-least-one-killed-in-pamirs-unrest (accessed 18 May 2022).

136 Jakub Jakóbowski (2018) 'Chinese-led regional multilateralism in Central and Eastern Europe, Africa and Latin America: 16+1, FOCAC, and CCF', *Journal of Contemporary China*, Vol. 27, Issue 113, p. 659.

137 Jakóbowski (2018), p. 659.

138 Emilian Kavalski (2010) 'Shanghaied into cooperation: framing China's socialization of Central Asia', *Journal of Asian and African Studies*, Vol. 45, Issue 2, pp. 131–45.

139 Catherine Owen (2017) '"The sleeping dragon is gathering strength": Causes of Sinophobia in Central Asia', *China Quarterly of International Strategic Studies*, Vol. 3, Issue 1, pp. 101–19.

140 Raffaello Pantucci and Alexandros Petersen (2022) *Sinostan: China's Inadvertent Empire*, Oxford: Oxford University Press, p. 266.

141 Pantucci and Petersen (2022), pp. 234–5.

142 *Reuters* (2016) 'China to build outposts for Tajik guards on Tajikistan-Afghanistan border', 26 September. Available at: https://www.reuters.com/article/us-tajikistan-china-border-idUSKCN11W0T1 (accessed 18 May 2022).

143 Gerry Shih (2019) 'In Central Asia's forbidding highlands, a quiet newcomer: Chinese troops', *The Washington Post*, 18 February. Available at: https://thehighasia.com/in-central-asias-forbidding-highlands-a-quiet-newcomer-chinese-troops/ (accessed 18 May 2022).

144 Pantucci and Petersen (2022), p. 185.

145 Wade Shepherd (2016) 'Khorgos: Why Kazakhstan is building a "new Dubai" on the Chinese border', Forbes, 28 February. Available at: https://www.forbes.com/sites/wadeshepard/2016/02/28/will-a-place-called-khorgos-become-the-next-dubai/?sh=2c6549e8f4b7 (accessed 19 May 2022).

146 Emily Feng and Henry Foy (2017) 'China-Kazakhstan border woes dent Silk Road ambitions', *Financial Times*, 21 December. Available at: https://www.ft.com/content/1606d70a-9c31-11e7-8cd4-932067fbf946 (accessed 19 May 2022).

147 Jonathan E. Hillman (2018) *The Rise of China-Europe Railways*, Washington, D.C.: Center for Strategic & International Studies, 6 March. Available at: https://www.csis.org/analysis/rise-china-europe-railways (accessed 27 May 2022).

148 Feng and Foy (2017).

149 Andrew Higgins (2018) 'China's ambitious new "port": Landlocked Kazakhstan', *The New York Times*, 1 January. Available at: https://www.nytimes.com/2018/01/01/world/asia/china-kazakhstan-silk-road.html (accessed 27 May 2022).

150 Hillman (2018).

151 *Al Jazeera* (2022) 'UN resolution against Ukraine invasion: full text', 3 March 2022. Available at: https://www.aljazeera.com/news/2022/3/3/unga-resolution-against-ukraine-invasion-full-text (accessed 27 May 2022).

152 An excellent summary of the Sino-Soviet split, including eye-witness testimonies by some of the principals, can be found in the documentary *Cold War: China 1949-1972* (minutes 16:08-21:42), Turner Original Productions (1998). Available at: https://www.youtube.com/watch?v=gSPIonMrLq0 (accessed 28 May 2022).

153 Pantucci and Petersen (2022), p. 180.

154 John Power (2022) 'As Russia's isolation grows, China hints at limits of friendship', *Al Jazeera*, 28 February. Available at: https://www.aljazeera.com/economy/2022/2/28/as-russias-isolation-grows-china-hints-at-limits-of-friendship (accessed 28 May 2022).

155 *Reuters* (2022) 'Russia fires official who said China refused to supply aircraft parts', 15 March. Available at: https://www.reuters.com/world/russia-fires-official-who-said-china-refused-supply-aircraft-parts-2022-03-15/ (accessed 28 May 2022).

156 *Hindustan News Hub* (2022) 'China closes airports to Boeings of Russian companies – The Moscow Times', 27 May. Available at: https://hindustannewshub.com/russia-ukraine-news/china-closes-airports-to-boeings-of-russian-companies-the-moscow-times/ (accessed 28 May 2022).

157 Vinay Kaura (2018) 'India's changing relationship with Russia', *The RUSI Journal*, Vol. 163, Issue 1, p. 50.

158 Jeremy Garlick (2017) 'An elusive synergy: the quest for cooperation on energy security between China and the European Union', *Issues and Studies*, Vol. 53, Issue 3, p. 4.

159 Simon Pirani (2019) *Central Asian Gas: Prospects for the 2020s*, OIES Paper NG 155, Oxford: Oxford Institute for Energy Studies, p. iii. Available at: https://a9w7k6q9.stackpathcdn.com/wpcms/wp-content/uploads/2019/12/Central-Asian-Gas-NG-155.pdf (accessed 5 March 2023).

160 Richard Pomfret (2019) *The Central Asian Economies in the Twenty-First Century: Paving a New Silk Road*, Princeton: Princeton University Press, p. 151.

161 Pirani (2019), p. 2.

162 Chris Rickleton (2021) 'Turkmenistan: big on gas, short on options', *Eurasianet*, 22 January. Available at: https://eurasianet.org/turkmenistan-big-on-gas-short-on-options (accessed 29 May 2022).

163 Pirani (2019), pp. 21, 30.

164 Komila Nabiyeva (2019) *Win-win or Win-lose? China-Kazakhstan Energy Cooperation within the Belt and Road Initiative*, Cologne: Stiftung Asienhaus, p. 3. Available at: https://fid4sa-repository.ub.uni-heidelberg.de/4176/1/Blickwechsel_China-Kazakhstan_Energy_Cooperation_within_the_Belt_and_Road_Initiative.pdf (accessed 3 June 2022).

165 Pomfret (2019), p. 243.

166 Nabiyeva (2019) p. 3.

167 Pirani (2019), p. 30.

168 Pirani (2019), p. 26.

169 Pirani (2019), pp. 21–2.

170 Pirani (2019), p. 31.

171 Pomfret (2019), pp. 188–9.

172 Pirani (2019), p. 31.

173 Lauren Johnston, Edmund Downie, Marina Rudyak and Joshua Mwakalikamo (2021) *China's Appetite for International Agricultural Investment: Case Studies of Kyrgyzstan, Myanmar and Tanzania*, London: ODI, p. 19. Available at: www.odi.org/publications/chinas-appetite-for-international-agricultural-investmentcase-studies-of-kyrgyzstan-myanmar-and-tanzania (accessed 2 June 2022).

174 Dreher et al (2022), p. 119.

175 Eurasianet (2022) 'Tajikistan: the cost of Chinese debt', 21 July. Available at: https://eurasianet.org/tajikistan-the-cost-of-chinese-debt (accessed 3 August 2022).

176 Eurasianet (2022) 'Tajikistan: the cost of Chinese debt'.

177 Pantucci and Petersen (2022), pp. 86–8.

178 Johnston et al (2021), p. 19.

179 Eurasianet (2022) 'Tajikistan: the cost of Chinese debt'.

180 Pantucci and Petersen (2022), p. 159.

181 Pantucci and Petersen (2022), p. 188–90.

182 Pantucci and Petersen (2022), p. 187.

183 Nabiyeva (2019), p. 5.

184 Pomfret (2019), p. 248.

185 Pantucci and Petersen (2022), p. 241.

186 Pantucci and Petersen (2022), p. 247.

187 Jos Boonstra (2015) 'Reviewing the EU's approach to Central Asia', *EUCAM Policy Brief No. 34*, 24 February. Available at: https://eucentralasia.eu/reviewing-the-eus-approach-to-central-asia/ (accessed 3 June 2022).

188 Pantucci and Petersen (2022), p. 249.

Chapter 6

1   Aaron L. Friedberg (2022) *Getting China Wrong*, Cambridge: Polity Press, p. 6.

2   Axel Dreher, Andreas Fuchs, Bradley Parks, Austin Strange, and Michael J. Tierney (2022) *Banking on Beijing: The Aims and Impacts of China's Overseas Development Program*, Cambridge: Cambridge University Press, p. 55.

3   Rush Doshi (2021) *The Long Game: China's Grand Strategy to Displace American Order*, New York: Oxford University Press.

4   See: Lee Jones and Shahar Hameiri (2022) *Fractured China: How State Transformation Is Shaping China's Rise*, Cambridge: Cambridge University Press; Kjeld Erik Brødsgaard (ed.) (2017) *Chinese Politics as Fragmented Authoritarianism: Earthquakes, Energy and Environment*, Abingdon: Routledge.

5   Jeremy Garlick (2019) 'China's principal-agent problem in the Czech Republic: the curious case of CEFC', *Asia Europe Journal*, Vol. 17, Issue 4, pp. 437–51.

6   Dreher et al (2022).

7   The data in the two columns were obtained from different sources, probably with distinct criteria for categorizing Chinese investments. The apparently enormous increase in Chinese investments in the Middle East after the advent of the BRI is presumably due to Dreher et al's (2022) methodology for categorizing Chinese investments in the Middle East during the pre-BRI era, which may have excluded Chinese investments not classified as 'development finance projects'. It is advisable not to read too much into the drastic difference in the amounts recorded in the two columns, although certainly they bear witness to an increase in Chinese investments in the region.

8   Matt Schrader and J. Michael Cole (2023) 'China hasn't given up on the Belt and Road', *Foreign Affairs*, 7 February. Available at: https://www.foreignaffairs.com/china/china-hasnt-given-belt-and-road (accessed 10 February 2023).

9   Lina Benabdallah (2020) *Shaping the Future of Power: Knowledge Production and Network-Building in China-Africa Relations*, Ann Arbor: University of Michigan Press, p. 137.

10 Benabdallah (2020), p. 148.

11 Dawn C. Murphy (2022) *China's Rise in the Global South: The Middle East, Africa, and Beijing's Alternative World Order*, Stanford: Stanford University Press, p. 264.

12 Murphy (2022), p. 264.

13 Murphy (2022), p. 255.

14 Dreher et al (2022), p. 127.

15 Murphy (2022), p. 271.

16 For instance, Jones and Hameiri (2022).

17 Jamie Monson (2021) 'Learning by heart: training for reliance on the TAZARA railway, 1968-1976', *Made in China Journal*, 9 November. Available at: https://madeinchinajournal.com/2021/11/09/learning-by-heart%E2%80%A8-training-for-self-reliance-on-the-tazara-railway-1968-1976/ (accessed 13 June 2022).

18 Dreher et al (2022), p. 15.

19 Zhangxi Cheng and Ian Taylor (2017) *China's Aid to Africa: Does Friendship Really Matter?* Abingdon: Routledge.

20 Guy C.K. Leung, Raymond Li, and Melissa Low (2011) 'Transitions in China's oil economy, 1990-2010', *Eurasian Geography and Economics*, Vol. 52, Issue 4, pp. 483–500.

21 Yike Fu (2021) 'The quiet China-Africa revolution: Chinese investment', *The Diplomat*, 22 November. Available at: https://thediplomat.com/2021/11/the-quiet-china-africa-revolution-chinese-investment/ (accessed 6 July 2022).

22 Daniel Workman (2021) 'Top 15 crude oil suppliers to China', World's Top Exports, 11 July. Available at: https://www.worldstopexports.com/top-15-crude-oil-suppliers-to-china/ (accessed 14 June 2022).

23   Jordan Link (2019) 'Neither tightening nor loosening the belt: Chinese lending to African BRI signatories', China Africa Research Initiative, Johns Hopkins School of Advanced International Studies, 24 April. Available at: http://www.chinaafricarealstory.com/2019/04/neither-tightening-or-loosening-belt.html (accessed 13 June 2022).

24   Abdi Latif Dahir (2019) 'Africa's resource-rich nations are getting even more reliant on China for their exports', *Quartz Africa*, 26 April. Available at: https://qz.com/africa/1605497/belt-and-road-africa-mineral-rich-nations-export-mostly-to-china/ (accessed 13 June 2022).

25   Austin Bodetti (2019) 'How China came to dominate South Sudan's oil', *The Diplomat*, 11 February. Available at: https://thediplomat.com/2019/02/how-china-came-to-dominate-south-sudans-oil/ (accessed 15 June 2022).

26   Vladimir Basov (2022) 'The world's largest cobalt producing countries in 2021 – report', Kitco News, 2 February. Available at: https://www.kitco.com/news/2022-02-02/Global-cobalt-production-hits-record-in-2021-as-mined-cobalt-output-in-DR-Congo-jumps-22-4.html (accessed 14 June 2022).

27   Wade Shepard (2019) 'What China is really up to in Africa', *Forbes*, 3 October. Available at: https://www.forbes.com/sites/wadeshepard/2019/10/03/what-china-is-really-up-to-in-africa/?sh=67b14bbb5930 (accessed 15 June 2022).

28   Chris Alden, Daniel Large, and Ricardo Soares de Oliveira (2008) 'Introduction', in Alden, Large, and de Oliveira (eds.) *China Returns to Africa: A Rising Power and a Continent Embrace*, New York: Columbia University Press, p. 11.

29   Carlos Mureithi (2022) 'Trade between Africa and China reached an all-time high in 2021', *Quartz Africa*, 8 February. Available at: https://qz.com/africa/2123474/china-africa-trade-reached-an-all-time-high-in-2021/ (accessed 14 June 2022).

30   Jevans Nyabiage (2022) 'China-Africa trade rises in first quarter, though coming months may see a flattening', *South China Morning Post*, 11 May. Available at: https://www.scmp.com/news/china/diplomacy/article/3177321/china-africa-trade-rises-first-quarter-though-coming-months (accessed 14 June 2022).

31   Eurostat (2022) 'Africa-EU – international trade in goods statistics'. Available at: https://ec.europa.eu/eurostat/statistics-explained/index.php?title=Africa-EU_-_international_trade_in_goods_statistics#:~:text=United%20Nations%20geoscheme.-,Africa's%20main%20trade%20in%20goods%20partner%20is%20the%20EU,exports%20and%2022%20%25%20of%20imports (accessed 15 June 2022).

32   Eric Olander (2021) 'China's Transsion dominates smartphone market in Africa', *The Africa Report*, 19 March. Available at: https://www.theafricareport.com/73472/chinas-transsion-dominates-smartphone-market-in-africa/ (accessed 14 June 2022).

33   Katja Scherer (2021) 'Music from Africa: the competition of the streaming services', Wirtschaft in Afrika (Economy in Africa) blog, 28 January. Available at: wirtschaftinafrika.de/musik-aus-afrika/ (accessed 6 July 2022).

34   Stuart Dredge (2022) 'Report: Africa's music streaming market to be $314.6m by 2026', musically.com, 6 June. Available at: https://musically.com/2022/06/06/report-africas-music-streaming-market-to-be-314-6m-by-2026/ (accessed 6 July 2022).

35   Mureithi (2022).

36   Carien du Plessis (2021) 'Eswatini, Taiwan's last partner in Africa', *The Diplomat*, 10 August. Available at: https://thediplomat.com/2021/08/eswatini-taiwans-last-partner-in-africa/ (accessed 14 June 2022).

37   Alden et al (2008), p. 9.

38 Peter Fabricius (2018) 'Taiwan has lost all its friends in Africa – except eSwatini', Institute for Security Studies, 31 May. Available at: https://issafrica.org/iss-today/taiwan-has-lost-all-its-friends-in-africa-except-eswatini (accessed 14 June 2022).

39 Obert Hodzi (2020) 'Bridging the asymmetries? African students' mobility to China', *Asian Ethnicity*, Vol. 21, Issue 4, p. 573.

40 Hodzi (2020), p. 579.

41 Richard Wike, Bruce Stokes, and Jacob Poushter (2015) 'Global publics back U.S. on fighting ISIS, but are critical of post-9/11 torture', Pew Research Center, 23 June, p. 28. Available at: file:///C:/Users/Jeremy/Downloads/Balance-of-Power-Report-FINAL-June-23-2015.pdf (accessed 15 June 2022).

42 Rhys Jenkins (2022) *How China Is Reshaping the Global Economy: Development Impacts in Africa and Latin America*, Oxford: Oxford University Press, p. 215.

43 Laura Silver, Kat Devlin, and Christine Huang (2019) 'Attitudes toward China', Pew Research Center, 5 December. Available at: https://www.pewresearch.org/global/2019/12/05/attitudes-toward-china-2019/ (accessed 15 June 2022).

44 Antony Sguazzin (2022) 'China surpasses US in eyes of young Africans, survey shows', *Bloomberg*, 13 June. Available at: https://www.bloomberg.com/news/articles/2022-06-12/china-surpasses-us-in-the-eyes-of-young-africans-survey-shows#xj4y7vzkg (accessed 15 June 2022).

45 Priya Gauttam, Bawa Singh, and Jaspal Kaur (2020) 'COVID-19 and Chinese global health diplomacy: Geopolitical opportunity for China's hegemony?' *Millennial Asia*, Vol. 11, Issue 3, p. 323.

46 Gauttam et al (2020), p. 325.

47 Katja Scherer (2021) 'Africa-China relationship: Started to stay', Economy in Africa (Wirtschaft in Afrika) blog, 18 November. Available at: wirtschaftinafrika.de/afrika-china-beziehung/ (accessed 6 July 2022).

48 *The Economist* (2022) 'How Chinese firms have dominated African infrastructure', 19 February. Available at: https://www.economist.com/middle-east-and-africa/how-chinese-firms-have-dominated-african-infrastructure/21807721 (accessed 15 June 2022).

49 Andrea Shalal (2022) 'Chinese funding of sub-Saharan African infrastructure dwarfs that of West, says think tank', *Reuters*, 9 February. Available at: https://www.reuters.com/markets/us/chinese-funding-sub-saharan-african-infrastructure-dwarfs-that-west-says-think-2022-02-09/ (accessed 15 June 2022).

50 Michael Monnerjahn (2021) 'German investments in Africa continue to rise', Germany Trade & Invest, 17 May. Available at: gtai.de/de/trade/afrika-uebergreifend/wirtschaftsumfeld/deutsche-investionen-in-afrika-steigen-weiter-650130 (accessed 6 July 2022).

51 Katja Scherer (2021) 'Africa-China relationship: started to stay', Economy in Africa (Wirtschaft in Afrika) blog, 18 November. Available at: wirtschaftinafrika.de/afrika-china-beziehung/ (accessed 6 July 2022).

52 Jean-Pierre Cabestan (2020) 'China's Djibouti naval base increasing its power', East Asia Forum, 16 May. Available at: https://www.eastasiaforum.org/2020/05/16/chinas-djibouti-naval-base-increasing-its-power/ (accessed 15 June 2022).

53 Shepard (2019).

54 Peter Hakim (2006) 'Is Washington losing Latin America?' *Foreign Affairs*, Vol. 85, Issue 1, p. 39.

55 Rhys Jenkins (2022) *How China Is Reshaping the Global Economy: Development Impacts in Africa and Latin America*, Oxford: Oxford University Press, p. 235.

56 See Martha L. Cottam (1994) *Images and Intervention: U.S. Policies in Latin America*, Pittsburgh: University of Pittsburgh Press, and Hakim (2006).

57 Carol Wise (2020) *Dragonomics: How Latin America Is Maximizing (or Missing Out on) China's International Development Strategy*, New Haven: Yale University Press, p. 230.

58 Jenkins (2022), *How China Is Reshaping*, p. 223.

59 Jenkins (2022), *How China Is Reshaping*, p. 231.

60 Wise (2020), p. 230.

61 Juan Carlos Gachúz (2012) 'Chile's Economic and Political Relationship with China', *Journal of Current Chinese Affairs*, Vol. 41, Issue 1, p. 136.

62 Shu G. Zhang and Ni Chen (2021) 'Beijing's institutionalised economic statecraft towards Brazil: a case study', *Journal of Current Chinese Affairs*, Vol. 50, Issue 3, pp. 339–65.

63 Zhang and Chen (2021), p. 356.

64 For instance, in the Czech Republic. See Jeremy Garlick (2019) 'China's principal-agent problem in the Czech Republic: the curious case of CEFC', *Asia Europe Journal*, Vol. 17, Issue 4, pp. 437–51.

65 Rhys Jenkins (2022) 'China's Belt and Road Initiative in Latin America: what has changed?' *Journal of Current Chinese Affairs*, Vol. 51, Issue 1, pp. 13–39.

66 Wise (2020), pp. 8–9.

67 Wise (2020), p. 9.

68 Jenkins (2022), *How China Is Reshaping*, p. 227.

69 Jenkins (2022), *How China Is Reshaping*, p. 229.

70 Jenkins (2022), *How China Is Reshaping*, p. 227.

71 R. Evan Ellis (2009) *China in Latin America: The Whats and Wherefores*, Boulder, CO: Lynn Rienner, p. 52.

72 Pedro Henrique Batista Barbosa (2021) 'Chinese economic statecraft and China's oil development finance in Brazil', *Journal of Current Chinese Affairs*, Vol. 50, Issue 3, p. 368.

73 Barbosa (2021), p. 373.

74 Emma Miriam Yin-Hang To and Rodrigo Acuña (2019) 'China and Venezuela: South-South cooperation or rearticulated dependency?', *Latin American Perspectives*, Vol. 46, Issue 2, pp. 127–8.

75 To and Acuña (2019), p. 127.

76 Jenkins (2022), *How China Is Reshaping*, p. 231.

77 To and Acuña (2019), pp. 127-128.

78 To and Acuña (2019), p. 134.

79 Eduardo Daniel Oviedo (2015) 'Actors in Argentina-China soybean trade and in Chinese immigration to Argentina', in Enrique Dussel Peters and Ariel C. Armony (eds.) *Beyond Raw Materials: Who Are the Actors in the Latin America and Caribbean-China Relationship?* Buenos Aires: Friedrich-Ebert Stiftung, p. 120.

80 Gachúz (2012), p. 137.

81 Gachúz (2012), p. 135.

82 R. Evan Ellis (2014) *China on the Ground in Latin America: Challenges for the Chinese and Impacts on the Region*, New York: Palgrave Macmillan, pp. 115–6.

83 Jenkins (2022), *How China Is Reshaping*, p. 310.

84 Jenkins (2022), *How China Is Reshaping*, pp. 312–4.

85 Jenkins (2022), *How China Is Reshaping*, p. 316.

86   Ministry of Foreign Affairs of China (2016) *Basic Information about China-CELAC Forum*. Available at: http://www.chinacelacforum.org/eng/ltjj_1/201612/P020210828094665781093.pdf (accessed 3 July 2022). Unintuitively, CELAC stands for 'Community of Latin American and Caribbean States'.

87   Sung-Han Kim and Sanghoon Kim (2022) 'China's contestation of the liberal international order', *The Pacific Review*, online first 9 April. Available at: https://www.tandfonline.com/doi/abs/10.1080/09512748.2022.2063367 (accessed 15 July 2022).

88   David Zweig and Bi Jianhai (2005) 'China's global hunt for energy', *Foreign Affairs*, Vol. 84, Issue 5, pp. 25–38.

89   Jeremy Garlick and Radka Havlová (2020) 'China's "Belt and Road" economic diplomacy in the Persian Gulf: strategic hedging amidst Saudi-Iranian regional rivalry', *Journal of Current Chinese Affairs*, Vol. 49, Issue 1, pp. 82–105.

90   Zahra Aghamohammadi and Ali Omidi (2018) 'The prospect of the United States and Saudi Arabia relations in light of Khashoggi murder', *World Sociopolitical Studies*, Vol. 2, Issue 4, pp. 605–32.

91   Marc Lanteigne (2020) *Chinese Foreign Policy: An Introduction (Fourth Edition)*, Abingdon: Routledge, p. 216.

92   Bethan McKernan (2022) 'Fist bumps as Joe Biden arrives to reset ties with "paria"' Saudi Arab'a', *The Guardian*, 15 July. Available at: https://www.theguardian.com/us-news/2022/jul/15/fist-bumps-as-joe-biden-arrives-to-reset-ties-with-pariah-saudi-arabia (accessed 15 July 2022).

93   Mohammadbagher Forough (2022) 'Biden's Middle East policy contradicts his China policy', *The Diplomat*, 19 July. Available at: https://thediplomat.com/2022/07/bidens-middle-east-policy-contradicts-his-china-policy/ (accessed 20 July 2022).

94   Jeremy Garlick and Radka Havlová (2021) 'The dragon dithers: assessing the cautious implementation of China's Belt and Road Initiative in Iran', *Eurasian Geography and Economics*, Vol. 62, Issue 4, pp. 454–80.

95   Garlick and Havlová (2021), p. 456.

96   Jeff Barron (2020) 'China's Crude Oil Imports Surpassed 10 Million Barrels per Day in 2019', U.S. Energy Information Administration (EIA), 23 March. Available at: https://www.eia.gov/todayinenergy/detail.php?id=43216 (accessed 16 July 2022).

97   Laura Silver, Kat Devlin, and Christine Huang (2019) 'People around the globe are divided in their opinions of China', Washington, D.C.: Pew Research Center, 5 December. Available at: https://www.pewresearch.org/fact-tank/2019/12/05/people-around-the-globe-are-divided-in-their-opinions-of-china/ (accessed 16 July 2022).

98   Michael Robbins (2021) 'Fragile popularity: Arab attitudes towards China', *Manara Magazine*, Cambridge Middle East and North Africa Forum (MENAF), 8 December. Available at: https://manaramagazine.org/2021/12/08/fragile-popularity-arab-attitudes-towards-china/ (accessed 16 July 2022).

99   The Middle East Monitor (2017) 'China is largest foreign investor in Middle East', *Middle East Monitor*, 24 July. Available at: https://www.middleeastmonitor.com/20170724-china-is-largest-foreign-investor-in-middle-east/ (accessed 16 July 2022).

100 Mordechai Chaziza (2021) 'Egypt in China's Maritime Silk Road Initiative: relations cannot surmount realities', in Jean-Marc F. Blanchard (ed.) *China's Maritime Silk Road Initiative, Africa, and the Middle East: Feats, Freezes, and Failures*, Singapore: Palgrave Macmillan, pp. 265–8.

101 Yoram Evron (2017) 'The economic dimension of China-Israel relations: political implications, roles and limitations', *Israel Affairs*, Vol. 23, Issue 5, p. 838–40.

102 Wang Yu (2018) 'Economic and cultural interactions between Israel and China: opportunities and challenges', in Anoushiravan Ehteshami and Niv Horesh (eds.) *China's Presence in the Middle East: The Implications of the One Belt, One Road Initiative*, Abingdon: Routledge, p. 139.

103 Garlick and Havlová (2021), pp. 471–2.

104 Tehran Times (2023) 'China launches direct shipping line to Iran's Chabahar port', 1 January. Available at: https://www.tehrantimes.com/news/480298/China-launches-direct-shipping-line-to-Iran-s-Chabahar-port (accessed 11 February 2023).

105 Mordechai Chaziza (2019) 'The significant role of Oman in China's Maritime Silk Road Initiative', *Contemporary Review of the Middle East*, Vol. 6, Issue 1, p. 50.

106 Angela Stanzel (2022) *China's Path to Geopolitics: Case Study on China's Iran Policy at the Intersection of Regional Interests and Global Power Rivalry*, SWP Research Paper 5, Berlin: German Institute for International and Security Affairs, p. 8.

107 Zvi Mazel (2022) 'China's growing economic impact on the Middle East', Geopolitical Intelligence Services, 21 April. Available at: https://www.gisreportsonline.com/r/china-middle-east/ (accessed 3 August 2022).

108 Stanzel (2022), p. 12.

109 Yahia H. Zoubir (2020) *China's 'Health Silk Road' Diplomacy in the MENA*, Med Dialogue Series No. 27, Tunis: Konrad-Adenauer-Stiftung, July, pp. 3–7. Available at: https://www.kas.de/documents/282499/282548/MDS_China+Health+Silk+Road+Di plomacy.pdf/ (accessed 3 August 2022).

110 Yahia H. Zoubir and Emilie Tran (2022) 'China's Health Silk Road in the Middle East and North Africa amidst COVID-19 and a contested world order', *Journal of Contemporary China*, Vol. 31, Issue 135, pp. 335–50.

111 Richard Turcsányi and Runya Qiaoan (2019) 'Friends or foes? How diverging views of communist past undermine the China-CEE "16+1 platform"', *Asia Europe Journal*, Vol. 18, Issue 3, pp. 397–412.

112 Twelve countries included by China in the regional cooperation platform are EU members: Poland, the Czech Republic, Hungary, Slovakia, Estonia, Latvia, Lithuania, Romania, Bulgaria, Croatia, Slovenia, and Greece. Five are outside the EU: Serbia, Montenegro, Albania, Macedonia, and Bosnia-Herzegovina.

113 Jeremy Garlick and Fangxing Qin (2023) 'China's Normative Power in Central and Eastern Europe: "16/17+1" Cooperation as a Tale of Unfulfilled Expectations', *Europe-Asia Studies* (online first).

114 Rudolf Fürst (2018) 'Czechia's relations with China: on a long road toward a real strategic partnership?' in Weiqing Song (ed.) *China's Relations with Central and Eastern Europe: From 'Old Comrades' to New Partners*, Abingdon: Routledge, p. 120.

115 Jakub Jakóbowski (2018) 'Chinese-led regional multilateralism in Central and Eastern Europe, Africa and Latin America: 16+1, FOCAC, and CCF', *Journal of Contemporary China*, Vol. 27, Issue 113, pp. 659–73.

116 Stefanie Bolzen and Johnny Erling (2012) 'Divide, conquer, aim east: China has a sharp new European trade strategy', *Die Welt*, 11 November. Available at: https://worldcrunch.com/world-affairs/divide-conquer-aim-east-china-has-a-sharp-new-european-trade-strategy (accessed 15 June 2022).

117 Richard Turcsányi (2021) 'An unrewarding show: online summit of China-CEE 17+1 platform', Italian Institute for International Political Studies, 26 February. Available at: https://www.ispionline.it/en/pubblicazione/unrewarding-show-online-summit-china-cee-171-platform-29431 (accessed 15 June 2022).

118 Aleksandar Vucic (2014) 'Guest post: the Serbia-China friendship bridge', *Financial Times*, 15 December. Available at: https://www.ft.com/content/97c3ee47-63cf-3966-9122-c653fc6cb4f3 (accessed 15 June 2022).

119 Nick Kampouris (2019) 'Greece officially joins China's "16+1" partnership with Central and Eastern Europe', Greek Reporter, 12 April. Available at: https://greekreporter.com/2019/04/12/greece-officially-joins-chinas-161-partnership-with-central-and-eastern-europe/ (accessed 18 June 2022).

120 Kateřina Menzelová (2017) 'Dohody za 60 miliard? Čínské investice slibované Zemanem zůstávají záhadou' ['Agreements for 60 billion? Chinese investment promised by Zeman remains a mystery'], *Lidové noviny*, 21 August. Available at: https://www.lidovky.cz/byznys/cinske-investice-zustavaji-zahadou.A170820_205549_statni-pokladna_ELE (accessed 20 June 2022).

121 Garlick (2019), p. 446.

122 Ido Vock (2020) 'When Chinese influence fails: how the rise and fall of a Chinese corporate giant turned the Czech Republic against Beijing', *The New Statesman*, 29 September. Available at: https://www.newstatesman.com/world/europe/2020/09/when-chinese-influence-fails (accessed 20 June 2022).

123 Rudolf Fürst (2022) 'Czech Republic: pendulum swings toward freezing ties based on overestimated fear of China', in John Seaman, Francesca Ghiretti, Lucas Erlbacher, Xiaoxue Martin, and Miguel Otero-Iglesias (eds.) *Dependence in Europe's Relations with China: Weighing Perceptions and Reality*, Paris: French Institute of International Relations (IFRI), p. 61.

124 Stuart Lau (2020) 'Czech president to skip Beijing summit over China "investment letdown"', *South China Morning Post*, 13 January. Available at: https://www.scmp.com/news/china/diplomacy/article/3045917/czech-president-skip-beijing-summit-over-china-investment (accessed 20 June 2022).

125 Andreea Brînză (2021) 'How China's 17+1 became a zombie mechanism', *The Diplomat*, 10 February. Available at: https://thediplomat.com/2021/02/how-chinas-171-became-a-zombie-mechanism/ (accessed 18 June 2022).

126 Richard Turcsányi, Kamil Liškutin, and Michal Mochtak (2022) 'Diffusion of influence? Detecting China's footprint in foreign policies of other countries', *Chinese Political Science Review* (online first). Available at: https://link.springer.com/article/10.1007/s41111-022-00217-5#citeas (accessed 18 June 2022).

127 Paulina Kanarek (2017) 'Perspectives for development of China-EU relations in the infrastructure investment sector: a case study of COVEC's investment in Poland', *The Journal of Political Risk*, Vol. 5, Issue 8, pp. 1–41.

128 Olivia Bizot (2021) 'Montenegro's highway to debt: unfinished Chinese road comes with strings attached', *France24*, 30 August. Available at: https://www.france24.com/en/tv-shows/focus/20210830-montenegro-s-highway-to-debt-unfinished-chinese-road-comes-with-strings-attached (accessed 20 June 2022).

129 Anita Komuves (2021) 'Hungarians protest against planned Chinese university campus', *Reuters*, 6 June. Available at: https://www.reuters.com/world/china/hungarians-protest-against-planned-chinese-university-campus-2021-06-05/ (accessed 20 June 2022).

130 Karl Wilson and Xu Weiwei (2022) 'Wang Yi's Pacific Islands tour boosts regional development', *Asia News Network*, 6 June. Available at: https://asianews.network/wang-yis-pacific-islands-tour-boosts-regional-development/ (accessed 5 July 2022).

131 Jonah Blank (2022) 'China's troubling new military strategy is coming into view', *The Atlantic*, 5 May. Available at: https://www.theatlantic.com/ideas/archive/2022/05/china-security-agreement-solomon-islands/629771/ (accessed 5 July 2022).

132 Kathrin Hille (2022) 'Pacific Islanders snub China by rejecting security pact', *Financial Times*, 30 May. Available at: https://www.ft.com/content/34b4842c-fafd-4144-b16b-3f379d82085d (accessed 5 July 2022).

133 The World Bank (2021) 'The World Bank in Pacific Islands'. Available at: https://www.worldbank.org/en/country/pacificislands/overview (accessed 5 July 2022).

134 Countryeconomy.com (2022) 'PIF – Pacific Islands Forum'. Available at: https://countryeconomy.com/countries/groups/pacific-islands-forum (accessed 5 July 2022).

135 Hiroyuki Umetsu (1996) 'Communist China's entry into the Korean hostilities and a U.S. proposal for a collective security arrangement in the Pacific offshore island chain', *Journal of Northeast Asian Studies*, Vol. 15, Issue 2, pp. 98–118.

136 Toshi Yoshihara (2012) 'China's vision of its seascape: the first island chain and Chinese seapower', *Asian Politics & Policy*, Vol. 4, Issue 3, pp. 293–314.

137 Transform Aqorau (2021) 'Solomon Islands' foreign policy dilemma and the switch from Taiwan to China', in Graeme Smith and Terence Wesley-Smith (eds.) *The China Alternative: Changing Regional Order in the Pacific Islands*, Acton: Australian National University Press, p. 337.

138 Lice Movono and Kate Lyons (2022) 'Solomon Islands PM rules out China military base and says Australia is "security partner of choice"', *The Guardian*, 14 July. Available at: https://www.theguardian.com/world/2022/jul/14/solomon-islands-pm-rules-out-chinese-military-base-china-australia-security-partner-manasseh-sogavare (accessed 15 July 2022).

139 Jonathan Pryke (2020) 'The risks of China's ambitions in the South Pacific', Washington, D.C.: The Brookings Institution, 20 July. Available at: https://www.brookings.edu/articles/the-risks-of-chinas-ambitions-in-the-south-pacific/ (accessed 5 July 2022).

140 Nick Sas (2022) 'China's influence hard to ignore in Solomon Islands' capital Honiara, as Australia warned it could be "left behind"', ABC News, 3 July. Available at: https://www.abc.net.au/news/2022-07-04/solomon-islands-and-china-influence-as-australia-watches-on/101204348 (accessed 5 July 2022).

141 Tsukasa Hadano and Fumi Matsumoto (2022) 'Kiribati runway project in focus as China's Wang Yi tours region', *Nikkei Asian Review*, 29 May. Available at: https://asia.nikkei.com/Politics/International-relations/Kiribati-runway-project-in-focus-as-China-s-Wang-Yi-tours-region (accessed 5 July 2022).

142 Geraldine Panapasa (2022) 'US announces new embassies in major Pacific push as it jostles with China for influence in region', *The Guardian*, 12 July. Available at: https://www.theguardian.com/world/2022/jul/12/us-to-open-two-new-embassies-in-pacific-as-it-jostles-with-china-for-influence-in-region (accessed 15 July 2022).

143 Kate Lyons (2022) 'Smiles and unity at the Pacific Islands Forum mask tough questions shelved for another day', *The Guardian*, 16 July. Available at: https://www.theguardian.com/world/2022/jul/16/smiles-and-unity-at-the-pacific-islands-forum-mask-tough-questions-shelved-for-another-day (accessed 16 July 2022).

144 Kate Lyons (2022) 'Kiribati withdraws from Pacific Islands Forum in blow to regional body', *The Guardian*, 10 July. Available at: https://www.theguardian.com/world/2022/jul/10/kiribati-withdraws-from-pacific-islands-forum-pif-micronesia (accessed 16 July 2022).

Chapter 7

1   Jason Karaian (2022) 'The Russian ruble keeps rising, hitting a seven-year high', *The New York Times*, 21 June. Available at: https://www.nytimes.com/2022/06/21/business/russian-ruble-ukraine.html (accessed 4 August 2022).

2   Victoria Kim and Clifford Krauss (2022) 'Asia is buying discounted Russian oil, making up for Europe's cutbacks', The New York Times, 21 June. Available at: https://www.nytimes.com/2022/06/21/world/asia/asia-is-buying-discounted-russian-oil-making-up-for-europes-cutbacks.html (accessed 4 August 2022).

3   Yanzhong Huang (2022) 'The Health Silk Road: how China adapts the Belt and Road Initiative to the COVID-19 pandemic', *American Journal of Public Health*, Vol. 112, Issue 4, pp. 567–9.

4   Al Jazeera (2022) 'China, Saudi Arabia strengthen partnership on energy, defence', 9 December. Available at: https://www.aljazeera.com/news/2022/12/9/china-saudi-arabia-strengthen-partnership-on-energy-defence (accessed 12 February 2023).

5   Dickson (2016).

6   Sébastien Peyrouse (2016) 'Discussing China: Sinophilia and Sinophobia in Central Asia', *Journal of Eurasian Studies*, Vol. 7, Issue 1, pp. 14–23.

7   Antonio Graceffo (2022) 'China's economy: more debt than meets the eye', *China Brief*, Vol. 22, Issue 21, pp. 18–21.

8   Garlick (2019).

9   See: Brautigam (2020).

10 Yasmeen Serhan (2022) 'A new U.N. vote shows Russia isn't as isolated as the West may like to think', *Time*, 13 October. Available at: https://time.com/6222005/un-vote-russia-ukraine-allies/ (accessed 12 February 2023).

11 Philip Oltermann (2022) 'Germany's Scholz heads to China amid questions over strategy', *The Guardian*, 3 November. Available at: https://www.theguardian.com/world/2022/nov/03/germany-olaf-scholz-china-visit-questions-over-strategy (accessed 12 February 2023).

12 Tanya Snyder (2022) 'Biden's incredible shrinking infrastructure plan', *Politico*, 17 June. Available at: https://www.politico.com/news/2022/06/17/democrats-shrinking-infrastructure-plan-00039588 (accessed 12 February 2023).

13 Clare Jim and Xie Yu (2022) 'China property developers' woes cast shadow over management units', *Reuters*, 10 August. Available at: https://www.reuters.com/world/china/china-property-developers-woes-cast-shadow-over-management-units-2022-08-10/ (accessed 13 August 2022).

14 Clare Jim and Xie Yu (2022) 'China vows timely home deliveries in wake of property protests', *Reuters*, 14 July. Available at: https://www.reuters.com/world/china/china-property-protests-threaten-dent-220-bln-banks-mortgage-loans-2022-07-14/ (accessed 13 August 2022).

15 Kevin Yao and Ellen Zhang (2022) 'China June industrial output rises 3.9 per cent, retail sales up 3.1 per cent', *Reuters*, 15 July. Available at: https://www.reuters.com/world/china/china-june-industrial-output-rises-39-retail-sales-up-31-2022-07-15/ (accessed 15 July 2022).

16 Evelyn Cheng (2022) 'China's consumer and factory data miss expectations in July', CNBC, 15 August. Available at: https://www.cnbc.com/2022/08/15/chinas-consumer-and-factory-data-miss-expectations-in-july.html (accessed 16 August 2022).

17 Vincent Ni (2022) 'Xi Jinping faces stumbling blocks as crucial Communist party meeting looms', *The Guardian*, 13 August 2022. Available at: https://www.theguardian.com/world/2022/aug/13/xi-jinping-faces-stumbling-blocks-as-crucial-communist-party-meeting-looms (accessed 13 August 2022).

18 Randall Hill, Phil Stewart, and Jeff Mason (2023) 'U.S. fighter shoots down suspected Chinese spy balloon', *Reuters*, 6 February. Available at: https://www.reuters.com/world/us/biden-says-us-is-going-take-care-of-chinese-balloon-2023-02-04/ (accessed 12 February 2023).

19 Dan Macklin (2022) 'Why a Xi Jinping third term looks secure', *The Diplomat*, 11 July. Available at: https://thediplomat.com/2022/07/why-a-xi-jinping-third-term-looks-secure/ (accessed 16 August 2022).

20 Frances Mao (2022) 'China abandons key parts of zero-Covid strategy after protests', *BBC News*, 7 December. Available at: https://www.bbc.com/news/world-asia-china-63855508 (accessed 12 February 2023).

21 Diego A. Cerdeiro and Sonali Jain-Chandra (2023) 'China's economy is rebounding, but reforms are still needed', International Monetary Fund, 3 February. Available at: https://www.imf.org/en/News/Articles/2023/02/02/cf-chinas-economy-is-rebounding-but-reforms-are-still-needed (accessed 12 February 2023).

22 Jamie Gaida, Jennifer Wong Leung, Stephan Robin, and Danielle Cave (2023) ASPI's Critical Technology Tracker – the Global Race for Future Power', Australian Strategic Policy Institute (ASPI), 2 March. Available at: ASPI's Critical Technology Tracker | Australian Strategic Policy Institute | ASPI (accessed 6 March 2023).

23 Dan Wang (2023) 'China's hidden tech revolution: how Beijing threatens U.S. dominance', *Foreign Affairs*, March/April issue. Available at: https://www.foreignaffairs.com/china/chinas-hidden-tech-revolution-how-beijing-threatens-us-dominance-dan-wang (accessed 6 March 2023).

24 Mearsheimer (2001).

SELECTED BIBLIOGRAPHY

Acharya, Amitav (2011) 'Norm subsidiarity and regional orders: sovereignty, regionalism, and rule-making in the Third World', *International Studies Quarterly*, Vol. 55, Issue 1, pp. 95–123.

Acharya, Amitav (2014) *Rethinking Power, Institutions and Ideas in World Politics: Whose IR?* Abingdon, UK: Routledge.

Aghamohammadi, Zahra, and Ali Omidi (2018) 'The prospect of the United States and Saudi Arabia relations in light of Khashoggi murder', *World Sociopolitical Studies*, Vol. 2, Issue 4, pp. 605–32.

Alden, Chris, Daniel Large, and Ricardo Soares de Oliveira (eds.) (2008) *China Returns to Africa: A Rising Power and a Continent Embrace*, New York: Columbia University Press.

Allison, Graham T. (2017) *Destined for War: Can America and China Escape Thucydides's Trap?* Boston: Houghton Mifflin Harcourt.

Allison, Graham, Robert D. Blackwill, and Ali Wyne (2013) *Lee Kuan Yew: The Grand Master's Insights on China, the United States, and the World*, Cambridge, MA: MIT Press.

Ang, Yuen Yuen (2016) *How China Escaped the Poverty Trap*, Ithaca and London: Cornell University Press.

Ang, Yuen Yuen (2018) 'Autocracy with Chinese characteristics: Beijing's behind-the-scenes reforms', *Foreign Affairs*, Vol. 97 (May/June), pp. 39–46.

Barbosa, Pedro Henrique Batista (2021) 'Chinese economic statecraft and China's oil development finance in Brazil', *Journal of Current Chinese Affairs*, Vol. 50, Issue 3, pp. 366–90.

Benabdallah, Lina (2020) *Shaping the Future of Power: Knowledge Production and Network-Building in China-Africa Relations*, Ann Arbor: University of Michigan Press.

Benedict, Ruth (1989) *The Chrysanthemum and the Sword: Patterns of Japanese Culture*, Boston: Houghton Mifflin.

Bhattacharya, Sumanta, Jayanta Kumar Ray, Shakti Sinha, and Bhavneet Kaur Sachdev (2021) 'Can India's necklace of diamonds strategy defeat the China's string of pearls', *International Journal of Recent Advances in Multidisciplinary Topics*, Vol. 2, Issue 11, pp. 105–8.

Blackmon, Pamela (2014) 'Determinants of developing country debt: the revolving door of debt rescheduling through the Paris Club and export credits', *Third World Quarterly*, Vol. 35, Issue 8, pp. 1423–40.

Blanchard, Jean-Marc F. (ed.) *China's Maritime Silk Road Initiative, Africa, and the Middle East: Feats, Freezes, and Failures*, Singapore: Palgrave Macmillan.

Brautigam, Deborah (2020) 'A critical look at Chinese "debt-trap diplomacy": the rise of a meme', *Area Development and Policy*, Vol. 5, Issue 1, pp. 1–14.

Brødsgaard, Kjeld Erik (ed.) (2017) *Chinese Politics as Fragmented Authoritarianism: Earthquakes, Energy and Environment*, Abingdon: Routledge.

Brown, Kerry (2016) *CEO China: The Rise of Xi Jinping*, London: I.B. Tauris.

Brown, Kerry (2018) *China's Dream: The Culture of Chinese Communism and the Secret Sources of Its Power*, Cambridge: Polity Press.

Burnett, Ipek S. (2020) *A Jungian Inquiry into the American Psyche: The Violence of Innocence*, Abingdon: Routledge.

Callahan, William A. (2008) 'Chinese visions of world order: post-hegemonic or a new hegemony?' *International Studies Review*, Vol. 10, Issue 4, pp. 749–61.

Callahan, William A. (2010) *China: The Pessoptimist Nation*, Oxford: Oxford University Press.

Carmody, Pádraig (2020) 'Dependence not debt-trap diplomacy', *Area Development and Policy*, Vol. 5, Issue 1, pp. 23–31.

Cemiloğlu, Sezgi (2015) *China's Economic Engagement in Africa: A Case Study of Angola*, Frankfurt: Peter Lang.

Chang, Gordon G. (2002) *The Coming Collapse of China*, London: Arrow.

Chaziza, Mordechai (2019) 'The significant role of Oman in China's Maritime Silk Road Initiative', *Contemporary Review of the Middle East*, Vol. 6, Issue 1, pp. 44–57.

Cheng, Zhangxi, and Ian Taylor (2017*) China's Aid to Africa: Does Friendship Really Matter?* Abingdon: Routledge.

Chomsky, Noam, and Andre Vltchek (2013) *On Western Terrorism: From Hiroshima to Drone Warfare*, London: Pluto Press.

Clementi, Marco, Matteo Dian, and Barbara Pisciotta (2018) *US Foreign Policy in a Challenging World: Building Order on Shifting Foundations*, Cham: Springer.

Clinton, Hilary (2011) 'America's Pacific century', *Foreign Policy*, 11 October. Available at: https://foreignpolicy.com/2011/10/11/americas-pacific-century/ (accessed 5 April 2022).

Cottam, Martha L. (1994) *Images and Intervention: U.S. Policies in Latin America*, Pittsburgh: University of Pittsburgh Press.

Cui, Lianbiao, and Malin Song (2019) 'Economic evaluation of the Belt and Road Initiative from an unimpeded trade perspective', *International Journal of Logistics Research and Applications*, Vol. 22, Issue 1, pp. 25–46.

Damasio, Antonio R. (1994) *Descartes' Error: Emotion, Reason, and the Human Brain*, London: Penguin.

De Long, J. Bradford, and Barry Eichengreen (1991) 'The Marshall Plan: History's Most Successful Structural Adjustment Program', Cambridge, MA: National Bureau of Economic Research. Available at: https://www.nber.org/papers/w3899 (accessed 27 August 2022).

Deudney, Daniel, and G. John Ikenberry (1999) 'The nature and sources of liberal international order', *Review of International Studies*, Vol. 25, Issue 2, pp. 179–96.

Dickson, Bruce J. (2016) *The Dictator's Dilemma: The Chinese Communist Party's Strategy for Survival*, New York: Oxford University Press.

Diez, Thomas (2013) 'Normative power as hegemony', *Cooperation and Conflict*, Vol. 48, Issue 2, pp. 194–210.

Doshi, Rush (2021) *The Long Game: China's Grand Strategy to Displace American Order*, New York: Oxford University Press.

Dreher, Axel, Andreas Fuchs, Bradley Parks, Austin Strange, and Michael J. Tierney (2022) *Banking on Beijing: The Aims and Impacts of China's Overseas Development Program*, Cambridge: Cambridge University Press.

Dunford, Michael, and Weidong Liu (2019) 'Chinese perspectives on the Belt and Road Initiative', *Cambridge Journal of Regions, Economy and Society*, Vol. 12, Issue 1, pp. 145–67.

Dunne, Timothy (1995) 'The social construction of international society', *European Journal of International Relations*, Vol. 1, Issue 3, pp. 367–89.

Ehrenberg, Alain (2010) *The Weariness of the Self: Diagnosing the History of Depression in the Contemporary Age*, Montreal & Kingston: McGill-Queen's University Press.

Ehteshami, Anoushiravan, and Niv Horesh (eds.) *China's Presence in the Middle East: The Implications of the One Belt, One Road Initiative*, Abingdon: Routledge.

Ellis, R. Evan (2009) *China in Latin America: The Whats and Wherefores*, Boulder, CO: Lynn Rienner.

Ellis, R. Evan (2014) *China on the Ground in Latin America: Challenges for the Chinese and Impacts on the Region*, New York: Palgrave Macmillan.

Evron, Yoram (2017) 'The economic dimension of China-Israel relations: political implications, roles and limitations', *Israel Affairs*, Vol. 23, Issue 5, pp. 828–47.

Fenby, Jonathan (2017) *Will China Dominate the 21st Century?*, Cambridge: Polity Press.

Feng, Huiyun (2009) 'Is China a Revisionist Power?', *Chinese Journal of International Politics*, Vol. 2, Issue 3, pp. 313–34.

Ferguson, Niall, and Xiang Xu (2018) 'Making Chimerica great again', *International Finance*, Vol. 21, Issue 3, pp. 239–52.

Fravel, M. Taylor (2019) *Active Defense: China's Military Strategy Since 1949*, Princeton: Princeton University Press.

Friedberg, Aaron L. (2022) *Getting China Wrong*, Cambridge: Polity Press.

Fürst, Rudolf (2018) 'Czechia's relations with China: on a long road toward a real strategic partnership?', in Weiqing Song (ed.) *China's Relations with Central and Eastern Europe: From 'Old Comrade'" to New Partners*, Abingdon: Routledge.

Fürst, Rudolf (2022) 'Czech Republic: pendulum swings toward freezing ties based on overestimated fear of China', in John Seaman, Francesca Ghiretti, Lucas Erlbacher, Xiaoxue Martin, and Miguel Otero-Iglesias (eds.) *Dependence in Europe's Relations with China: Weighing Perceptions and Reality*, Paris: French Institute of International Relations (IFRI), pp. 56–61.

Gachúz, Juan Carlos (2012) 'Chile's economic and political relationship with China', *Journal of Current Chinese Affairs*, Vol. 41, Issue 1, pp. 133–54.

Galtung, Johan (1969) 'Violence, peace, and peace research', *Journal of Peace Research*, Vol. 6, Issue 3, pp. 167–91.

Galtung, Johan (1980) 'A structural theory of imperialism', in Richard A. Falk, and Samuel S. Kim (eds.) *The War System: An Interdisciplinary Approach*, New York: Routledge.

Garlick, Jeremy (2013) 'A critical analysis of EU-China relations: towards improved mutual understanding', *Contemporary European Studies*, Vol. 1, pp. 51–70.

Garlick, Jeremy (2018) 'Deconstructing the China-Pakistan Economic Corridor: pipe dreams versus geopolitical realities', *Journal of Contemporary China*, Vol. 27, Issue 112, pp. 519–33.

Garlick, Jeremy (2019) 'China's principal-agent problem in the Czech Republic: the curious case of CEFC', *Asia Europe Journal*, Vol. 17, Issue 4, pp. 437–51.

Garlick, Jeremy (2020) *The Impact of China's Belt and Road Initiative: From Asia to Europe*, Abingdon: Routledge.

Garlick, Jeremy (2022) *Reconfiguring the China-Pakistan Economic Corridor: Geo-Economic Pipe Dreams Versus Geopolitical Realities*, Abingdon: Routledge.

Garlick, Jeremy, and Radka Havlová (2020) 'China's "Belt and Road" economic diplomacy in the Persian Gulf: strategic hedging amidst Saudi-Iranian regional rivalry', *Journal of Current Chinese Affairs*, Vol. 49, Issue 1, pp. 82–105.

Garlick, Jeremy, and Radka Havlová (2021) 'The dragon dithers: assessing the cautious implementation of China's Belt and Road Initiative in Iran', *Eurasian Geography and Economics*, Vol. 62, Issue 4, pp. 454–80.

Garlick, Jeremy, and Fangxing Qin (2023) 'China's Normative Power in Central and Eastern Europe: "16/17+1" Cooperation as a Tale of Unfulfilled Expectations', *Europe-Asia Studies*, Vol. 75, Issue 4, pp. 583–605 (online first, 7 March 2023).

Garver, John W., and Fei-Ling Wang (2010) 'China's anti-encirclement struggle', *Asian Security*, Vol. 6, Issue 3, pp. 238–61.

Gauttam, Priya, Bawa Singh, and Jaspal Kaur (2020) 'COVID-19 and Chinese global health diplomacy: geopolitical opportunity for China's hegemony?', *Millennial Asia*, Vol. 11, Issue 3, pp. 318–40.

Gelfand, Michele J., et al (2011) 'Differences between tight and loose cultures: a 33-nation study', *Science*, Vol. 332, Issue 6033, pp. 1100–4.

Gelfand, Michele (2018) *Rule Makers, Rule Breakers: Tight and Loose Cultures and the Secret Signals That Direct Our Lives*, New York: Scribner.

Gerstl, Alfred (2020) 'Malaysia's hedging strategy towards China under Mahathir Mohamad (2018–2020): direct engagement, limited balancing, and limited bandwagoning', *Journal of Current Chinese Affairs*, Vol. 49, Issue 1, pp. 106–31.

Gerstl, Alfred, and Ute Wallenböck (eds.) (2021) *China's Belt and Road Initiative: Strategic and Economic Impacts on Central Asia, Southeast Asia, and Central Eastern Europe*, *Abingdon*: Routledge.

Gertz, Bill (2000) *The China Threat: How the People's Republic Targets America*, Washington, D.C.: Regnery.

Godement, François, and Abigael Vasselier (2017) *China at the Gates: A New Power Audit of EU-China Relations*, London: European Council on Foreign Relations.

Goh, Evelyn, and Cheng-Chwee Kuik. See: Evelyn Goh (2005) *Meeting the China Challenge: the U.S. in Southeast Asian Regional Security Strategies*, Washington, D.C.: East-West Center.

Golden, Sean (2011) 'China's perception of risk and the concept of comprehensive national power', *The Copenhagen Journal of Asian Studies*, Vol. 29, Issue 2, pp. 79–109.

Griffiths, Richard T. (2017) *Revitalising the Silk Road: China's Belt and Road Initiative*, Leiden: HIPE Publications.

Grow, Michael (2008) *U.S. Presidents and Latin American Interventions: Pursuing Regime Change in the Cold War*, Lawrence, Kansas: University Press of Kansas.

Hakim, Peter (2006) 'Is Washington losing Latin America?', *Foreign Affairs*, Vol. 85, Issue 1, pp. 39–53.

Hameiri, Shahar, and Lee Jones (2016) 'Rising powers and state transformation: the case of China', *European Journal of International Relations*, Vol. 22, Issue 1, pp. 72–98.

Han, Byung-Chul (2017) *In the Swarm: Digital Prospects*, Cambridge, Mass.: The MIT Press.

Han, Rongbin (2015) 'Manufacturing consent in cyberspace: China's "fifty-cent army"', *Journal of Current Chinese Affairs*, Vol. 44, Issue 2, pp. 105–34.

Hayton, Bill (2014) *The South China Sea: The Struggle for Power in Asia*, New Haven: Yale University Press.

Heath, Timothy R. (2016) 'China's evolving approach to economic diplomacy', *Asia Policy*, Vol. 11, Issue 22, pp. 157–92.

Hillman, Jonathan E. (2018) *The Rise of China-Europe Railways*, Washington, D.C.: Center for Strategic & International Studies, 6 March. Available at: https://www.csis.org/analysis/rise-china-europe-railways.

Hillman, Jonathan (2020) *The Emperor's New Road: China and the Project of the Century*, New Haven and London: Yale University Press.

Hillman, Jonathan (2021) *The Digital Silk Road: China's Quest to Wire the World and Win the Future*, London: Profile Books.

Hoadley, Stephen, and Jian Yang (2007) 'China's cross-regional FTA initiatives: towards comprehensive national power', *Pacific Affairs*, Vol. 80, Issue 2, pp. 327–48.

Hobson, John (2012) *The Eurocentric Conception of World Politics: Western International Theory, 1760–2010*, Cambridge: Cambridge University Press.

Hodzi, Obert (2020) 'Bridging the asymmetries? African students' mobility to China', *Asian Ethnicity*, Vol. 21, Issue 4, pp. 566–84.

Hofstede, Geert, and Gert Jan Hofstede (2005) *Cultures and Organizations: Software of the Mind*, New York: McGraw-Hill.

Holslag, Jonathan (2015) *China's Coming War with Asia*, Cambridge: Polity.

Holslag, Jonathan (2017) 'How China's New Silk Road Threatens European Trade', *The International Spectator*, Vol. 52, Issue 1, pp. 46–60.

Huang, Yanzhong (2022) 'The Health Silk Road: how China adapts the Belt and Road Initiative to the COVID-19 pandemic', *American Journal of Public Health*, Vol. 112, Issue 4, pp. 567–9.

Huntington, Samuel P. (2005) *Who Are We?: The Challenges to America's National Identity*, New York: Simon & Schuster.

Hurley, John, Scott Morris, and Gailyn Portelance (2018) *Examining the Debt Implications of the Belt and Road Initiative from a Policy Perspective*, Washington, D.C.: Center for Global Development, Policy Paper 121.

Islam, Iyanatul, and Anis Chowdhury (1997) *Asia-Pacific Economies: A Survey*, London and New York: Routledge.

Islam, Shahidul, Wuyi Wang, and Laping Sheng (2022) 'The construction of Bangladesh-China-India-Myanmar Economic Corridor: current situation, problem, and countermeasures', *Asian Journal of Social Science Studies*, Vol. 7, Issue 4, pp. 10–24.

Jackson, Sukhan, and Adrian Sleigh (2000) 'Resettlement for China's Three Gorges Dam: socio-economic impact and institutional tensions', *Communist and Post-Communist Studies*, Vol. 33, Issue 2, pp. 223–41.

Jacques, Martin (2009) *When China Rules the World: The Rise of the Middle Kingdom and the End of the Western World*, London: Allen Lane.

Jäger, Siegfried (2001) 'Discourse and knowledge: theoretical and methodological aspects of a critical discourse and dispositive analysis', in Ruth Wodak, and Michael Meyer (eds.) *Methods of Critical Discourse Analysis*, London: Sage.

Jakóbowski, Jakub (2018) 'Chinese-led regional multilateralism in Central and Eastern Europe, Africa and Latin America: 16+1, FOCAC, and CCF', *Journal of Contemporary China*, Vol. 27, Issue 113, pp. 659–73.

Jenkins, Rhys (2022) 'China's Belt and Road Initiative in Latin America: what has changed?', *Journal of Current Chinese Affairs*, Vol. 51, Issue 1, pp. 13–39.

Jenkins, Rhys (2022) *How China is Reshaping the Global Economy: Development Impacts in Africa and Latin America*, Oxford: Oxford University Press.

Jervis, Robert (1997) *System Effects: Complexity in Political and Social Life*, Princeton: Princeton University Press.

Jian, Junbo, and Donata Frasheri (2014) 'Neo-colonialism or de-colonialism? China's economic engagement in Africa and the implications for world order', *African Journal of Political Science and International Relations*, Vol. 8, Issue 7, pp. 185–201.

Johnson, Steven (2002) *Emergence: The Connected Lines of Ants, Brains, Cities and Software*, London: Penguin.

Johnston, Lauren, Edmund Downie, Marina Rudyak, and Joshua Mwakalikamo (2021) *China's Appetite for International Agricultural Investment: Case Studies of Kyrgyzstan, Myanmar and Tanzania*, London: ODI. Available at: www.odi.org/publications/chinas-appetite-for-international-agricultural-investmentcase-studies-of-kyrgyzstan-myanmar-and-tanzania.

Jones, David Martin, and Nicole Jenne (2022) 'Hedging and grand strategy in Southeast Asian foreign policy', *International Relations of the Asia-Pacific*, Vol. 22, Issue 2, pp. 205–35.

Jones, Lee, and Shahar Hameiri (2020) *Debunking the Myth of 'Debt-Trap Diplomac'': How Recipient Countries Shape China's Belt and Road Initiative*, London: Chatham House.

Jones, Lee, and Shahar Hameiri (2022) *Fractured China: How State Transformation Is Shaping China's Rise*, Cambridge: Cambridge University Press.

Jones, Lee, and Jinghan Zeng (2019) 'Understanding China's "Belt and Road Initiative": beyond "grand strategy" to a state transformation analysis', *Third World Quarterly*, Vol. 40, Issue 8, pp. 1415–39.

Jünemann, Annette, Nikolas Scherer, Nicolas Fromm (eds.) (2017) *Fortress Europe? Challenges and Failures of Migration and Asylum Policies*, Wiesbaden: Springer VS.

Kanarek, Paulina (2017) 'Perspectives for development of China-EU relations in the infrastructure investment sector: a case study of COVEC's investment in Poland', *The Journal of Political Risk*, Vol. 5, Issue 8, pp. 1–41.

Kavalski, Emilian (2010) 'Shanghaied into cooperation: framing China's socialization of Central Asia', *Journal of Asian and African Studies*, Vol. 45, Issue 2, pp. 131–45.

Kavalski, Emilian (2012) 'Waking IR up from its "deep Newtonian slumber"', *Millennium: Journal of International Studies*, Vol. 41, Issue 1, pp. 137–50.

Kavalski, Emilian (2013) 'The struggle for recognition of normative powers: normative power Europe and normative power China in context', *Cooperation and Conflict*, Vol. 48, Issue 2, pp. 247–67.

Kavalski, Emilian (2015) 'Complexifying IR: disturbing the "deep Newtonian slumber" of the mainstream'. In Emilian Kavalski (ed.) *World Politics at the Edge of Chaos: Reflections on Complexity and Global Life*, Albany: State University of New York Press, pp. 253–72.

Kavalski, Emilian (2015) 'Introduction: Inside/outside and around: observing the complexity of global life'. in Emilian Kavalski (ed.) *World Politics at the Edge of Chaos: Reflections on Complexity and Global Life*, Albany: State University of New York Press, pp. 1–27.

Keay, John (2008) *China: A History*, London: HarperPress.

Kenderdine, Tristan, and Han Ling (2018) 'International capacity cooperation: financing China's export of industrial overcapacity', *Global Policy*, Vol. 9, Issue 1, pp. 41–52.

Khurana, Gurpreet S. (2008) 'China's "string of pearls" in the Indian Ocean and its security implications', *Strategic Analysis*, Vol. 32, Issue 1, pp. 1–39.

Kim, Sung-Han, and Sanghoon Kim (2022) 'China's contestation of the liberal international order', *The Pacific Review*, online first 9 April. Available at: https://www.tandfonline.com/doi/abs/10.1080/09512748.2022.2063367.

King, Gary, Robert O. Keohane, and Sidney Verba (1994) *Designing Social Inquiry: Scientific Inference in Qualitative Research*. Princeton: Princeton University Press.

Kironska, Kristina, and Jeremy Garlick (2022) 'Pakistanis perceive China as their "best frien"', *The Diplomat*, 14 October. Available at: https://thediplomat.com/2022/10/pakistanis-perceive-china-as-their-best-friend/ (accessed 9 February 2023).

Kissinger, Henry (2012) *On China*, London: Penguin.

Kroeber, Arthur R. (2016) *China's Economy: What Everyone Needs to Know*, New York: Oxford University Press.

Kuhn, Robert Lawrence (2011) *How China's Leaders Think* (revised edition), Singapore: John Wiley & Sons.

Kuik, Cheng-Chwee (2008) 'The essence of hedging: Malaysia and Singapore's response to a rising China', *Contemporary Southeast Asia*, Vol. 30, Issue 2, pp. 159–85.

Kynge, James (2006) *China Shakes the World: The Rise of a Hungry Nation*, London: Weidenfeld & Nicolson.

Langan, Mark (2018) *Neo-Colonialism and the Poverty of Development in Africa*, Cham: Palgrave Macmillan.

Lanteigne, Marc (2020) *Chinese Foreign Policy: An Introduction (Fourth Edition)*, Abingdon: Routledge.

Lavin, Franklin L. (1996) 'Isolationism and U.S. foreign policy', *The Brown Journal of World Affairs*, Vol. 3, Issue 1, pp. 271–7.

Le Corre, Philippe, and Alain Sepulchre (2016) *China's Offensive in Europe*, Washington, D.C.: Brookings Institution Press.

Lee, Ching Kwan (2017), *The Specter of Global China: Politics, Labor, and Foreign Investment in Africa*, Chicago: University of Chicago Press.

Lee, Erika (2007) 'The "yellow peril" and Asian exclusion in the Americas', *Pacific Historical Review*, Vol. 76, Issue 4, pp. 537–62.

Lee, Kai-Fu (2018) *AI Superpowers: China, Silicon Valley, and the New World Order*, New York: Mariner Books.

Leung, Guy C.K., Raymond Li, and Melissa Low (2011) 'Transitions in China's oil economy, 1990–2010', *Eurasian Geography and Economics*, Vol. 52, Issue 4, pp. 483–500.

Li, Xing (ed.) (2019) *Mapping China's 'One Belt One Road' Initiative*, Cham: Palgrave Macmillan.

Liu, Siyang, Jeremy Garlick, and Fangxing Qin (2021) 'Towards guanxi? Reconciling the "relational turn" in Western and Chinese international relations scholarship', *All Azimuth*, Vol. 11, Issue 1, pp. 67–85.

Lu, Shulin (2014/2015) 'China-Pakistan Economic Corridor: a flagship and exemplary project of "One Belt and One Road"', *Strategic Studies*, Vol. 34, Issue 4/Vol. 35, Issue 1, pp. 165–73.

Maçães, Bruno (2018) *Belt and Road: A Chinese World Order*, London: Hurst & Co.

Mackinder, Halford J. (1904) 'The geographical pivot of history', *The Geographical Journal*, Vol. 23, Issue 4, pp. 421–37.

Mahbubani, Kishore (2022) *The Asian 21st Century*, Singapore: Springer.

Manners, Ian (2002) 'Normative power Europe: a contradiction in terms?', *Journal of Common Market Studies*, Vol. 40, Issue 2, pp. 235–58.

Martin, Peter (2021) *China's Civilian Army: The Making of Wolf Warrior Diplomacy*, New York: Oxford University Press.

Mearsheimer, John J. (2001) *The Tragedy of Great Power Politics*, New York: W.W. Norton.

Mearsheimer, John J. (2019) 'Bound to fail: the rise and fall of the liberal international order', *International Security*, Vol. 43, Issue 4, pp. 7–50.

Mertha, Andrew (2009) '"Fragmented authoritarianism 2.0": political pluralization in the Chinese policy process', *The China Quarterly*, Vol. 200, pp. 995–1012.

Miller, John H., and Scott E. Page (2007) *Complex Adaptive Systems: An Introduction to Computational Models of Social Life*, Princeton: Princeton University Press.

Moravcsik, Andrew (2005) 'The European constitutional compromise and the neofunctionalist legacy', *Journal of European Public Policy*, Vol. 12, Issue 2, pp. 349–86.

Morgan, Stephen L. (2021) *The Chinese Economy*, Newcastle upon Tyne: Agenda Publishing.

Murphy, Dawn C. (2022) *China's Rise in the Global South: The Middle East, Africa, and Beijing's Alternative World Order*, Stanford: Stanford University Press.

Nabiyeva, Komila (2019) *Win-win or Win-lose? China-Kazakhstan Energy Cooperation within the Belt and Road Initiative*, Cologne: Stiftung Asienhaus. Available at: https://fid4sa-repository.ub.uni-heidelberg.de/4176/1/Blickwechsel_China-Kazakhstan_Energy_Cooperation_within_the_Belt_and_Road_Initiative.pdf.

Navarro, Peter (2008) *The Coming China Wars: Where They Will Be Fought and How They Can Be Won*, Upper Saddle River, NJ: FT Press.

Nie, Wenjuan (2015) 'Dengmeng duihua de shenfen dingwei yu zhanlue fenxi' ['An analysis of ASEAN views of and strategies towards China'], *Dangdai Yatai* (Journal of Contemporary Asia-Pacific Studies), Vol. 1, pp. 21–37.

Norris, William J. (2016) *Chinese Economic Statecraft: Commercial Actors, Grand Strategy, and State Control*. Ithaca, NY: Cornell University Press.

Norris, William J. (2021) 'China's post-Cold War economic statecraft: a periodization', *Journal of Current Chinese Affairs*, Vol. 50, Issue 3, pp. 294–316.

Nye, Joseph S., Jr. (1990) 'Soft power', *Foreign Policy*, pp. 153–71.

Nye, Joseph S. (2004) *Soft Power: The Means to Success in World Politics*, New York: Public Affairs.

Nye, Joseph S., Jr. (2011) *The Future of Power*, New York: Public Affairs.

Nyíri, Pál, and Danielle Tan (2017) *Chinese Encounters in Southeast Asia: How People, Money, and Ideas from China Are Changing a Region*, Seattle: University of Washington Press.

Owen, Catherine (2017) '"The sleeping dragon is gathering strength": causes of Sinophobia in Central Asia', *China Quarterly of International Strategic Studies*, Vol. 3, Issue 1, pp. 101–19.

Pande, Aparna Pande (ed.) (2018) *Routledge Handbook of Contemporary Pakistan*, Abingdon: Routledge.

Pantucci, Raffaello, and Alexandros Petersen (2022) *Sinostan: China's Inadvertent Empire*, Oxford: Oxford University Press.

Parry, William T., and Edward A. Hacker (1991) *Aristotelian Logic*, Albany, NY: State University of New York Press.

Pavlićević, Dragan (2018) '"China threat" and "China opportunity": politics of dreams and fears in China-Central and Eastern European relations', *Journal of Contemporary China*, Vol. 27, Issue 113, pp. 688–702.

Pei, Minxin (2006) *China's Trapped Transition: The Limits of Developmental Autocracy*, Cambridge, MA: Harvard University Press.

Perkins, Richard, and Eric Neumayer (2010) 'The organized hypocrisy of ethical foreign policy: human rights, democracy and Western arms sales', *Geoforum*, Vol. 41, Issue 2, pp. 247–56.

Peters, Enrique Dussel, and Ariel C. Armony (eds.) *Beyond Raw Materials: Who are the Actors in the Latin America and Caribbean-China Relationship?* Buenos Aires: Friedrich-Ebert Stiftung.

Peyrouse, Sébastien (2016) 'Discussing China: Sinophilia and Sinophobia in Central Asia', *Journal of Eurasian Studies*, Vol. 7, Issue 1, pp. 14–23.

Pillsbury, Michael (2015) *The Hundred-Year Marathon: China's Secret Strategy to Replace America as the Global Superpower*, New York: Henry Holt.

Pirani, Simon (2019) *Central Asian Gas: Prospects for the 2020s*, OIES Paper NG 155, Oxford: Oxford Institute for Energy Studies. Available at: https://a9w7k6q9.stackpathcdn.com/wpcms/wp-content/uploads/2019/12/Central-Asian-Gas-NG-155.pdf.

Polanyi, Karl (1957) *The Great Transformation: The Political and Economic Origins of Our Time*, Boston: Beacon Press.

Pomfret, Richard (2019) *The Central Asian Economies in the Twenty-First Century: Paving a New Silk Road*, Princeton: Princeton University Press.

Pye, Lucian W. (1997) 'Chinese democracy and constitutional development', in Fumio Itoh (ed.) *China in the Twenty-First Century: Politics, Economy, and Society*, Tokyo: United Nations University Press.

Qin, Yaqing (2016) 'A relational theory of world politics', *International Studies Review*, Vol. 18, Issue 1, pp. 33–47.

Rae, Alastair I.M. (2005) *Quantum Physics: A Beginner's Guide*, Oxford: Oneworld.

Ramalingam, Ben (2013) *Aid on the Edge of Chaos: Rethinking International Cooperation in a Complex World*, Oxford: Oxford University Press.

Rippa, Alessandro (2019) 'Cross-border trade and "The Market" between Xinjiang (China) and Pakistan', *Journal of Contemporary Asia*, Vol. 49, Issue 2, pp. 254–71.

Rogelja, Igor, and Konstantinos Tsimonis (2020) 'Narrating the China threat: securitising Chinese economic presence in Europe', *The Chinese Journal of International Politics*, Vol. 13, Issue 1, pp. 103–33.

Rogelja, Igor, and Konstantinos Tsimonis (2023) *Belt and Road: The First Decade*, Newcastle Upon Tyne: Agenda Publishing.

Rolland, Nadège (2017) *China's Eurasian Century? Political and Strategic Implications of the Belt and Road Initiative*, Seattle: The National Bureau of Asian Research.

Said, Edward W. (1978) *Orientalism*, New York: Pantheon.

Schrader, Matt, and J. Michael Cole (2023) 'China hasn't given up on the Belt and Road', *Foreign Affairs*, 7 February. Available at: https://www.foreignaffairs.com/china/china-hasnt-given-belt-and-road.

Scissors, Derek (2022) *China Global Investment Tracker*, Washington, D.C.: American Enterprise Institute. Available at: https://www.aei.org/china-global-investment-tracker/.

Shambaugh, David (2008) *China's Communist Party: Atrophy and Adaptation*, Washington, D.C.: Woodrow Wilson Center Press.

Shambaugh, David (2013) *China Goes Global: The Partial Power*, New York: Oxford University Press.

Shambaugh, David (2021) *China's Leaders: From Mao to Now*, Cambridge: Polity.

Shambaugh, David (2021) *Where Great Powers Meet: America & China in Southeast Asia*, New York: Oxford University Press.

Shirk, Susan L. (2007) *China: Fragile Superpower*, New York: Oxford University Press.

Siddiqa, Ayesha (2007) *Military Inc.: Inside Pakistan's Military Economy*, London: Pluto Press.

Sil, Rudra, and Peter J. Katzenstein (2010) *Beyond Paradigms: Analytic Eclecticism in the Study of World Politics*, Houndmills, UK: Palgrave Macmillan.

Silver, Laura, Kat Devlin, and Christine Huang (2019) 'Attitudes toward China', Pew Research Center, 5 December. Available at: https://www.pewresearch.org/global/2019/12/05/attitudes-toward-china-2019/.

Singh, Ajit (2021) 'The myth of "debt-trap diplomacy" and realities of Chinese development finance', *Third World Quarterly*, Vol. 42, Issue 2, pp. 239–53.

Small, Andrew (2015) *The China-Pakistan Axis: Asia's New Geopolitics*, Oxford: Oxford University Press.

Smith, Graeme, and Terence Wesley-Smith (eds.) (2021) *The China Alternative: Changing Regional Order in the Pacific Islands*, Acton: Australian National University Press.

Spence, Jonathan (1980) *To Change China: Western Advisers in China*, New York: Penguin.

Spence, Jonathan (1990) *The Search for Modern China*, New York: W.W. Norton.

Stanzel, Angela (2022) *China's Path to Geopolitics: Case Study on China's Iran Policy at the Intersection of Regional Interests and Global Power Rivalry*, SWP Research Paper 5, Berlin: German Institute for International and Security Affairs.

Stone, Dan (2017) *Concentration Camps: A Short History*, Oxford: Oxford University Press.

Storey, Ian (2011) *Southeast Asia and the Rise of China: The Search for Security*, Abingdon: Routledge.

Storey, Ian (2015) *Thailand's Post-Coup Relations with China and America: More Beijing, Less Washington* (Trends in Southeast Asia, no. 20), Singapore: ISEAS-Yusof Ishak Institute.

Strange, Susan (1988) *States and Markets*, London: Bloomsbury.

Taleb, Nicholas Nassim (2008) *The Black Swan: The Impact of the Highly Improbable*, London: Penguin.

Tang, Shiping (2013) *The Social Evolution of International Politics*, Oxford: Oxford University Press.

To, Emma Miriam Yin-Hang, and Rodrigo Acuña (2019) 'China and Venezuela: South-South cooperation or rearticulated dependency?', *Latin American Perspectives*, Vol. 46, Issue 2, pp. 126–40.

Toktomushev, Kemel (2018) 'Understanding cross-border conflict in post-Soviet Central Asia: the case of Kyrgyzstan and Tajikistan', *Connections*, Vol. 17, Issue 1, pp. 21–41.

Turcsányi, Richard, and Eva Kachlíková (2020) 'The BRI and China's soft power in Europe: why Chinese narratives (initially) won', *Journal of Current Chinese Affairs*, Vol. 49, Issue 1, pp. 58–81.

Turcsányi, Richard, and Runya Qiaoan (2019) 'Friends or foes? How diverging views of communist past undermine the China-CEE "16+1 platform"', *Asia Europe Journal*, Vol. 18, Issue 3, pp. 397–412.

Umetsu, Hiroyuki (1996) 'Communist China's entry into the Korean hostilities and a U.S. proposal for a collective security arrangement in the Pacific offshore island chain', *Journal of Northeast Asian Studies*, Vol. 15, Issue 2, pp. 98–118.

Vangeli, Anastas (2019) 'A framework for the study of the One Belt One Road initiative as a medium of principle diffusion', in Li Xing (ed.) *Mapping China's 'One Belt One Road' Initiative*, Cham: Palgrave Macmillan, pp. 57–89.

Waldrop, M. Mitchell (1993) *Complexity: The Emerging Science at the Edge of Order and Chaos*, London: Viking.

Wallerstein, Immanuel (1979) *The Capitalist World-Economy*, Cambridge: Cambridge University Press.

Walt, Stephen M. (2021) 'The myth of American exceptionalism', *Foreign Policy*, 11 October. Available at: https://foreignpolicy.com/2011/10/11/the-myth-of-american-exceptionalism/ (accessed 28 December 2021).

Walt, Stephen M. (2021) 'What comes after the forever wars', *Foreign Policy*, 28 April. Available at: https://foreignpolicy.com/2021/04/28/what-comes-after-the-forever-wars/.

Walter, Carl E., and Fraser J.T. Howie (2011) *Red Capitalism: The Fragile Financial Foundation of China's Extraordinary Rise*, Singapore: John Wiley & Sons.

Waltz, Kenneth (1979) *Theory of International Politics*, New York: Addison-Wesley.

Wang, Yuzhu (2021) 'Hedging strategy: concept, behavior, and implications for China-ASEAN relations', *East Asian Affairs*, Vol. 1, Issue 2, pp. 1–36.

Wang, Zheng (2008) 'National humiliation, history education, and the politics of historical memory: patriotic education campaign in China', *International Studies Quarterly*, Vol. 52, Issue 4, pp. 783–806.

Watson, Burton (trans.) (2013) *The Complete Works of Zhuangzi*, New York: Columbia University Press.

West, Cornel (2005) *Democracy Matters: Winning the Fight against Imperialism*, New York: Penguin Books.

Wise, Carol (2020) *Dragonomics: How Latin America Is Maximizing (or Missing Out on) China's International Development Strategy*, New Haven: Yale University Press.

Wodak, Ruth (2001) 'The discourse-historical approach', in Ruth Wodak, and Michael Meyer (eds.) *Methods of Critical Discourse Analysis*, London: Sage, pp. 63–94.

Wolf, Siegfried O. (2020) *The China-Pakistan Economic Corridor of the Belt and Road Initiative: Concept, Context and Assessment*, Cham: Springer.

Wood, Robert E. (1986) *From Marshall Plan to Debt Crisis: Foreign Aid and Development Choices in the World Economy*, Berkeley: University of California Press.

Wucker, Michele (2016) *The Gray Rhino: How to Recognize and Act on the Obvious Dangers We Ignore*, New York: St Martin's Press.

Xi, Jinping (2014) *The Governance of China*, Beijing: Foreign Languages Press.

Yang, Zhenjie (2013) '"Fragmented authoritarianism" – the facilitator behind the Chinese reform miracle: a case study in central China', *China Journal of Social Work*, Vol. 6, Issue 1, pp. 4–13.

Yoshihara, Toshi (2012) 'China's vision of its seascape: the first island chain and Chinese seapower', *Asian Politics & Policy*, Vol. 4, Issue 3, pp. 293–314.

Yu, George T. (1971) 'Working on the railroad: China and the Tanzania-Zambia railway', *Asian Survey*, Vol. 11, Issue 11, pp. 1101–17.

Zawacki, Benjamin (2021) *Thailand: Shifting Ground between the US and a Rising China* (2nd ed.), London: Zed Books.

Zeng, Ming, Liu Ximei, Li Yulong, and Peng Lilin (2014) 'Review of renewable energy investment and financing in China: status, mode, issues and countermeasures', *Renewable and Sustainable Energy Reviews*, Vol. 31, pp. 23–37.

Zhang, Shu G., and Ni Chen (2021) 'Beijing's institutionalised economic statecraft towards Brazil: a case study', *Journal of Current Chinese Affairs*, Vol. 50, Issue 3, pp. 339–65.

Zhang, Shuxiu (2016) *Chinese Economic Diplomacy: Decision-Making Actors and Processes*, London and New York: Routledge.

Zhang, Weiying (2018) *Game Theory and Society*, Abingdon: Routledge.

Zhang, Xiaoming (2005) 'China's 1979 war with Vietnam: a reassessment', *The China Quarterly*, Vol. 184, pp. 851–74.

Zhang, Yibing (2011) *The Subjective Dimension of Marxist Historical Dialectics* (2nd ed.), London: Canut Publishers.

Zhao, Tingyang (2006) 'Rethinking empire from a Chinese concept "All-under-Heaven" (Tian-xia, 天下)', *Social Identities*, Vol. 12, Issue 1, pp. 29–41.

Zhou, Weifeng, and Mario Esteban (2018) 'Beyond Balancing: China's approach towards the Belt and Road Initiative', *Journal of Contemporary China*, Vol. 27, Issue 112, pp. 487–501.

Zoubir, Yahia H., and Emilie Tran (2022) 'China's Health Silk Road in the Middle East and North Africa amidst COVID-19 and a contested world order', *Journal of Contemporary China*, Vol. 31, Issue 135, pp. 335–50.
Zweig, David, and Bi Jianhai (2005) 'China's global hunt for energy', *Foreign Affairs*, Vol. 84, Issue 5, pp. 25–38.

INDEX